# Entrepreneurship and Local Economic Development

# Entrepreneurship and Local Economic Development

Edited by Norman Walzer

LEXINGTON BOOKS

A division of
ROWMAN & LITTLEFIELD PUBLISHERS, INC.
Lanham • Boulder • New York • Toronto • Plymouth, UK

LEXINGTON BOOKS

A division of Rowman & Littlefield Publishers, Inc.
A wholly owned subsidary of The Rowman & Littlefield Publishing Group, Inc.
4501 Forbes Boulevard, Suite 200
Lanham, MD 20706

Estover Road
Plymouth PL6 7PY
United Kingdom

British Library Cataloguing in Publication Information Available

**Library of Congress Cataloging-in-Publication Data**

Entrepreneurship and local economic development / edited by Norman Walzer.
    p. cm.
  1. Entrepreneurship—United States. 2. New business enterprises—United States.
3. Small business—United States. 4. Community development—United States.
5. Rural development—United States. I. Walzer, Norman.
  HB615.E6268 2007
  338′.040973—dc22                                                2007022032

  ISBN-13: 978-0-7391-1712-5 (cloth : alk. paper)
  ISBN-13: 978-0-7391-1713-2 (pbk. : alk. paper)
  ISBN-13: 978-0-7391-4121-2 (electronic)

Printed in the United States of America

To Emma and Brennen, future entrepreneurs

# Contents

# Preface

For many years, local elected officials and development practitioners have tried to stimulate business activity in their areas. Retention and attraction of businesses, especially industrial firms, have been popular approaches. Increased competition from off-shore locations and the smaller number of large firms that relocate, however, have brought pressures to find other strategies, especially in rural areas.

While starting and promoting small businesses has been recognized as an important development strategy for more than a quarter century, in the past decade more attention has been paid to creating a local climate that promotes entrepreneurship. More research has been devoted to identifying people, including youth, with entrepreneurship potential, creating a system in which education and technical assistance is available to entrepreneurs at all experience levels, and developing financing alternatives when traditional sources are not available.

A huge literature on entrepreneurship topics has developed in recent years as various disciplines have studied this issue. This literature is sometimes conflicting and confusing to practitioners and students alike. Scholars and practitioners come to the issue from different perspectives and immediate need for application that can widen the gap in discussions of entrepreneurship.

This book is intended to assemble current thinking on important aspects of entrepreneurship as it relates to use as a local economic development strategy. Important concepts are presented initially followed by practical examples of places that have successfully applied the principles. We certainly have not exhausted the important topics; rather, we have tried to organized the discussions in such a way that students and practitioners can evaluate whether an entrepreneurship strategy is suitable in their community.

Many people have contributed to this project. Dr. Joseph Rallo, Provost and Academic Vice-President, Western Illinois University, provided seed money for the project and supported the endeavor throughout. Karen Poncin, Illinois Institute for Rural Affairs (IIRA), handled the editing and manuscript preparation tasks. Karin Spader, Lori A. Sutton, and other members of the IIRA assisted with the process in many ways. Without the help of these individuals and others, this project could not have been completed.

—Norman Walzer

# 1

# Introduction and Overview

*Norman Walzer and Adee Athiyaman*

Finding and implementing successful local economic development strategies, especially in rural areas, has become more important in recent years as local officials struggle to stimulate stagnant or declining economies and stem population losses. Rural areas, in general, have experienced a significant restructuring as higher paying manufacturing jobs are replaced by lower-paying service jobs (Walzer 2003). While local development practitioners are concerned about these changes, they all too often have neither the staff nor expertise to mount a successful business recruiting campaign and find it hard to compete with larger centers for relocation jobs.

High school graduates leave rural areas for better employment opportunities and there are too few high-paying economic opportunities to bring them back to their home areas later in life (Goetz and Rupasingha 2005). While they realize that youth represent the future of rural communities and their ability to prosper, or at least survive, rural community leaders and development practitioners are often unsure how to change the local economic climate and policies to successfully deal with this issue.

Rural communities often pursue policies or strategies that were successful in the past, hoping that these efforts will succeed in the future. Industrial attraction practices, based on offering low-cost sites and wages, attracted many businesses and jobs in earlier times. However, this approach is becoming less effective now because of even lower costs in offshore locations and increased competition among states to lure the relatively few large businesses seeking to relocate.

Promoting small business start-ups and development has been recognized as a strategy for many years following research showing that a majority of the employment growth was in small companies. An aging population in rural

areas and smaller markets than in large regional centers can mean less interest and fewer opportunities for business starts. Young families have migrated
to larger centers which, in and of itself, can mean a smaller pool of potential
people interested in starting businesses.

At the same time, an in-migration of early retirees with considerable
wealth and growing numbers of foreign-born populations can offer potential opportunities for new part-time business ventures either directly or
through financial investment. Hispanics and other groups with limited incomes may be survival entrepreneurs if they can access capital to start an enterprise.

The importance of small businesses in generating employment in rural
areas is well-known (Bruce et al. 2007). For many years, large corporations
have not grown at rates sufficient to propel national and local economies.
Birch and others documented the employment increases contributed by
small businesses laying the groundwork for supporting this group as a development strategy since the 1980s (Birch 1987; Acs and Armington 2005;
Shaffer 2002, 2006).

The changing economic environment, combined with increased pressures on rural areas to replace lost jobs or create additional jobs, forced local development practitioners to seek alternative strategies. Entrepreneurship as a development strategy is one such approach that has become
prominent especially in the past decade as practitioners recognize the limited number of firms relocating and the resulting competition for these
businesses.

## BACKGROUND RESEARCH

The importance of entrepreneurship in business and regional development
can be traced to Schumpeter and others early in the twentieth century
(Schumpeter 1934; Wilkens 1979) but research on entrepreneurship has
grown rapidly in recent years (Low 2001; Schenkel 2006). For instance, a
survey of the *Academy of Management Journal* shows more articles published
on entrepreneurship since 2000 than in all previous periods combined (Ireland, Reutzel, and Webb 2005). The recent growth in entrepreneurship research raises the question of "how the field got a start," and "why the sud-
den interest in the study of entrepreneurship?" The next several pages
briefly summarize major research directions leading to the current interest.

Economic changes in the late eighteenth century to the mid-nineteenth
century with the growth of industry from agriculture to shop assembly fostered the role of entrepreneurs in assembling capital and organizing production processes (McDaniel 2005). Classical economists such as Ricardo

and Malthus writing during this period analyzed economic growth through a dynamic lens involving the effects of capital accumulation and population growth (Harrod 1948). While this dynamic conceptualization of economies left room to study efforts by entrepreneurs, for example, in producing new products to satisfy the needs of a growing population, later economists especially in the Marginal Utility School, posited little direct role for entrepreneurs in the conditions for economic equilibrium (Demsetz 1997).

Schumpeter's (1934) theory of economic development revived interest in dynamic accounts of economic growth. In this view, economic development starts endogenously with entrepreneurs who destroy the static economic equilibrium by introducing innovations in the market place.

According to Soltow (1968), the first academic effort to study entrepreneurship began in the late 1920s with N. S. B. Gras pioneering the "business history studies" at Harvard University. Although several valuable works such as the study of Standard Oil emerged under Gras's leadership, the focus in the 1940s shifted from entrepreneurship to business policy studies and management of individual firms.

The interest in entrepreneurship was revived again in 1948 with the creation of the Research Center in Entrepreneurial History at Harvard. Under the direction of A. H. Cole, the Center approached the study of entrepreneurship from a multidisciplinary perspective with concepts drawn from economics, sociology, and history. For instance, the sociological concepts of social role and social sanction were used to understand the behavior of entrepreneurs guided by societal norms (Research Center in Entrepreneurial History 1949).

Evans (1949) summarized the then seminal developments in the field by highlighting the motives of an entrepreneur (for example, adventure) and the actions resulting from the motives (for example, innovative products). Specifically, the motivating forces include financial security (triggered by fear of bankruptcy or fear of financial embarrassment), adventure (joy of creating), and power (being one's own master; controlling one's own destiny).

Generalizations about entrepreneurial behavior based on past research can be organized into seven topics as follows:

1. *Division of Labor*. The owner of the stock (that is, an entrepreneur) which employs a large number of laborers attempts, for personal gain, to allocate employment so as to produce the largest quantity of work possible.
2. *Limits of Investment within a Given Field*. Each entrepreneur makes capital investments to push the business to the outer limit of profitability.

3. *Combination of Factors of Production.* Entrepreneurs deploy equipment to gain the highest productivity and least cost per unit.
4. *Shifting of Entrepreneurial Activity from One Industry to Another.* An entrepreneur will shift into new businesses or industries to improve the prospects for profit.
5. *Attitudes toward the Supply of a Product.* Entrepreneurs expand production and supply more at higher prices in an attempt to maximize profits.
6. *Bases of Entrepreneurial Expectations.* Entrepreneurs assume that the most recently realized results will continue, except when there are definite reasons to expect change.
7. *Actions Associated with Different Phases of the Business Cycle.* When business is slack, entrepreneurs sell surplus goods outside of a specific market at prices that little more than cover basic costs, while within that market still try to sell at prices that nearly cover both basic and supplementary costs.

In closing, Evans (1949) claims that entrepreneurial research focuses minimally on the following domains with a view to generating rules that guide entrepreneurial action: choice of products, methods of production, size and location of plant, mobility of investments, relations with competitors, marketing procedures, and relations with government. The following pages explore developments in these areas since the mid-twentieth century.

## RECENT ENTREPRENEURSHIP THEMES

Economics is only one discipline in which entrepreneurship research is conducted but even a cursory examination of research in the past several decades shows the diversity of topics and issues studied (Low 2001). A literature search was conducted using *EconLit*: the American Economic Association database that references 750 publications (see www.econlit.org). The period from January 1969 to January 2007 was chosen to provide a representative sample of publications pertaining to the latter half of the twentieth century. A simple keyword search using the term "entrepreneur" resulted in 1,388 records (table 1.1). Since the interest is in generalizations about entrepreneurial behavior, the search was limited to one macro keyword (entrepreneurial orientation) and several micro or specific keywords suggested by Evans (1949).

Of the 49 hits resulting from the keyword *entrepreneurial orientation*, 19 studies focused on entrepreneurial traits or culture. For entrepreneurs, the stable traits include innovativeness, proactiveness, and risk-taking (Todor-

Table 1.1.  Terms Employed to Search for Entrepreneurship Papers

| Keywords | Justification | No. of "Hits" | Percent |
|---|---|---|---|
| Entrepreneurial orientation | This catchall phrase is expected to uncover research related to entrepreneurial innovations in production processes, and marketing activities. In fact, the entire system of entrepreneurial initiatives is expected to be the outcome of this search. | 49 | 94 |
| Entrepreneur and size and location of plant | Keyword abstracted from Evan's (1949) paper on entrepreneurial theory. | 0 | |
| Entrepreneur and mobility of investments | Keyword abstracted from Evan's (1949) paper on entrepreneurial theory. | 2 | 4 |
| Entrepreneur and relations with competitors | Keyword abstracted from Evan's (1949) paper on entrepreneurial theory. | 0 | |
| Entrepreneur and marketing procedures | Keyword abstracted from Evan's (1949) paper on entrepreneurial theory. | 1 | 2 |
| Entrepreneur and relations with government and other institutions | Keyword abstracted from Evan's (1949) paper on entrepreneurial theory. | 0 | |

ovic 2004). The higher the number of people with these traits in a population, the greater the chance of success in entrepreneurial initiatives such as starting firms and succeeding in business (Maritz and Nieman 2006; Schlosser and Todorovic 2006; De Clercq, Sapienza, and Crijns 2005; Kyriakopoulos, Muelenberg, and Nilsson 2004).

The remaining papers are not easy to classify and range in topics from corporate entrepreneurship (Grozdanic 2006) to university start-ups (O'Shea et al. 2005). Low (2001) encountered the same problem in trying to classify and analyze trends in entrepreneurial research. He described entrepreneurship research as a potpourri. While the subject areas covered by entrepreneurship are broad, it is possible to abstract the scattered findings into a few generalizations that can help lay the groundwork for practical applications in the following chapters.

## Community-Specific Generalizations

The existence of a population with specific environmental traits or characteristics prone to entrepreneurship has a positive impact on the potential for entrepreneurship-induced economic development in a region (Lumpkin and Dess 2000). This is not to say that entrepreneurial ability cannot be modified through education and experiences. Lyons, Lichenstein, and Kutzhanova (chapter 6) examine these issues.

Likewise, the economic, political/legal, and social factors in the region are important in promoting successful entrepreneurship (Lee and Peterson 2000; Ibeh 2003). Creating an environment that encourages risk-taking and investment is key to success as discussed by Hustedde (chapter 3).

An entrepreneurial culture or environment involves the public sector directly because public policies can seriously affect investor attitudes and approaches. An entrepreneurial public sector creates a climate that encourages and enhances the potential of business investors to succeed. This type of climate is also likely to attract innovators. The role of entrepreneurial strategies in managing the public sector was recognized early by Osborne and Gaebler (1993).

## Firm-Specific Generalizations

An entrepreneurial culture when combined with market orientation, i.e., a strong customer focus, recognition of competitors' sources of advantage, and a strong cross-functional team approach to providing customer solutions, results in higher start-up success rates (Schlosser and Todorovic 2006; Bhuian and Habib 2004; Kyriakopoulos, Muelenberg, and Nilsson 2004).

Banks or financial institutions are less likely to finance new start-ups especially in industries with which they are unfamiliar. While entrepreneurs typically provide much of the start-up capital from their own funds, they need access to other avenues of support. Venture capital funds can finance innovative and growth-oriented firms (Cosh, Cummings, and Hughes 2005; Lindsay 2004) but areas with a variety of financing sources more often succeed as discussed by Markley (chapter 7).

## Public Policy

Successful entrepreneurship requires public policies that emphasize greater competition, provide at least a level playing field, and actively promote entrepreneurial behavior (Parker 2002; Mody 1999). During the past decade or so, entrepreneurship has become recognized in its own right as a distinct development approach rather than as a minor part of other development strategies. Practitioners realize that a mission-driven approach within an agency or unit to promote entrepreneurship and innovation succeeds more often than when it is included in a unit with many other assigned responsibilities. The result has been that many states now have entrepreneurial networks, centers, and other initiatives to stimulate job creation using an entrepreneurship strategy (NGA 2004; Williams 2004).

The diversity of programs and approaches used by development agencies in the name of entrepreneurship has made these strategies difficult to define precisely. Paramount to success is creating an environment in which investors take risks; function in a flexible environment allowing them to react quickly to market changes; and adopt innovative problem-solving approaches. Fortunately, this type of environment can exist in both rural and metro areas.

On the other hand, local development practitioners may see entrepreneurship as a specific or narrow development strategy focusing directly on identifying potential business investors, helping them find ways to take existing business ventures to higher levels or identify new business opportunities. These programs may be distinct from more traditional business attraction strategies or even Small Business Development Centers that help potential investors with business plans and internal management issues.

The two approaches to entrepreneurship just described are somewhat complementary, but successful communities or regions will adopt both. As later discussions in this book show, the greatest success in stimulating entrepreneurship is likely in communities with a climate and a system of education and technical assistance that address the needs of entrepreneurs at all levels. This environment promotes innovation and new ventures, interactions among business investors, and includes population groups prone to business investment.

## PURPOSES OF THIS BOOK

Entrepreneurship is hard to define and two distinct groups have been engaged in discussions of ways to promote the process. As noted previously, researchers have spent considerable energy trying to identify common characteristics of successful entrepreneurs and outlining the conditions that will advance entrepreneurial efforts and maximize success.

Practitioners, on the other hand, have focused more on designing programs aimed at starting businesses such as business plan competitions, networking seminars among interested groups, and small grants to help launch business ventures. In some instances these efforts are independent of other technical assistance or education efforts.

Scholars and researchers may tend to dismiss some of these programs as less effective because they are not grounded in theory or are not sufficiently supported by research. Practitioners, on the other hand, may find the scholarly literature of little direct application in daily operations since they must deal with potential business investors interested in immediate results.

This volume tries to link both groups and bridge some gaps in the thinking about the role of entrepreneurship in community and economic development. Presenting the current thinking about the importance of entrepreneurship approaches in local development strategies, especially in rural areas, can help practitioners evaluate them as a community or economic development strategy.

The entrepreneurship literature is huge and ranges from psychological characteristics of entrepreneurs to a very practical issue of the best way to help business entrepreneurs finance ventures. It would be naïve to think that the literature can be summarized in one volume; however, key components of successful programs can be distilled to help guide practitioners in their efforts.

The book is organized into two main sections to accommodate the needs of both groups. The first section addresses conceptual issues that local development practitioners should consider in evaluating entrepreneurship as a strategy. These chapters review the academic and professional literature and, in general, make a strong case for entrepreneurship initiatives. The second section discusses the role of small businesses in local economic development, specific needs for assistance, and successful programs that have been initiated. The discussion concludes with questions that can guide practitioners interested in launching a local entrepreneurship effort.

Because creating and implementing a successful entrepreneurship strategy requires involvement and participation by many groups and agencies within a community, this book contains several broad themes of interest to local elected officials, volunteers, and community or economic development practitioners. The discussions are designed to help community leaders and professionals decide whether, and how, they might incorporate entrepreneurship practices into local development strategies.

The treatment in subsequent chapters runs from purely objective analyses of entrepreneurial processes and environments to detailed examples of how similar concepts have been used successfully in rural areas. The latter examples have been selected to illustrate how basic principles have been incorporated and have led to success. They do not represent an objective evaluation of entrepreneurship as a strategy. Rather, they identify important considerations underlying successes so that practitioners can more readily implement these principles or practices.

The local development and job creation literature can be confusing in its use of terms related to entrepreneurs, entrepreneurship, small businesses, and microenterprises, so several definitions are especially important in this volume.

First, entrepreneurship does not relate only to business start-ups. Large businesses can be just as entrepreneurial in approach, and managers of these businesses can be considered entrepreneurs. Perhaps the deciding criterion in defining entrepreneurship or an entrepreneurial approach, as discussed by Brian Dabson in chapter 2, is that an investor or manager takes an innovative approach to addressing an issue and does something differently from past practices.

Also true is that small businesses can be started and can even succeed without following especially entrepreneurial practices. The market may adopt some businesses when the timing is right for a specific product or service. While this differentiation may not seem important, it does mean that practitioners must try to identify and foster potential business investors who are willing to take risks, have an innovative approach, and who are willing to do something markedly different and/or better than what previously was done. These entrepreneurs may already be in business or may be launching a new venture.

Second, the terms *small businesses* and *microenterprises* are used frequently in this volume. The Small Business Administration considers *small businesses* those with 500 or fewer employees (Crain 2005). Devins (1999) and Kangasharju (2001) use ten employees as a cut-off. The terms *microenterprise* or *microbusiness* are used in subsequent discussions to describe very small businesses such as those in which the owner has no employees or has four employees or less according to the Association of Enterprise Opportunity (AEO) (2006). Woods and Muske (chapter 10) discuss the issue of business size in more detail and show how microbusinesses should be considered a subset of small businesses with special needs for assistance.

## BOOK THEMES

Discussions in this volume address several main themes of interest to local practitioners considering an entrepreneurship development approach. Clearly not all of the issues surrounding entrepreneurship are discussed but, to the extent possible, those important for local practitioners are identified and applied in the best practices section.

### Innate Ability versus Training

For many years, the prevailing view was that entrepreneurs are born rather than trained. To some extent, this attitude may have slowed the acceptance of entrepreneurship as a development strategy because it implies that relatively little could be done to promote or develop entrepreneurs.

This view is now open to serious debate with solid research support on both sides.

Lyons, Lichtenstein, and Kutzhanova (chapter 6) make a strong case that local institutions can, in fact, provide entrepreneurs with the skills needed to help them succeed, but this process requires an integrated approach by service providers. A system must work with entrepreneurs at their levels of development to provide training, finance, or other assistance in a timely fashion based on the needs of entrepreneurs. Communities often already have many, if not most, of the relevant service providers, but lack a system that makes service providers function as a team responding to the needs of entrepreneurs rather than focusing on programs required by funding agencies.

## Culture of Entrepreneurship

Creating a scenario to foster entrepreneurial activities in the private or public sector is difficult because many factors, personalities, and circumstances are involved. Entrepreneurial activity requires motivation and opportunities and, in this respect, it involves both talent and skills. A climate conducive to innovation and sharing among entrepreneurs may also lure people with similar talents to an area and further enhance entrepreneurial efforts. The concept of Open-Source Entrepreneurship where everyone gains from more interaction and networking among entrepreneurs is the basis of several successful programs.

Fairfield, Iowa (pop. 9,509), is a prime example of the evolution and development of an entrepreneurial climate (Chojnowski 2006). The location of Maharisi University in a relatively small midwestern community changed the culture and ways of approaching issues. The result was the attraction of people willing to start businesses or engage in other innovations not often found in small rural communities. The immigrants and Fairfield residents created a synergy that fosters innovation and creativity. The outcome is a small community with an impressive list of innovations, inventions, diverse new businesses, and philanthropy that would be the envy of most communities of similar size. Whether a similar experience and outcomes can be easily replicated in other communities is unknown. What is clear is that an entrepreneurial environment, however created, underlies these successes.

Hustedde (chapter 3) describes the importance of culture(s) within a community and its role in fostering entrepreneurship. Designing and shaping an environment in which people take risks, share resources, and otherwise assist each other in fostering innovation is important, and public agencies can have a major impact on building and shaping this environment. Hustedde describes seven strategies used successfully to create an environment in which entrepreneurship can prosper. These strategies are based on a shared vision and a systems thinking approach. Examples of communities or regions that have effectively used these strategies or practices are provided.

## Focus on Youth

There is no disagreement about the importance of youth in the future of rural areas but it is increasingly difficult to attract high school graduates and young adults back to their home communities as differentials in wages and economic opportunities between urban and rural areas widen. Successful entrepreneurship strategies can be an effective strategy to retaining and/or attracting youth.

Entrepreneurship development offers several opportunities to help slow the loss of youth and integrate them more fully into the future of rural areas. If students become interested in starting businesses, they will invest in their community and, at the same time, provide employment opportunities for peers. This commitment enhances the likelihood that they will remain in the community as adults.

Past studies have shown a strong interest among students in owning a business (Gallup Organization and NCREE 1994). All too often, because of other pressures on the curriculum and a shortage of resources, schools have not focused on entrepreneurship or business ownership as a career choice; instead, they prepare students for higher education and careers not readily available in rural areas. Fortunately, programs that can prepare students for entrepreneurship exist and there is considerable evidence of programs such as REAL that have taken root with positive results.

Two chapters are devoted to the role that education plays in preparing entrepreneurs, especially youth, and successful ways in involving youth in entrepreneurship activities. Schroeder (chapter 8) describes ways communities across the United States have fostered youth entrepreneurship. He also discusses the setting or climate in a community that encourages students to engage and succeed in these efforts, followed by best practices to illustrate these approaches. An important message is the need for an integrated youth entrepreneurship development strategy that engages students, equips them to undertake entrepreneurial efforts, and then supports their efforts and outcomes.

Since a major issue in designing local entrepreneurship development initiatives involves identifying potential entrepreneurs and motivating them, Kayne (chapter 9) describes the basic practices and principles involved in designing programs to attract youth. A main point is that students should be introduced to entrepreneurship skills in their educational pursuits, as early as in elementary school. This approach, rather than focusing on business involvement per se, should recognize, foster, and reward student creativity in a variety of ways.

Students who find satisfaction in their individualism and creativity during the early years are more likely to pursue entrepreneurial ventures, including businesses, when they reach adolescence and young adulthood. Equally important is that entrepreneurship principles are best taught not as an add-on to the school curriculum; rather, they should be incorporated into other subjects. Kayne also describes resources available for schools to use in incorporating entrepreneurship into the classroom.

### Financial Support

Increasing residents' interest in entrepreneurship, creating a positive environment or culture to promote business start-ups, and working with population segments such as youth is only part of the equation. New business entrepreneurs must have access to financial capital, of which, much or most, comes from their own savings and those of their families and friends.

It is important for communities considering entrepreneurship as a development strategy to empower and encourage local financial institutions to actively support local efforts. This is true of all business starts, not only those involving entrepreneurs in the sense used here. Financial institutions in rural areas do not always have a staff with the resources or expertise to evaluate business opportunities, especially in emerging markets. These institutions also follow more conservative lending strategies, requiring collateral that is difficult for entrepreneurs to provide. Likewise, small financial institutions with minimal staff may be less willing to participate in guaranteed loan programs available from the Small Business Administration or other agencies.

Alternative funding arrangements such as angel investors or venture capital funds used by urban entrepreneurs typically are not as readily available in rural areas. Markley (chapter 7) describes several options for rural areas to consider in increasing the availability of start-up funds for prospective entrepreneurs. The fact that local economic development agencies in most communities have limited resources places a special burden on policymakers to make a strong case for entrepreneurship initiatives.

Financing entrepreneurship programs often means reallocating resources from other more established efforts such as industrial attraction. Adequate funding may also require involvement by philanthropic organizations and civic groups. As is true in starting any new endeavor, policymakers must demonstrate the potential for positive impacts of entrepreneurship efforts on a community. This justification can build on best practices in other communities and on a serious assessment of the potential for local entrepreneurship efforts. Discussions in this volume can help community leaders make a strong case for a variety of local entrepreneurship efforts.

## Potential and Role of Microenterprises in Local Development

The point was made earlier that entrepreneurship can exist in virtually any size establishment as well as in the public sector. Small businesses, however, are especially important in rural areas with small markets. For this reason, special attention is paid to the importance of small businesses, entrepreneurial or otherwise, in local development.

Henderson, Low, and Weiler (chapter 5) examine the breadth (quantity of entrepreneurs) and depth (value created) of self-employment in regional economies across the United States. They also examine spatial variations in the importance and effects of entrepreneurship in metro and nonmetro counties, testing for the effects of human capital, amenities, financial capital, and infrastructure based on proprietor employment and income data. The results from this national study demonstrate that entrepreneurship, as measured by proprietors, is influenced by, among other factors, the concentration of foreign-born residents, amenities, financial capital, infrastructure, region of the United States, and whether a county is micro- or metropolitan.

Small businesses, however measured, are a mainstay of many rural counties and often represent one-third or more of the total employment in rural areas (Walzer, Athiyaman, and Hamm, chapter 4). Walzer, Athiyaman, and Hamm examine microenterprises, when defined as those with either no employees (other than the owner) or four employees or fewer. They study the percentage of total nonfarm employment represented by these establishments in rural counties in six midwestern states and the rate of change in the number of these businesses in recent years. The authors address several issues such as identifying the likelihood of potential sources of entrepreneurs. For instance, the impact of county business structure on attracting entrepreneurial talents to the county is examined as is the effect of natural amenities such as perceptions about quality of life on entrepreneurship. While the midwestern and the national studies differ in approach and region, they both offer insights to practitioners regarding groups to target in entrepreneurship initiatives, and shed light on the potential impact of successful entrepreneurship programs on local economies. This information can help find or reallocate resources to these initiatives along with other development pursuits.

Once businesses start, owners and managers often need considerable assistance with marketing and daily operations such as financing. This need has been documented many times by the high closure rate of small businesses (Macke and Kayne 2001). Woods and Muske (chapter 10) examine the reported needs of small business owners and managers along with options for providing assistance. The issues with which small business owners require assistance often involve daily operations from such issues as health insurance and governmental regulations to identifying potential customer bases and marketing products or services.

While many local sources of technical assistance on these issues may be available, they often are not interconnected or, as mentioned previously, are not provided in a systematic way. The research by Woods and Muske reinforces the view that successful entrepreneurship programs should involve an integrated approach where entrepreneurship is part of an organized local economic development strategy. This system must be community-wide with full support from both public and private agencies.

## Best Practices

Successful entrepreneurship efforts differ, depending on community size, location, economic base, and population characteristics. Some use broad development approaches while others target specific industries or population groups. Regardless of approach, the important point in designing or starting a local initiative is that many successful models can work in a community.

Best practices, including one statewide and one regional, are provided to illustrate how the entrepreneurship concepts outlined previously have been, or can be, incorporated into successful local initiatives. Macke (chapter 11) describes several statewide initiatives, including HomeTown Competitiveness (HTC). These programs have several common characteristics that maximize the possibilities of success in launching a local effort.

The HTC, started in Nebraska in 2000, is especially useful because it is a broad, community-wide effort that incorporates many, if not most, of the principles for successful programs set forth earlier in this volume. It helps communities raise local funds and support through community foundations that foster an integrated approach to community development. The program focuses on youth entrepreneurs as well as building leadership capacity in other groups to make economic development sustainable. The HTC approach is only one of several successful statewide initiatives across the United States that illustrate the types of efforts to consider in designing a local strategy.

Not all successful entrepreneurship programs are organized statewide; in some cases, it is more reasonable to consider a regional effort, building on local assets such as used in Ohio. Holley (chapter 12) describes the Appalachian Center for Economic Networks (ACEnet) which created a Regional Innovation Economy in the rural Appalachian region of southern Ohio. This highly acclaimed entrepreneurship program started with a community kitchen incubator where residents can experiment and develop local recipes and market them to a regional and national markets.

The ACEnet strategy builds on local assets, namely specialty foods using local agricultural inputs, and is aptly called Entrepreneurship with a Local

Flavor. The initial approach is a model in design since it networks a broad range of residents with special skills, helps arrange financing, and focuses on building a sustainable initiative.

The kitchen incubator program has since broadened to a Regional Innovation Economy that promotes a Regional Flavor for a relatively rural area. Participating businesses serve a regional, rather than local, market which is often essential to success in rural areas. Community involvement has been high, and a successful "buy local" approach is key in the successes. A regional innovation fund and support services have been created to provide access to capital and technical assistance for start-ups and expansions. The region is also marketed using a recognizable brand.

## GETTING STARTED

The need for a community approach to entrepreneurship in rural areas and basic principles or practices underlying successful approaches are documented throughout this volume. The relative importance of small businesses in rural economies was documented with a wealth of experience on various facets of entrepreneurial approaches and best practices provided.

The final chapter helps local leaders determine whether a community is ready for an entrepreneurial approach and ways to identify strengths or gaps. Loveridge (chapter 13) incorporates discussions throughout this volume into a set of guidelines that practitioners can use in evaluating readiness and ways to proceed.

Specifically, Loveridge focuses on three main topics: (1) Community and Networks, (2) Finance and Regulations, and (3) Training and Mentoring. These areas are crucial in designing an effective system, although each can be addressed in many ways depending on unique local characteristics. Community leaders can score their potential for a successful entrepreneurship initiative and use these questions as guides to build capacity. The questions in this chapter are not meant to prescribe how a community should proceed; instead, they help practitioners assess the directions that a community might take in formulating a program or initiative. An overriding and compelling point is that the ultimate aim of undertaking a community-based entrepreneurial initiative is to improve the quality of life and prosperity of residents rather than focusing solely on starting business ventures.

## CONCLUDING OBSERVATIONS

Major economic transitions affecting rural areas have forced community leaders and development practitioners to find alternative and innovative ways to rebuild the economic base and improve the quality of life for residents.

Industrial attraction models have been less successful in smaller and remote areas than in the past, causing leaders to consider a stronger emphasis on finding ways to start or expand businesses.

Entrepreneurship programs in rural areas have shown impressive results. While certainly no panacea, they represent a solid economic development strategy that can be used along with other approaches. Entrepreneurship offers potential in both community and economic development but must be community-wide with an integrated delivery system aimed at building a sustainable initiative.

This book provides an overview of principles and practices that can help local practitioners design a successful system. While an entrepreneurship approach may not be the best alternative for all rural areas, the discussions in this volume support that this approach can work and should at least be considered by local development practitioners.

## REFERENCES

Acs, Zoltan C., and Catherine Armington. 2005. Using census BITS to explore entrepreneurship, geography, and economic growth. *Small Business Research Summary* 248 (February): 1–45.

Association for Enterprise Opportunity (AEO). 2006. *About microenterprises.* AEO. www.miroenterworks.org/index.asp?sid=17 (December 6, 2006).

Bhuian, Shahid, and Moshin Habib. 2004. The relationship between entrepreneurship, market orientation and performance: A test in Saudi Arabia. *Journal of Transnational Management* 10(1): 79–98.

Birch, David L. 1987. *Job creation in America: How our smallest companies put the most people to work.* New York: Free Press.

Bruce, Donald, John A. Deskins, Brian C. Hill, and Jonathan C. Rork. 2007. *Small business and state growth: An econometric investigation (Report #292).* Washington, DC: Small Business Administration.

Bygrave, William D., and Stephen A. Hunt. 2005. *Global Entrepreneurship Monitor 2004 financing report.* Babson Park, MA and London: Babson College and London Business School. www.gemconsortium.org/download/1174354235250/GEM _2004_Financing_Report.pdf (August 18, 2006).

Chojnowski, Burt. 2006. Open-source rural entrepreneurial development. *Rural Research Report* 17(2). Macomb: Illinois Institute for Rural Affairs, Western Illinois University.

Corporation for Enterprise Development (CED). 2006. *REAL entrepreneurship education: A history.* www.cfed.org/focus.m?parentid=32&siteid=341&id=343 (August 18, 2006).

Cosh, Andy, Douglas Cumming, and Alan Hughes. 2005. *Outside entrepreneurial capital,* Working Paper: ESRC Centre for Business Research.

Crain, W. Mark. 2005. *The impact of regulatory costs on small firms.* Washington, DC: U.S. Small Business Administration, Office of Advocacy.

De Clercq, Dirk, Harry Sapienza, and Hans Crijns. 2005. The internationalization of small and medium-sized firms. *Small Business Economics* 24(4): 409-19.

Demsetz, Harold. 1997. The firm in economic theory: A quiet revolution. *AEA Papers and Proceedings*: 426-29.

Devins, David. 1999. Supporting established micro businesses: Policy issues emerging from an evaluation. *International Small Business Journal* 18(1): 86-97.

Evans, George H. 1949. The entrepreneur and economic theory: A historical and analytical approach. *American Economic Review* 39(3): 336-48.

Flora, J. L. 1998. Social capital and communities of place. *Rural Sociology* 63(4): 481-506.

Florida, Richard. 2002. *The rise of the creative class, and how it's transforming work, leisure and everyday life*. New York: Basic Books.

Gallup Organization, Inc. and National Center for Research in Economic Education (NCREE). 1994. *Entrepreneurship and small business in the United States: A survey report on the views of the general public, high school students, and small business owners and managers*. Kansas City, MO: Center for Entrepreneurial Leadership, Inc., Ewing Marion Kauffman Foundation.

Goetz, Stephan, and Anil Rupasingha. 2005. How the returns to education in rural areas vary across the nation. In *The role of education: Promoting the economic and social vitality of rural America*, ed. Lionel J. Beaulieu and Robert Gibbs, 6-9. Mississippi State, MS: Southern Rural Development Center.

Grozdanic, Radmilla. 2006. Staff restructuring at public companies and entrepreneurial tools. *Tourism and Hospitality Management* 12(1): 119-130.

Harrod, Roy F. 1948. *Toward a dynamic economics*. London: Macmillan Publishers, Ltd.

Ibeh, Kevin. 2003. Toward a contingency framework of export entrepreneurship: Conceptualizations and empirical evidence. *Small Business Economics* 20(1): 49-68.

Ireland, Duane, Christopher Reutzel, and Justin Webb. 2005. Entrepreneurship research in AMJ: What has been published, and what might the future hold. *Academy of Management Journal* 48(4): 556-64.

Kangasharju, A. 2001. Growth of the smallest: Determinants of small firm growth during strong macroeconomic fluctuations. *International Small Business Journal* 19(1): 28-43.

Kyriakopoulos, Kyriakos, Matthew Muelenberg, and Jerker Nilsson. 2004. The impact of cooperative structure and firm culture on market orientation and performance. *Agribusiness* 20(4): 379-96.

Lee, Sang M., and Suzanne Peterson. 2000. Culture, entrepreneurial orientation, and global competitiveness. *Journal of World Business* 35(4): 401-16.

Lindsay, Noel. 2004. Do business angels have an entrepreneurial orientation? *Venture Capital* 6(2-3): 197-210.

Low, Murray. 2001. The adolescence of entrepreneurship research: Specification of purpose. *Entrepreneurship Theory and Practice* 25(4): 17-25.

Lumpkin, G. T., and Gregory Dess. 2000. Clarifying the entrepreneurial orientation construct and linking it to performance. *Advances in Entrepreneurship* 1: 136-73, Elgar Reference Collection, Cheltenham, UK and Northampton, MA: Elgar.

Lyons, T. S. 2001. Building social capital for sustainable enterprise development in country towns and regions: Successful practices from the United States. In *The future of Australia's country towns.* ed. M. F. Rogers and Y. M. J. Collins, 94–112. Bendigo, Victoria, Australia: Centre for Sustainable Regional Communities, La Trobe University.

Macke, Don, and Joseph Kayne. 2001. *Rural entrepreneurship: Environmental scan.* Columbia, MO: Center for Rural Entrepreneurship.

Maritz, A., and G. Nieman. 2006. Entrepreneurial orientation in a franchised home entertainment system. *South African Journal of Economic and Management Sciences* 9(1): 1–16.

McDaniel, Bruce A. 2005. A contemporary view of Joseph A. Schumpeter's theory of the entrepreneur. *Journal of Economic Issues* 29(2): 485–89.

Mody, Ashoka. 1999. *Industrial policy after the East Asian crisis: From outward orientation to new internal capabilities?* The World Bank, Policy Research Working Paper Series 2112.

Munnich, Lee W., Jr. 2002. Rural knowledge clusters: The challenge of rural economic prosperity. *Reviews of Economic Development Literature and Practice.* No. 12. Washington, DC: Economic Development Administration.

National Governor's Association (NGA). 2004. *A governor's guide to strengthening state entrepreneurship policy.* Washington, DC: NGA Center for Best Practices.

Osborne, David and Ted Gaebler. 1993. *Reinventing Government: How the Entrepreneurial Spirit Is Transforming the Public Sector.* New York: Penguin Books, Inc.

O'Shea, Rory, Thomas Allen, Arnaud Chevalier, and Frank Roche. 2005. Entrepreneurial orientation, technology transfer and spin-off performance of US universities. *Research Policy* 34(7): 994–1009.

Parker, Rachel. 2002. Coordination and competition in small business policy: a comparative analysis of Australia and Denmark. *Journal of Economic Issues* 36(4): 935–52.

Research Center in Entrepreneurial History. 1949. *Change and the entrepreneur: Postulates and patterns of entrepreneurial history.* Cambridge, MA: Harvard University.

Schenkel, Mark T. 2006. Book Review: *Pioneers in entrepreneurship and small business research.* By Hans Landstrom. New York: Springer Science + Business Media, 2005.

Schlosser, Francine K., and William Todorovic. 2006. Entrepreneurial charisma: a key to employee identification? *Journal of Small Business and Entrepreneurship* 19(1): 49–62.

Schumpeter, Joseph Alois. 1934. *The theory of economic development: an inquiry into profits, capital, credit, interest, and the business cycle.* Harvard economic studies, vol. XLVI. Cambridge, MA: Harvard University Press.

Schumpeter, Joseph Alois. 1950. *Capitalism, socialism, and democracy* (3rd ed.). New York: Harper and Row.

Shaffer, Sherrill. 2006. Establishment size and local employment growth. *Small Business Economics* 26: 439–54.

Shaffer, Sherrill. 2002. Firm size and economic growth. *Economics Letters* 76: 195–203.

Soltow, James H. 1968. The entrepreneurship in economic history. *American Economic Review* 58(2): 84–92.

Todorovic, Zelimir. W. 2004. The framework of static and dynamic components: An examination of entrepreneurial orientation and university ability to teach entrepreneurship. *Journal of Small Business and Entrepreneurship* 17(4): 301–16.

Walzer, Norman (Ed.). 2003. *The American Midwest: Managing change in rural transition.* Armonk, NY: M. E. Sharpe, Inc.

Williams, Lori E. 2004. Entrepreneurial education: Creating a usable economic base. *Rural Research Report* 15(8). Macomb: Illinois Institute for Rural Affairs.

Wilkens, Paul H. 1979. *Entrepreneurship: A comparative and historical study.* Norwood, NJ: Ablex Publishing Corporation.

# 2

# Entrepreneurship as Rural Economic Development Policy: A Changing Paradigm

*Brian Dabson*

## DEFINING ENTREPRENEURSHIP FOR POLICYMAKERS

Across the United States and indeed across the world, entrepreneurship has become an article of faith, reflecting a confidence and certainty that its facilitation will lead to positive economic outcomes. Although scholars and researchers worry about how to appropriately define the terms *entrepreneur* and *entrepreneurship*, growing numbers of policymakers and grassroots community developers are exploring how entrepreneurship can transform local and regional economies and provide solutions to poverty and inequitable development.

An impetus for the interest in entrepreneurship is the recognition that, for many communities and regions, traditional approaches to economic development do not seem to be working, even though substantial resources continue to be devoted to or set aside for recruiting corporations interested in relocating or expanding. Increasingly, the conversation is about how local assets can be engaged to create homegrown economic opportunities as opposed to importing them from elsewhere.[1] Thus, the role of entrepreneurs as the catalyst that transforms assets into opportunity has become a topic of intense practical interest.

Academic discussions about entrepreneurship usually begin by tracing its roots back to Say, Schumpeter, Knight, Hayek, Drucker, and Baumol.[2] These discussions focus on trying to determine what distinguishes entrepreneurs and entrepreneurship from other economic actors and activities. Economists, sociologists, anthropologists, psychologists, and political scientists have weighed in with their disciplinary perspectives, and it is clear that entrepreneurship has become a legitimate and fruitful area of scholarly inquiry (see Lyons, Lichtenstein, and Kutzhanova, chapter 6). These discussions are important to the policymaking process because they may eventually help to identify where public policy can best encourage and foster entrepreneurship. As David Hart (2003) argues, "entrepreneurship ought to be an explicit focus of policy design, choice, and implementation. Analysts can and should do a much better job of assisting policy-makers in making it so" (4).

One of the main challenges for entrepreneurship policy is to be clear about what is meant by *entrepreneurship* as distinct from small business development. For most purposes, it is sufficient to apply a broad definition such as "entrepreneurs are people who create and grow enterprises" (Dabson et al. 2003) or "entrepreneurship is any attempt to create a new business enterprise or to expand an established business" (Zacharakis, Bygrave, and Shepard 2000, 5) or "the processes of starting and continuing to expand new businesses" (Hart 2003, 5).

As Peter Drucker (1985) observes, however, not every new small business is entrepreneurial or represents entrepreneurship—most repeat what has already been done before, creating "neither a new satisfaction nor new consumer demand" (21). Entrepreneurs, he continues, "create something new, something different; they change or transmute values" (22). Drucker also helpfully points out that not every entrepreneurial venture is small; indeed, large corporations can be and often are entrepreneurial. Further, he adds, not every entrepreneurial venture is an economic institution, it can be a university or a nonprofit agency; not all entrepreneurs are capitalists, some are pursuing social causes; and not all entrepreneurs are employers, they can also be employees.

What Drucker (1985) sees as the defining characteristic of an entrepreneur is not the venture size, nor its newness, nor its institutional form, but the willingness and ability to innovate: "Innovation is the specific instrument of entrepreneurship. It is the act that endows resources with a new capacity to create wealth" (30).

It would be a mistake for policy purposes, however, to narrow the definition to particular types of entrepreneurs—for instance, those which are deemed innovative or are to be found in a specific high-technology sector. It is impossible to identify in advance which entrepreneur will grow and have a significant economic impact. The policy goal should be to mobilize a diverse pool of people wanting to create new businesses from which a steady stream of growth entrepreneurs will drive the local and regional economy (Dabson 2003).

To amplify this assertion, it is necessary to turn to data about the nature and characteristics of entrepreneurship and small business development. In 2000, there were about 21 million employer and nonemployer firms in the United States, of which some 76 percent were nonemployer firms.[3] In spite of their large numbers, these firms accounted for only 4 percent of total business revenues, however. *Small* businesses with annual revenues of less than $90,000 represent 95 percent of nonemployer firms and just 38 percent of business revenues; whereas, small businesses account for 25 percent of employer firms but less than 5 percent of business revenues. Similarly, *young* businesses (less than four years old) represent just over 40 percent of nonemployer businesses with some 37 percent of business revenues, and about 35 percent of employer businesses accounting for less than 20 percent of revenues.

Although their economic impact is relatively small compared with longer-established employer businesses, Davis et al. (2005) claim that these small and young enterprises are important because they are a critical part of U.S. business dynamics. They support the notion that small nonemployers are a seedbed for future employment growth because over a three-year time frame, about 5 percent of nonemployer businesses (accounting for 10 percent of nonemployer business revenues) became employer businesses or were acquired by, or absorbed into, employer businesses. This equates to 750,000 businesses. Moreover, these newer firms that are transitioning to employer businesses are the fastest growing in the economy.

As part of the Global Entrepreneurship Monitor (GEM) program, Autio and Hancock (2005) analyzed what they termed *High Expectation Entrepreneurial Activity* or HEE. They defined HEE as all start-ups and newly formed businesses which expect to have at least 20 employees within 5 years. Their findings showed that these businesses represent just 9.8 percent of the total pool (and that only 4.9 percent expected to employ more than 50 people in that timeframe). Even so, they estimate that HEE will be responsible for 75 percent of the jobs created by all start-ups and newly formed businesses.

These studies make clear that the return in terms of jobs and wealth from entrepreneurship development will come only from between 1 in 10 to 1 in 20 ventures. Although there have been many attempts to isolate predictors of these high-flying entrepreneurs, including suggestions by Autio and Hancock (2005), *picking winners* is inherently risky and not a recommended basis for public policy. One factor to consider is that people creating enterprises have different motivations, which might limit or shape their aspirations, or which may evolve over time with experience.

A typology used in a recent Kellogg Foundation/CFED report (Dabson et al. 2003) on rural entrepreneurship identifies five types of entrepreneurs. *Aspiring* entrepreneurs are those who are attracted to the idea of creating an enterprise but have yet to launch a venture. Of those already in business, *survival* entrepreneurs have resorted to creating enterprises either to supplement existing, inadequate incomes or are those with few other options for obtaining employment; and *lifestyle* entrepreneurs are those who create enterprises in order to pursue a certain lifestyle or live in a specific community.

It is generally assumed that although survival and lifestyle enterprises, without doubt, make significant contributions to their local economies, only a very small fraction will evolve into companies that will become economic drivers based on some form of innovation. It would be a mistake, however, to dismiss these enterprises as unimportant in policy terms—not only because of their local economic impact, but also because they do still provide a seedbed for potential economic drivers, and they contribute to an overall entrepreneurial climate in their community and region.

There are two more types of entrepreneur: (1) *growth* entrepreneurs, who are motivated to grasp opportunities and to develop and grow their businesses that create jobs and wealth, and (2) *serial* entrepreneurs, who make a career out of creating businesses, often selling them once they are successful, and sometimes assembling multienterprise holding companies. Obviously, growth and serial entrepreneurs are of most interest to policymakers because they are likely to yield the highest return on investments—ironically, it is these entrepreneurs who are the least likely to want or need assistance from formal sources.

## THE GLOBAL CONTEXT FOR ENTREPRENEURSHIP

A slightly different distinction is made by the GEM, which classifies entrepreneurs both by their stage in the *entrepreneurial life cycle* and by two primary motivations (Minitti 2006). GEM is an annual cross-national assessment of entrepreneurial activity, which for the 2005 edition had 35 participating countries. Its purpose is to measure differences in the level of entrepreneurial activity between countries, to uncover factors determining the levels of entrepreneurial activity, and to identify policies that may enhance the level of entrepreneurial activity.

Data is collected over the life cycle of the entrepreneurship process with three critical points examined: (1) when an entrepreneur (ages 18 to 64) commits resources or starts a business, termed a *nascent* entrepreneur; (2) when she or he owns and manages a business that has paid salaries for more than 3 months but less than 42 months, known as a *new business owner*; and (3) when she or he owns and manages an established business that has been in operation for more than 42 months, known as an *established business owner*. Nascent entrepreneurs and new business owners can be combined into a category of *early-stage entrepreneurs*. Established business owners have survived the liability of newness at which point the focus shifts from the individual to the businesses.

The other distinction made by GEM is between early-stage entrepreneurs who are either opportunity or necessity entrepreneurs. *Opportunity* entrepreneurs are those who start businesses because they recognize an opportunity which they think they can turn into a business venture; *necessity* entrepreneurs, on the other hand, start businesses because of a lack of better job alternatives—similar to the survival entrepreneurs referred to earlier.

GEM is especially useful in providing an indication of how the United States compares with other countries, and the key measure here is *entrepreneurial activity*, expressed as a percentage of the population, ages 18 to 64 who are engaged in early stage entrepreneurship and established business ownership (Minitti 2006). The argument is made that there is a systematic relationship between the per capita GDP of a country, its economic growth, and its level and type of entrepreneurial activity.

The United States ranks sixth in entrepreneurial activity in early-stage entrepreneurship with 12.4 percent of the population engaged—the average across the 35 countries is 8.4 percent. For established business ownership, the United States drops to 26th (4.7 percent), well below the average rate of 6.6 percent. The critical *dynamic* measurement is the survival rate expressed as the ratio of established businesses to early-stage enterprises, however: here, the United States ranks 31st of 35. Another important ratio is the one that shows the proportion of opportunity entrepreneurs to necessity entrepreneurs. The average ratio across the 35 countries is 5.9 to 1; the ratio for the United States is 7.2 to 1, giving it a ranking of 8th.

The position of the United States with high levels of early-stage entrepreneurship and a low survival rate can perhaps be explained by two factors. First, the United States's opportunity-oriented culture and high incomes spur entrepreneurship even if chances of success are relatively poor. This is helped by the fact that failure is less stigmatized than in many countries.

Second, poorer regions across the United States have higher levels of necessity entrepreneurship—people without many viable alternatives start businesses even though long-term prospects may not be too favorable. From an entrepreneurship policy viewpoint, it seems clear that the issue is less about encouraging more people to consider entrepreneurship, although this undoubtedly has critical importance in certain parts of the country, and more about how to increase the survival rate of businesses that are created.

The comparative entrepreneurial performance of the United States has increased relevance in considering the impacts of global competition. Thomas Friedman's (2005) recent book, *The World Is Flat*, based largely on visits to India and China, provided his assessment that the world has changed almost beyond recognition in the past decade and that the days of the United States having global economic supremacy are numbered. His analysis has been the subject of considerable debate, but there are some useful specific contextual implications for U.S. entrepreneurship development.

In considering how American workers and communities can prepare for and withstand the impact of increasing global competition on their economic opportunities, Friedman (2005) has identified three categories of people who will be largely protected from outsourcing of their jobs and future job prospects: (1) *specialized* workers are knowledge workers whose skills are in high demand and hard to replicate; (2) *anchored* workers are those who are tied to a specific location and who rely on face-to-face contacts with customers, clients, and patients; and (3) *adaptable* workers, who are able to change as jobs change and who accordingly acquire new skills. This emphasis on knowledge and adaptability tracks well with entrepreneurial skills and underscores the point that entrepreneurship can be both a strategy for survival in, and for grasping opportunities that may arise from, the disturbances that are associated with a flattening world. An interesting point about anchored workers is that Friedman seems to be acknowledging that place does still have relevance and meaning in the global economy.

## Regional Competitiveness as Economic Driver

But how does *place* play out in entrepreneurship development policy? As the debates have raged about the costs and benefits of global trade, it has become apparent that the distribution of its consequences and opportunities is not evenly spread, and that approaches to economic development must reflect this new reality. The essence of these new approaches is that economic regions are now the basic unit of global competitiveness, that competitiveness is founded on the identification and leverage of a unique combination of regional assets, and that innovation and entrepreneurship are the keys to translating these regional assets into global competitiveness.

An advisory committee appointed by the U.S. Secretary of Commerce recently reported its findings on the federal role in economic development. The committee's review of the evolution of economic development during the past half-century and of the forces that are currently shaping local and national economies concluded that "In the 21st century, America's communities will derive economic strength by acting regionally to compete globally. Innovation and entrepreneurship are the new engines for job creation, productivity, growth, economic prosperity, and healthy communities" (Strengthening America's Communities Advisory Committee 2005, 8).

A 2001 Council on Competitiveness report prepared by Michael Porter (2001) suggested that thinking on regional competitiveness was undergoing a significant transition. In many regions, the emphasis still focused on holding down wages, reducing taxes, and recruiting new companies using financial incentives. This emphasis, the Council argued, was self-defeating because cheap labor and natural resources are widely (globally) available, low wages do not yield competitiveness but hold down the standard of living, and financial incentives are easily matched by competing regions and only serve to undermine the tax base needed to invest in education and infrastructure.

If the aim is to increase regional prosperity, the focus must be on sustained productivity growth, which is at the very heart of competitiveness. The Council asserts that sustained productivity growth requires an understanding and adoption of several key principles.

Productivity does not depend on in *which* industries a region competes but on *how* it competes—the challenge is not to pick winners but to upgrade the sophistication and productivity of its industries. The most important sources of productivity are *created* not inherited—competitiveness is not the exploitation of location, natural resources, or low-cost workers; rather, it is converting these assets into intellectual capital and added value.

Regional prosperity depends on the productivity of *all* its industries and assets—even local services and infrastructure can have considerable impact on the performance of exporting industries. There are no low-tech industries, only low-tech firms—innovation can drive productivity in any industry so a sole focus on high-tech companies misses major opportunities to increase regional competitiveness.

Richard Florida's (2005) work has suggested that the most successful regional economies are those which have a combination of assets that attract creative talent such as the presence of other creative people, access to technology and technological advances, and the tolerance of the community to diversity and difference. He also argues that place matters, and those places which offer a quality of life—both urban and outdoors—sought by creative people will become the new centers of economic competitiveness.

Florida (2005) believes that the ascendancy of certain professions and occupations associated with the new economy has given rise to a *Creative Class* that now drives the competitive economy. The core of this class includes the fields of computers and math, architecture and engineering, the social sciences, education, arts, design, entertainment, sports, and the media. He estimates that the Creative Class now numbers 38 million people and that this class will grow by a further 10 million people in the next ten years.

At the same time, there are two other classes—one comprising those working in the traditional manufacturing and agricultural industries that will continue to decline in their relative share of the economy, and the other being the Service Class, which is and will continue to be the largest group by numbers of jobs, but which will only pay one-third of what jobs in the Creative Class are paid. In other words, Florida sees a growing cleavage between the well-educated and well-paid with global opportunities on the one hand and the less-educated and poorly-paid with limited prospects on the other.

Florida (2005) sees these trends playing out regionally and globally, with successful regional economies having a combination of assets that attract creative people, what he calls the three Ts—talent, technology, and tolerance. Metropolitan regions with concentrations of creative talent, access to technology and technological advances, and which welcome diversity and difference, he argues, will be the leaders in the global economy.

## Entrepreneurship for Competitive Rural Regions

The key to rural competitiveness is to pursue entrepreneurship as *the* core rural economic development strategy. There are several reasons for this. First and foremost, the traditional reliance on recruiting companies to relocate or expand into rural communities is just not working for most places, and leaders are looking for viable alternatives. Second, there is a growing awareness of the body of evidence, as referred to earlier, on the critical role played by entrepreneurs and small businesses in driving local and national economies. Third, the structure of rural economies is essentially composed of small enterprises, which are responsible for job growth and innovation, and which represent an appropriate scale of activity for rural places.

A recent review of entrepreneurship programs across rural America concluded that there is "ample evidence of organizations, institutions, and agencies pursuing all manner of programs and initiatives that are meant to encourage greater entrepreneurship in rural America" (Dabson et al. 2003, 59). From all this experience, three important policy principles are beginning to emerge that focus on regionalism, systems, and assets.

### Principle 1. Regionalism

If Friedman and Florida are correct in their analyses, the future for large parts of the United States, and especially for rural America, looks bleak. Already, the increasingly competitive global economy has forced major restructuring in rural regions and communities in many painful ways—from volatile prices for farm commodities to the collapse of textile and carpet manufacturing, to the structure of the retail sector.

Moreover, there have been dramatic changes on the rural landscape as some regions experience continuing net population loss, while others are seeing substantial immigration, whether it is the healthy and wealthy moving to high amenity areas or the poor and the aspiring looking for affordable living conditions and opportunity. Still other regions are dealing with the warm embrace of metropolitan expansion and increasing suburbanization.

The obvious point to stress is that America comprises multiple regions, each with its own competitive strengths and weaknesses, and that economic development policies must be crafted to appropriately reflect this diversity. To underscore one of the Council on Competitiveness's principles for sustained productivity growth referred to earlier, regional prosperity depends on the productivity of *all* its industries and assets, including capitalizing on the connections and flows of people, goods, services, ideas, and information within regions. Thus, policies to promote and sustain regional competitiveness must include policies to promote and sustain the competitiveness of all the *places,* both urban and rural, within any given region.

In assessing rural regional competitiveness, Porter concluded, among other things, that, "economic development in rural regions is often framed as an activity inherently different from economic development more generally. This has created policies and institutions that are not well integrated with regional development activities in metropolitan regions" (Porter 2004, 61).

Mark Drabenstott (2003), a leading proponent of regional approaches to economic development, makes a related point:

> Regional thinking is driven by the realization that competing successfully in global markets requires a critical mass that single cities or counties cannot muster on their own. Thinking regionally does not come naturally, though, when regions are shot through with jurisdictional lines laid down a century ago or more. When the lines separate cities, counties, or even states, they rarely define new economic opportunities. (2)

In recent testimony to the House Committee on Agriculture, Drabenstott (2006a) stressed the importance of rural regions being able to craft effective competitiveness strategies across the public and private sectors. Such strategies, he argued, would require preinvestments in leadership capacity to facilitate regional dialogue, the identification of new sources of competitive advantage, and the building of a consensus vision in terms of better regional economic information and new tools for regional governance.

This regional imperative has been given practical expression across rural America. The Sierra Nevada is a 400-mile-long mountain range that spans parts of 23 counties in California and Nevada. It faces huge increases in population and growth driven by the climate, environment, and quality of life, but its success threatens to undermine these very same factors. The Sierra Business Council (2003), a unique alliance of business, property, ranching, residents, and government interests, has created a regional community and economic development strategy. Central to this strategy is a nurturing environment for entrepreneurs, supporting the belief that entrepreneurship creates enduring economic growth, strengthens communities, creates more high-paying jobs, and is especially effective in rural regions.

Only by communities working together in a regional collaborative context can this be realized.

Another mountain region, Appalachia, provides a second example of regional framing for entrepreneurship. The Central Appalachian Network (2005), an alliance of nonprofit, community-based organizations and academic institutions straddling four states, has developed a series of strategies for what it calls *sustainable entrepreneurship*. Emerging clusters of entrepreneurial activity need regionally based expertise and infrastructure to encourage and support value-added production and services and to connect individual businesses to regional markets. Many of these needs cannot be met locally except through regional collaborations across public and private sectors and through the efforts of regional catalysts and networks.

## Principle 2. Systems

The second principle is that any strategy must be *systems-based*. In most parts of rural America, there is no shortage of programs and agencies to support small business development. These initiatives provide advice, training, technical assistance, and capital access but often are disconnected, categorical, competing, underresourced, and altogether too confusing for entrepreneurs to bother to navigate. The most comprehensive critique of these programs has been provided by Lichtenstein and Lyons (2001) who note that programs are generally funder-driven rather than client-driven, and focus on the business activity or on offering specific products rather than on the needs and circumstances of entrepreneurs (see chapter 6).

Lichtenstein and Lyons (2001) were pioneers in advocating a systems approach to entrepreneurship development based on tailoring services that are both responsive to the various levels of skill, education, and motivation to be found among entrepreneurs and aligned with the capacities and resources of the service providers. A national competition sponsored by the Kellogg Foundation in 2004, designed by CFED (Dabson 2005a), built on this thinking and invested in a variety of approaches that would create or enhance systems approaches to entrepreneurship development.

The desired programs were defined as a coordinated infrastructure of public and private supports that facilitate entrepreneurship with an effective system that integrates a wide range of programs and tailors products and services to the diverse needs of entrepreneurs. These systems, it was determined, would be comprehensive, flexible, culturally sensitive, and integrated, and should require providers to collaborate rather than operate independently or in isolation.

The resulting Kellogg-funded project, *Entrepreneurship Development Systems in Rural Development* (Dabson 2005a), looked for collaborative efforts that would embrace entrepreneurship education, training and technical assistance, capital access, networks, and entrepreneurial culture in self-defined multicounty rural regions. There were 182 submissions from rural regions in 47 states with more than 2,000 organizations directly involved in the process as part of collaboratives.

### Principle 3. Assets

The third principle is that entrepreneurship strategy must be *assets-based*. Although Kretzman and McKnight (1993) published their groundbreaking and widely adopted and adapted guide in the early 1990s to encourage communities to stop thinking in terms of deficits and shortcomings and start focusing on their assets and potentials, it still remains a challenge for many rural regions to identify and accept that they may have real assets that can yield entrepreneurial opportunities.

Nevertheless, the building blocks for competitive rural regions must be their assets that can be leveraged for vitalization efforts. There are many different categorizations of such assets. For instance, Flora and Flora (2004) refer to seven types of capital—cultural, social, human, political, natural, financial, and built capital—which they define as a resource invested to create new resources, and which can be identified in rural communities. The policy challenge is which of these disparate assets can be translated into entrepreneurial opportunities and what is the most effective means of doing so.

For many scholars and observers, the main drivers of regional economies are to be found primarily in large metropolitan centers or at least close to centers of knowledge investment and creation. For instance, David Audretsch (2005), a leading entrepreneurship theorist, suggests that entrepreneurship will be greater and will lead to higher levels of economic growth in geographically delimited areas around sources of knowledge spillover such as research universities and technology companies.

Much depends, however, on the extent to which these spillovers present opportunities attractive to entrepreneurs and to the strength of the entrepreneurial capital available. This approach supports Florida's (2005) ideas mentioned earlier about the concentration of creativity around certain centers, but it does not necessarily preclude rural participation through land grant universities and colleges or certain research institutions.

A new study that recasts the Florida (2005) Creative Class formulation for rural America (McGranahan and Wojan 2006) supports the notion that creativity in both urban and rural contexts is indeed a factor in economic growth, and that certain rural characteristics can attract workers in creative occupations. Amenity-based rural development strategies not only attract tourists, vacation home residents, and retirees, but also creative workers who see outdoor amenities as enhancing their quality of life.

Local opportunities for outdoor recreation, such as biking, hiking, skiing, water sports, hunting, or fishing, can be strong magnets for talent. In addition, Creative Class members in rural locations tend to be somewhat older than their counterparts in metropolitan hubs and are interested in ensuring good quality educational opportunities for their children. Nevertheless, the evidence from the McGranahan and Wojan (2006) study also shows that it is the higher density rural areas that are the most attractive because high levels of social interaction and a degree of diversity are still important.

The implication appears to be that only some well-endowed rural regions will benefit from entrepreneurial activity leading to economic growth and competitiveness. There seems to be some basis for cautious optimism coming from practical, on-the-ground experience, however, which over time must be confirmed by rigorous research.

The Central Appalachian Network's (2005) report on sustainable entrepreneurship cited earlier focused much emphasis on Appalachia's natural assets and the heritage of the people and the place:

> Natural capital entrepreneurship is based on the sustainable use of forests, farmland, rivers, lakes and mountains of our region. Organic and niche crops, ecotourism, wood products made from sustainable harvested timber, and non-timber forest products such as ginseng are all products of entrepreneurship based on natural capital. Placed-based entrepreneurship draws on the beauty and heritage of our region through development of traditional crafts, music, foods, and natural treasures such as historic bed and breakfasts. (31)

The report goes on to provide evidence of the income generation that flows from these activities and to reinforce the point that these natural assets are the region's competitive advantage. Similar messages are contained in an Association for Enterprise Opportunity report (Keiser and Herd 2003), which resulted from a two-year Rural Microenterprise Successful Practices Project examining what improves effectiveness and impact. The project focused on entrepreneurial development in the food, tourism, and artisan sectors and concluded, among other things, that collaboration and innovation go hand in hand in successful entrepreneurial rural communities. Again, the entrepreneurial opportunities arose from an understanding and valuing of available rural assets.

Many ideas and approaches were generated by the previously mentioned Kellogg Foundation project, including unusual partnerships among institutions that rarely, if ever, work together. Nearly 40 collaboratives were led by universities or community colleges reaching out to communities and other agencies to offer the possibility of the transfer of skills and technologies across rural regions. Some included major research and development facilities such as NASA in New Mexico and the National Surface Warfare Center in Indiana. Others focused on facilitating entrepreneurship and innovation in specific sectors such as sustainable agriculture, life sciences, or alternative energy. Still others saw new technologies as central to connecting entrepreneurs and their ideas to markets.

In Kentucky, the Innovation Group, an initiative of the Kentucky Science and Technology Corporation, manages a network of six Innovation and Commercialization Centers housed in universities across the state (see Dabson 2005b). Three of these centers serve primarily rural regions and assist entrepreneurs with refining business strategies and commercialization plans, and they, in turn, are supported by seven regional Innovation Centers that provide initial assistance to entrepreneurs geared to the special challenges faced by rural communities in the new economy.

By assisting with the application of appropriate technologies and providing access to a statewide network of capital, Web-based resources, and technical guidance, these centers are the first step in fostering entrepreneurial opportunities. The Innovation Group manages a Rural Innovation Fund designed to help small, rural firms convert their inventions and ideas into investment-quality ventures and access private equity markets.

### Research Agenda

Early in this chapter, reference was made to the importance of aligning entrepreneurship research to the policymaking process. From the various publications and research findings cited, it is possible to assert what is known and/or agreed about entrepreneurship and what has yet to be evaluated.

There seems to be a large measure of agreement on the following:

- Entrepreneurs are diverse with different levels of education, skill, and motivation. They can be identified in many different contexts, but the critical defining characteristic is a willingness and ability to innovate.
- Innovation can be found in many different contexts and is not restricted to high-technology sectors.
- Only one in ten entrepreneurs will succeed in creating enterprises that will create significant numbers of jobs and wealth but even this small proportion equates to 750,000 businesses a year.
- It would be unwise from a policy standpoint to attempt to identify which entrepreneurs will eventually be these job creators, so a prudent approach is to facilitate the creation of a large and diverse pool of aspiring and early-stage entrepreneurs.
- The main challenge is to increase the conversion rate from early-stage entrepreneurs to established business owners through appropriate policies and supports.
- The broader economic context for entrepreneurship has changed dramatically through globalization and related threats and opportunities.

People with entrepreneurial characteristics are more likely to be able to grasp these opportunities. Globalization places a high premium on effective regional competitiveness and the ability of regions to make full use of all their assets. For rural areas, the identification of competitive assets and the recognition of interrelationships with metropolitan centers in a regional context are of paramount importance.

- Some rural areas are better endowed than others in terms of sources of innovation or climate for entrepreneurship, especially those with universities and research establishments and those with natural assets that can be parlayed into entrepreneurship opportunities.

What policymakers still need is input from the research and evaluation community in respect to the following assertions and emerging initiatives and practices:

- Entrepreneurship yields equivalent or greater returns to public investment than more conventional economic development approaches such as recruitment and investment in infrastructure.
- Regional frameworks that explore the connections between urban and rural areas provide the necessary policy context for entrepreneurship and economic development.
- With appropriate investments in leadership capacity, tools to identify competitive advantage, and regional consensus building, governments, academic institutions, the private sector, and nongovernmental organizations can build lasting regional collaborations.
- Given the dearth of financial and knowledge resources in many rural areas, the focus should be on system-building to align available resources and efforts to meet the differing needs and characteristics of entrepreneurs.
- Incentives for collaboration and system-building to facilitate entrepreneurship development are more effective than categorical programs.
- The route to rural competitiveness is through the identification of assets and that most, if not all, communities possess assets that entrepreneurs can transform into economic opportunity. Creativity and innovation can be found and encouraged in all rural regions—even those with few obvious endowments.

Entrepreneurship is by acclamation becoming the strategy of choice for a growing number of regions and communities across rural America, but the national, regional, and state policy contexts are still works in progress. Even though the above assertions seem to have merit, one of the stumbling blocks to their wider acceptance and action is the lack of hard evidence to support them. To paraphrase David Hart (2003), analysts can and should do a much better job of assisting policymakers by testing these assertions and by designing policy tools for effective implementation.

## NOTES

1. For some examples, see Schweke and Dabson 1994; Henderson 2002; National Commission for Entrepreneurship 2002; Sierra Business Council 2003; Central Appalachian Network 2005; and Drabenstott 2006b.

2. A useful summary timeline is given on page 7 of *Understanding Entrepreneurship: A Research and Policy Report* by the Ewing Marion Kauffman Foundation (2005).

3. The data presented in this section comes from the Integrated Longitudinal Business Database as interpreted in Davis, Haltiwanger, and Jarmin (2005).

## REFERENCES

Audretsch, David B. 2005. The knowledge spillover theory of entrepreneurship and economic growth. In *The emergence of entrepreneurial economics. Volume 9: Research on technological innovation, management and policy,* ed. G. T. Vining and R. C. W. Van Der Voort, 37–54. Oxford, UK: Elsevier Jai.

Autio, Erkko, and Mick Hancock. 2005. *Global entrepreneurship monitor high expectation entrepreneurship 2005 summary report.* London: Mazars, London Business School and Babson College. www.mazars.de/download/studien/GEM%20full%20report.pdf (December 19, 2006).

Central Appalachian Network. 2005. *Strategies for sustainable entrepreneurship.* Central Appalachian Network. www.cannetwork.org/roundtable/strategies.pdf (February 20, 2007).

Dabson, Brian. 2005a. *Fostering entrepreneurship development systems in rural America: First review of the results of the request for proposals.* CFED/RUPRI Report to the W. K. Kellogg Foundation. www.energizinentrepreneurs.org (February 20, 2007).

Dabson, Brian. 2005b. Innovation and entrepreneurship in rural America. *Economic Development America* (Winter). www.eda.gov/EDAmerica/winter2005/.html (February 20, 2007).

Dabson, Brian, with Kent Marcoux. 2003. *Entrepreneurial Arkansas: Connecting the dots.* Little Rock, AR: Winthrop Rockefeller Foundation.

Dabson, Brian, Jennifer Malkin, Amy Mathews, Kimberly Pate, and Sean Stickle. 2003. *Mapping rural entrepreneurship.* Battle Creek, MI: W. K. Kellogg Foundation, and Washington, DC: CFED.

Davis, Steven J., John A. Haltiwanger, and Ron S. Jarmin. 2005. Understanding U.S. business dynamics: What can young, small firms add? In *Understanding entrepreneurship: A research and policy report,* 34–38. Kansas City, MO: Ewing Marion Kauffman Foundation.

Drabenstott, Mark. 2003. Top ten ways to reinvent rural regions. In *The Main Street Economist.* Kansas City, MO: Center for the Study of Rural America, Federal Reserve Bank of Kansas City.

Drabenstott, Mark. 2006a. *A new rural economy: A new role for public policy.* Testimony prepared for House Committee on Agriculture, Subcommittee on Conservation, Credit, Rural Development, and Research, March 30.

Drabenstott, Mark. 2006b. *A review of the federal role in regional economic development.* Kansas City, MO: Federal Reserve Bank of Kansas City.

Drucker, Peter F. 1985. *Innovation and entrepreneurship.* New York: Harper Perennial Library.

Ewing Marion Kauffman Foundation. 2005. *Understanding entrepreneurship: A research and policy report.* Kansas City, MO: Ewing Marion Kauffman Foundation.

Flora, Cornelia Butler, and Jan L. Flora, with Susan Fey. 2004. *Rural communities: Legacy and change* (2nd ed.) Boulder, CO: Westview Press.

Florida, Richard. 2005. *The flight of the creative class.* New York: HarperCollins.

Friedman, Thomas L. 2005. *The world is flat: A brief history of the twenty-first century.* New York: Farrar, Strauss, and Giroux.

Hart, David M. 2003. Entrepreneurship policy: What it is and where it came from. In *The emergence of entrepreneurship policy: governance, start-ups, and growth in the U.S. knowledge economy,* ed. David M. Hart, 3–19. Cambridge, UK: Cambridge University Press.

Henderson, Jason. 2002. Are high growth entrepreneurs building the rural economy. *The Main Street Economist.* Kansas City, MO: Center for the Study of Rural America, Federal Reserve Bank of Kansas City.

Keiser, Natallie, and Jennifer Herd. 2003. *Innovations in microenterprise development form the rural experience.* Arlington, VA: Association for Enterprise Opportunity.

Kretzman, John P., and John L. McKnight. 1993. *Building communities from the inside out: A path toward finding and mobilizing a community's assets.* Chicago, IL: ACTA Publications.

Lichtenstein, Gregg A., and Thomas S. Lyons. 2001. The entrepreneurship development system: Transforming business talent and community economies. In *Economic Development Quarterly* 15 (February): 3–30.

McGranahan, David A., and Timothy R. Wojan. 2006. Recasting the creative class to examine growth processes in rural and urban counties. Forthcoming in *Regional Studies.*

Minitti, Maria, with William D. Bygrave and Erkko Autio. 2006. *Global Entrepreneurship Monitor 2005 executive report.* London: Babson College and London Business School.

National Commission for Entrepreneurship (NCOE). 2002. *Entrepreneurship: A candidate's guide: Creating good jobs in your community.* Washington, DC: NCOE.

Porter, Michael E. 2001. *Clusters of innovations: Regional foundations of U.S. competitiveness.* Washington, DC: Council on Competitiveness.

Porter, Michael E., with Christian H. M. Ketels, Kaia Miller, and Richard T. Bryden. 2004. *Competitiveness in rural U.S. regions: Learning and research agenda.* Cambridge, MA: Institute for Strategy and Competitiveness, Harvard Business School.

Schweke, F. William, and Brian Dabson. 1994. *Bidding for business: How cities and states sell themselves short.* Washington, DC: Corporation for Enterprise Development.

Sierra Business Council. 2003. *Investing for prosperity: Building successful communities and economies in the Sierra Nevada.* Truckee, CA: Sierra Business Council.

*Strengthening America's Communities Advisory Committee.* 2005. Report submitted to Carlos M. Gutierrez, U.S. Secretary of Commerce.

Zacharakis, Andrew L., William D. Bygrave, and Dean A. Shepard. 2000. Global Entrepreneurship Monitor: National Entrepreneurship Assessment, United States of America, 2000 Executive Report. www.gemconsortium.org/download/1174415970390/GEM2000USA.pdf (January 20, 2007).

# 3

# What's Culture Got to Do with It? Strategies for Strengthening an Entrepreneurial Culture

*Ron Hustedde*

Think of a community or region as an entrepreneurial venture. Entrepreneurs transform ideas into something of value that people want or need. They tend to be curious; they question the status quo; they listen to their customers and find ways to satisfy them. They change behavior and thought patterns to create new market opportunities. If a community or region can be viewed as an entrepreneurial venture, one would expect to find similar characteristics: behaviors and attitudes that are open to new ideas and opportunities with a supportive environment that encourages new ventures. This is part of what is meant by an entrepreneurial culture.

This chapter addresses two major questions: (1) What does culture have to do with entrepreneurship? and, (2) How does one foster an entrepreneurial-friendly culture in a rural setting? Subsequent discussions will define entrepreneurial culture and various types of entrepreneurs. The chapter will explore seven major practices for building an entrepreneurial culture: (1) creating opportunities to learn, question, and think about entrepreneurship; (2) welcoming fresh voices and embracing diversity; (3) mobilizing resources for entrepreneurs; (4) cultivating networks for entrepreneurs to thrive; (5) focusing on assets; (6) developing a shared vision about entrepreneurship; and (7) creating entrepreneurial advocates and leaders.

## DEFINING AN ENTREPRENEURIAL CULTURE

There are cultures within a community that nurture, tolerate, or discourage the creation of new enterprises. Communities with cultures that value independence, innovation, diversity, and wealth creation can be viewed as entrepreneurial-friendly while those that place higher values on conformity and homogeneity or that tend to be overwhelmed by their deficits and problems can be viewed as entrepreneurial tolerant or resistant.

Typically, a community has several cultures within a dominant culture. These cultures can be ethnic, gender, or values-based clusters of people with shared interests. For example, a group of Hispanic entrepreneurs, small manufacturing firm owners, or pro-environment entrepreneurs may have their own informal networks, values, and resources that are shared. They don't necessarily oppose the dominant culture but operate within it on their own terms.

There are also entrepreneurial countercultures within rural communities, which can be expressed in a variety of ways. For example, when tourism-based firms question the location of a potential polluter, they could be viewed as counterculture. When a group of small business leaders create their own organization apart from the local Chamber, that action could be viewed as counterculture.

Indeed, culture shapes and molds the entrepreneurs that emerge in rural spaces. Culture can be defined as a type of *collective mind programming* (Hofstede and Hofstede 2005, 4). It includes value judgments and social behavior. A community's culture defines what is acceptable and what is not. Culture isn't rigid and fixed; it evolves. It is shaped and reshaped by internal and external forces, including entrepreneurs (Williams 1983). The closure of a manufacturing plant, government regulations, the opening of a major retail discount store, or the success of a youth entrepreneurship fair can contribute to attitudes, values, and behavior about entrepreneurship.

Culture is also influenced by factors such as settlement patterns, religion, and other historical conditions. For example, Appalachian coal towns have typically been dominated by a single firm, which influenced thinking in subtle and visceral ways that discouraged entrepreneurship and innovation. In other Appalachian settings, such as Ivanhoe, Virginia, traditional industrial recruitment has been replaced with an informal patchwork of income sources, including nontraditional approaches such as bartering and finding creative ways to meet local needs and to sell to external markets.

Entrepreneurial cultures can inspire entrepreneurs to emerge. This type of culture is expressed through a can-do attitude that is manifested in symbols and behavior that value entrepreneurship; it can include award ceremonies, value statements, community-minded visions, local policy, investments, and other approaches.

Culture is so pervasive that it tends to be forgotten as it fades into the background as a part of economic development strategies. Some communities have cultures in which they feel victimized by external forces while others build on those forces and adapt them to create opportunities for new enterprises (Shaffer, Deller, and Marcouiller 2004). A nonentrepreneurial culture fails to recognize the forces that maintain the status quo such as entrepreneurs in Appalachia who believe there is a perceived negative attitude toward success (Taylor, Dees, and Swanson 2003).

A community that only tolerates entrepreneurs and doesn't welcome them could be viewed as having a nonentrepreneurial culture. The focus on the collective rather than individual success is one of several factors hindering an entrepreneurial culture in aboriginal Canada along with inadequate access to financing and capital, lack of educational opportunities, and limited access to external markets (Levitte 2004). This results in little questioning about current economic strategies and more focus on problems rather than assets.

Some scholars assert that an entrepreneurial culture is about a framework in which entrepreneurs have the potential to emerge and local economic resilience is promoted (Krueger 2003). Others argue that an entrepreneurial community has three major characteristics: (1) a critical mass of entrepreneurs who are capturing new market opportunities; (2) a group of entrepreneurs with a distinct community within the community characterized by a strong support network and mutual self-help; and (3) the community as a whole is open to change (Lichtenstein, Lyons, and Kutzhanova 2004). Richard Florida (2002) views entrepreneurial-friendly communities as places that appeal to creative individuals. That is, they nurture the arts, promote a healthy civic life, honor diversity, and celebrate their cultural uniqueness.

Thornton (1999) asserts that the entrepreneurship literature has placed too much emphasis on the supply side perspective, with a focus on the individual characteristics of entrepreneurs. She points to the limitations of studies about entrepreneurs as a class and suggests an examination of the newer work on the demand side perspective—a focus on the context in which entrepreneurship occurs.

In this view, demand is triggered by several factors such as the emergence of generalist and dominant firms that create new market niches for specialist organizations and shocks in markets which trigger the founding of new ventures. Thornton (1999) believes more research should be directed towards a multilevel analysis about how, where, and why new ventures are founded. That is, what are the unique institutions, environment, values, and other aspects embedded within a specific setting that creates a demand for entrepreneurs?

In essence, an entrepreneurial-friendly culture cannot be defined simplistically; however, even this brief literature review suggests some clear patterns that can help communities to broaden the supply and demand for entrepreneurs.

## ENTREPRENEURS AREN'T JUST SMALL BUSINESSES

Before further discussing an entrepreneurial culture, one must examine entrepreneurship more closely as is undertaken by Dabson in the previous chapter. Although there isn't a universal definition for entrepreneurs, there are some common threads in the literature. Entrepreneurs are innovators who create new products, new services, or new markets which are manifested in new organizations. Entrepreneurs are not high risk takers; rather, they tend to share risks with investors. They bear the risks of failures but also reap the rewards of success.

Entrepreneurs come in many forms. First, civic or social entrepreneurs seek to strengthen the arts, recreation, health, environment, or other aspects of public life and thus are crucial in forming and maintaining an entrepreneurial culture. These rural social entrepreneurs are innovators whose new services, products, or markets are expressed in forms such as nonprofit, civic, or governmental organizations or through informal networks. Like business entrepreneurs, they are creative; however, they don't necessarily focus on profit. Rather, they concentrate on public outcomes such as minimizing poverty, educating children, or supporting entrepreneurs.

Rural social entrepreneurs are valued for four major reasons: (1) they improve the quality of life in a region; (2) they are critical leaders within rural places; (3) they engage in building entrepreneurial environments, which are essential for business innovators; and (4) they may directly support business entrepreneurs (Markley and Macke 2003).

Business entrepreneurs seek profits, but they can also be interested in social issues such as reducing pollution, providing more accessible health care, or offering better recreation opportunities. As Dabson notes in the previous chapter, entrepreneurs can be classified in several ways, including aspiring, start-ups, and growth-oriented (Dabson 2003). Aspiring entrepreneurs are actively considering going into business and are engaged in researching a business idea. They may be motivated by a job loss or other changes in their lives.

Start-up entrepreneurs have an idea, have formulated a plan, and have made a decision to start a business or have already started one. Both aspiring and start-ups tend to have a modest early impact. In some cases, start-ups emerge because of a necessity; it is the only alternative to a job and income loss. Those attracted to opportunities (versus necessities) are more likely to grow.

Growth-oriented entrepreneurs tend to represent a relatively small group of enterprises that are already successful and are motivated to grow. They have the opportunity for high impact growth such as increasing the number of employees, market expansion, and profit growth. While some state and regional strategies focus exclusively on high growth firms, one can argue that this approach merely "skims the cream from the top" and ignores other viable forms of entrepreneurship.

## WHY ENTREPRENEURSHIP?

Community leaders must make a case for entrepreneurship before investing time and energy in building an entrepreneurial environment. For the most part, rural communities should pursue a broad-based approach to social and business entrepreneurship—those with high growth potential as well as those who can meet local needs.

Microenterprises, those that employ four people or less, should be considered part of a rural development strategy for three major reasons: (1) they allow the disadvantaged to build assets and accumulate wealth; (2) they create the bulk of new jobs; and (3) microenterprise entrepreneurs tend to become more involved as leaders in their community (Dabson 2003).

Both social and business entrepreneurs are essential for the quality of life in rural areas. They often offer essential services and products such as grocery stores, automobile repair, and health care. They also make life more vibrant and interesting for rural residents in fields such as recreation, retail, and financial services. They often provide leadership to stimulate social and business ventures and can create more philanthropic opportunities to strengthen local life. Rural entrepreneurs can also provide a laboratory for business and social innovation; produce high-quality, locally controlled food and fiber resources; protect and restore the environment; and provide new opportunities for immigrants and the disadvantaged (Shuman 2006).

Social and business entrepreneurs provide other economic benefits as well. They increase wealth in a community through external grants and investments and through links with external markets. Small enterprises account for half of the new jobs created (Headd, Ou, and Clark 2004). One can argue that entrepreneurial organizations are more efficient and dynamic because they can respond more quickly to change than highly structured large organizations.

Entrepreneurship should be a centerpiece for rural economic development. Large businesses often ignore local needs and create a sense of dependency while local entrepreneurs are more closely tied to place, less resistant to relocation, and have a tendency to be good neighbors (Shuman 2006).

While entrepreneurship is a logical economic development strategy for rural communities, one should note that entrepreneurship tends to be a long-term solution to economic issues rather than a panacea that easily translates into family-supporting wages and benefits. It can also be part of a broader economic development strategy that includes increasing the re-circulation of dollars in the community, such as though public services, and community and regional facilities; expanding purchases by nonlocal people; and recognizing the role of retirement benefits and unemployment compensation as a flow of income into the community.

## BUILDING AN ENTREPRENEURIAL CULTURE

What can a community do to encourage entrepreneurship or to strengthen or build an entrepreneurial culture? The answer is multifaceted. An entrepreneurial culture is based on two premises: (1) shared learning and (2) a systems approach.

The first premise, shared learning, is about building a learning community. Learning isn't simply the act of acquiring information; it is about developing the capacity to produce the results that are truly desired. A learning community can be defined by its ability to learn new knowledge, discover new insights, share this knowledge with the community, and modify its behavior so as to reflect this learning (Gruidl and Hustedde 2003).

The second premise is about strengthening the entrepreneurial system. A major shortcoming of local economic development is that it does not consider which critical components are missing or how they operate in isolation from each other (Lichtenstein, Lyons, and Kuthanova 2004). An entrepreneurial culture cannot be imposed from the top down nor can it be isolated from other aspects of community life, especially community goals and visions or programs involving the arts, health care, or education.

Essentially, a human system can be characterized by three criteria: (1) the whole is greater than the sum of its parts, (2) all parts are interdependent and affect each other, and (3) a living system perpetuates itself by self-adapting to its context (Moffitt 1999).

An abstract discussion about the core themes of shared learning and a systems approach is likely to be a frustrating exercise for action-oriented economic developers and community leaders who prefer visceral approaches. Consequently, the remainder of this chapter focuses on seven practical strategies and examples for building an entrepreneurial climate:

1. Create opportunities to learn, question, and think differently about entrepreneurship
2. Welcome fresh voices and embrace diversity
3. Mobilize resources for entrepreneurs
4. Cultivate networks for entrepreneurs to thrive
5. Focus on assets instead of deficits

6. Build a shared vision about entrepreneurship
7. Foster entrepreneurial leaders and advocates

Each strategy is rooted in theoretical and empirical research about building an entrepreneurial culture.

## STRATEGY 1. CREATE OPPORTUNITIES TO LEARN, QUESTION, AND THINK DIFFERENTLY ABOUT ENTREPRENEURSHIP

Leaders can create opportunities for people to learn, to question, and to get out of old ruts. Some scholars argue that an entrepreneurial culture places a significant value on storytelling (Lounsbury and Glynn 2001). Stories serve as an inspiration for aspiring entrepreneurs and also legitimize individual entrepreneurs to investors, competitors, and others who make resource decisions based on their interpretation of the stories presented to them. The stories about the ups and downs of entrepreneurship are especially valuable for understanding the complexities of finance, product development, marketing, and management. When aspiring entrepreneurs tell their stories, they get to the heart of the issues with which they are wrestling. The metaphors associated with the entrepreneurial stories also provide insights into the entrepreneurs' own perspectives and aspirations and can inspire others in the community (Dodd 2002). The conventional American metaphors of entrepreneurship as a journey, parenting, building, passion, race, or war illustrate the multifaceted, even paradoxical, process. Storytelling provides meaning to the entrepreneurial process; it can be manifested in celebrations, awards, and testimonials.

The Fairfield (Iowa) Entrepreneurs Association (FEA) is a volunteer group that "taps into the collective wisdom of other businesses" (Chojnowski 2005). A leader of the group asserted that "90 percent of what local entrepreneurs learn is from other entrepreneurs" (Chojnowski 2005). The FEA makes use of significant storytelling. Failure is often incorporated into the entrepreneurial stories because failure is "the compost that supports the startup of new companies or builds the second generation startups—those who have had one business failure and started another" (Chojnowski 2005). It does not have the negative stigma one finds in other communities (Chojnowski 2005).

Like other entrepreneurial-friendly communities, Fairfield celebrates entrepreneurs by recognizing success stories with awards ceremonies such as *Entrepreneur of the Year*. These entrepreneurial stories and events have stimulated a solid entrepreneurial culture. Since 1990, more than $250 million has been invested in 50 new Fairfield firms in fields such as software development, marketing, financial services, media, and telecommunications.

This investment has provided Fairfield with 3,000 new jobs and nearly $1 billion in equity. Local residents view their community as the "Entrepreneurial Capital of Iowa."

Self-assessment surveys can also trigger new conversations and reflections about attitudes, capacity, and the climate for entrepreneurship. The RUPRI Center for Rural Entrepreneurship (2006) has several surveys in its toolkit for *Energizing Entrepreneurs: Charting a Course for Rural Entrepreneurs*. The Rural Community Entrepreneurship Survey and other tools have been posed to elected leaders, economic development professionals, and social and business entrepreneurs to foster different perspectives about the entrepreneurial capacities of the community. Even a simple question such as "Where has entrepreneurship succeeded in our area?" or "Are we entrepreneurial-friendly?" have engaged communities in soul-searching conversations about attitudes, technical and financial assistance, infrastructure, and a range of other issues associated with an entrepreneurial culture.

## STRATEGY 2. WELCOME FRESH VOICES AND EMBRACE DIVERSITY

A systems approach to entrepreneurship includes *symbolic diversity*—a community-level orientation that inspires communities to engage in constructive controversy. Rural communities provide settings in which people see each other in a variety of roles; however, rural communities tend to suppress controversy such as the need for a new landfill to avoid feeling uncomfortable when meeting the person concerned at church or the bowling alley. Absence of controversy can be as dangerous for communities as conflict.

Communities can depersonalize politics where controversy is accepted: people can still disagree with one another but still respect each other. Symbolic diversity can be stimulated by a focus on process rather than on winning. It calls for a broader definition of group identity which expands the "we" with fewer "theys" and with more permeable group boundaries (Flora and Flora 1993).

The Washington Policy Center is an example of symbolic diversity. It cooperated with 60 organizations, including the Washington State Hispanic Chamber of Commerce, the PNW Black Chamber of Commerce, and the Latino Business Association, to bring 350 diverse small business leaders together to discuss how to improve the state's business climate. Discussion guidelines created a safe space for various perspectives to be heard and to reach consensus about small business issues such as regulatory uncertainty, lack of government accountability, and actual or perceived antibusiness attitudes. After a 2003 conference, 5 small business recommendations and 15 other bills were signed into law that directly reflected conference outcomes (U.S. Small Business Administration, Office of Advocacy 2005).

Symbolic diversity is also achieved by welcoming fresh voices, especially those of the young, artisans, teachers, healthcare workers, and entrepreneurs. Some researchers argue that communities are likely to become more prosperous if they welcome diverse viewpoints and become a haven for creative workers (Florida 2002). One study suggests that natural resource amenities such as hiking trails, water sports, hunting, and fishing as well as a cluster of arts, humanities, and educational opportunities provide the creative juices to attract entrepreneurs and other innovators (McGranahan and Wojan 2006).

Welcoming fresh and diverse perspectives can be part of stimulating an entrepreneurial culture. Take the case of Palestine, a small municipality in southern Illinois. Their economic development dream includes encouraging all residents to enjoy and experience the arts; stimulating cooperation among artists, patrons, and enthusiasts; and promoting the development of individual artists. The Palestine Artists Relocation Project (2006) is an attempt to attract artists of all genres to the city. Those artists eligible for relocation can benefit from commercial and historical sites, a co-op art gallery, access to Websites, revolving loan funds, and other incentives. The artist relocation initiative complements other economic development approaches.

## STRATEGY 3. MOBILIZE RESOURCES
## FOR ENTREPRENEURS

Resource mobilization is a key aspect of an entrepreneurial social infrastructure. Rural America is faced with slow growing or decreasing real incomes and a decreasing tax base in some instances, and they are increasingly being asked to rely on their own resources for rural development and entrepreneurship. Entrepreneurship is facilitated when communities can share some of the entrepreneurs' risks in the form of money, space, communications, and equipment. Entrepreneurial communities are willing to commit funds, through additional taxes or reallocation, to provide the physical or human capital resources for entrepreneurs to succeed.

The Douglas-Coffee County Chamber and Economic Development Authority in Georgia created 240 additional jobs in 1 year through an entrepreneurial initiative. They saw the region in an economic slump, questioned the Chamber of Commerce's role, and made changes. First, they worked with county leaders to start a new entrepreneur and small business program. They prepared a *How to Start and Grow a Business* publication, which was available electronically and in print. To make it clear that the county was serious about entrepreneurship, it offered tax abatements for small business entrepreneurs and created an informal retail incubator where potential retailers could lease space on a monthly basis to test their ideas. Those businesses with a viable concept leased permanent space and started operations. These and other efforts led to their designation as an "entrepreneurial friendly community" by the Georgia Department of Commerce (Greenway 2005).

The IDEA Center Incubator in Tupelo, Mississippi, serves new business entrepreneurs in manufacturing and professional services. It was developed after lengthy negotiations and includes more than $1.5 million in funding from 11 government agencies for construction and first-year operations. The incubator provides 40 spaces for entrepreneurs with high-speed Internet access, Voice-Over-Internet-Protocol phone service, faxing and copying services, and customer parking. More importantly, it provides one-stop services such as business counseling, training, and networking to help entrepreneurs successfully launch businesses. The National Business Incubation Association (NBIA) states that publicly supported incubators create jobs at a cost of $1,000 each while other job creation incentives cost more than $10,000 per job created (Averett 2005).

## STRATEGY 4. CULTIVATE NETWORKS
## FOR ENTREPRENEURS TO THRIVE

An entrepreneurial culture fosters networks for entrepreneurs to prosper. Both formal and informal networks are essential for information flows and key linkages (Flora and Flora 1993). It is essential that voices other than traditional elites be heard in these networks. Diverse leadership, including men and women, different ethnic backgrounds, and different income levels, must be nurtured during this process. While some people may find it uncomfortable to be around others unlike themselves, an entrepreneurial culture needs diversity.

Hispanic-owned businesses increased from 5 percent of the total number of firms in 1995 to 7.4 percent in 2002 (Headd, Ou, and Clark 2004). Those in the 55 to 64 age category also increased from 15.9 percent to 19.9 percent of businesses during this period. African Americans and Hispanic Americans exhibited higher rates of opportunity-based entrepreneurship than Asian Americans and white Americans. Women continue to represent about 34 percent of the self-employed.

A community must reach out to these diverse constituencies and include them in leadership networks to stimulate new social and business ventures. A noteworthy example is the Rural Enterprise Assistance Project (REAP)

Hispanic Rural Business Center in Nebraska. In its first year of operation, the center helped more than 100 Hispanic entrepreneurs receive significant technical assistance and training.

In addition, the pilot communities of Schuyler, South Sioux City, Crete, and Madison formed REAP Rural Business Roundtable groups and completed the five-session basic business training course in Spanish. These pilot communities were chosen because of their high population Hispanics. REAP plans to expand its outreach to Hispanic entrepreneurs and will continue to research, develop, and build strategic partners (REAP Business Update 2006).

Entrepreneurial communities are able to grapple with difficult problems and rephrase them in more inclusive ways that allow diverse voices to be heard. They think about issues from a systems perspective rather than isolate entrepreneurship from the broader community.

Horizontal networks are also essential. Entrepreneurs tend to learn best from those most like themselves, rather than experts. For example, small business owners and civic leaders founded the Business Alliance for Local Living Economies (BALLE) to create more humane and sustainable local communities. Some BALLE groups train new social entrepreneurs while others push for greater state commitment in renewable energy and health care (Schuman 2006).

The Community Progress Initiative in the Wisconsin Rapids area involved more than 130 individuals in industry clustering networks along with entrepreneur mentoring teams and study tours. Because of these and other entrepreneurial-friendly initiatives more than 1,000 jobs have been created or retained (U.S. Small Business Administration, Office of Advocacy 2005).

Vertical networks encourage a two-way flow of information. Entrepreneurial communities cannot depend exclusively on local resources but need to link with others outside the community for information and resources. Vertical networks are created at different systems levels. The Northern Iowa Area Community College Pappajohn Entrepreneurial Center cooperated with the Iowa Department of Economic Development to identify informal investors, *angels*, to create a community-based venture capital fund and to develop an investor-entrepreneur network in northern Iowa. Sixty-one investors from 16 communities started a $1.7 million for-profit venture capital fund (Zanios 2006).

This network has a stake in the entrepreneur's success; they offer expertise, not just money, and often become part of the entrepreneur's board of directors. The group has reviewed 81 business proposals, has assisted 51 of those with technical and educational assistance, and has provided start-up funds for 5 firms. This networking involves more than capital; it is a critical connection between those with investment and business expertise and entrepreneurs in the region.

Tupelo, Mississippi, is an example of a classical approach to internal and external entrepreneur networks. Tupelo was the nation's poorest county in 1940 (Grisham 1999); however, the local newspaper editor, George McLean, believed that rich and poor alike could work to improve the quality of life in the community. This social entrepreneur viewed the rural area around Tupelo as part of the community. His first initiative involved local businessmen who bought one bull to inseminate dairy cows; that modest action led to a cluster of small dairy businesses for poor farmers in the county. In 1948, he persuaded 151 local business leaders to invest in the Community Development Foundation, which provided the structure for major changes to occur.

Tupelo's success was linked to residents who were seen as responsible for creating new alternatives. The surrounding rural areas were integrated into the Tupelo initiative; new rural development councils were created along with business incubators, worker training programs, and an upgrade of the educational infrastructure. Tupelo's leaders visited and learned from other regions that diversified their economies. Equal access was encouraged for all races prior to Civil Rights legislation, and other efforts were made to find economic alternatives and enterprises that eventually led the county to become the second wealthiest county in Mississippi (Grisham 1999).

In essence, an entrepreneurial culture cannot be viewed in isolation from other parts of a community or region or as distinct from other initiatives. Systems thinking involves quality networks in which entrepreneurs are linked with each other as well as outsiders. It is a mind-set that can become a habitual form of thought in a community.

## STRATEGY 5. FOCUS ON ASSETS INSTEAD OF DEFICITS

There are two major approaches to economic development. One is known as the deficit or needs-based model in which the community is viewed as a collection of needs or crises (Wade 1989). Under this model, the community concentrates on what it lacks and seeks external resources to correct those needs. Unfortunately, the deficit approach can demoralize residents because they can often feel overwhelmed with the task at hand.

The alternative approach is known as asset-based community development (Kretzmann and McKnight 1993). It is also known as *asset mapping* because a community's assets are mapped, including individuals, organizations, and other community characteristics. In the asset approach, the primary building block for entrepreneurship or other community initiatives includes those community assets most readily available, especially those resources located in and controlled by residents.

Each community can map its individual assets, including skills, talents, experiences, income, and individual and home-based businesses. There are also organizational assets: business and citizen associations, religious groups, and other informal networks. Secondary building blocks include those assets which are within the community but controlled by outsiders.

An asset-based approach to entrepreneurship begins with a comprehensive analysis of a community's positive core and then links that knowledge to the heart of any strategic change. It is a discovery of everything which brings a system to life. An asset-based approach links people to the hidden and obvious potentials in their community. They can see changes they never thought possible, and people can be mobilized with enthusiasm, confidence, and energy. It tends to bring out the best of "what is" and "what can be." For example, compare the following two questions. The deficit-based approach question might ask, "Why don't we have many entrepreneurs in our community?" In contrast, the asset-based approach question might be, "What makes extraordinary entrepreneurship possible in our community?" The former question encourages self-doubt while the latter can trigger spontaneity, discovery, dreams, and innovation.

If Mora, New Mexico (pop. 5,000), was examined from a deficit perspective in the mid-1990s, one would see low-income rural families and a declining textile industry. Mora's leadership concentrated on local assets—the natural beauty of their surroundings, a vibrant rural way of life in spite of low income, a history of working in textiles for almost 300 years, people wanting to stay in their ancestral homes, and the potential for an increase in cultural tourism.

*Tapetes de Lana* was created in Mora in 1998 to revive the lost tradition of weaving and to subsidize the incomes of low-income families. It started with $20,000 and a newly formed nonprofit agency to offer job training alternatives for families on welfare. History and tradition played an important role as residents learned to do hand spinning, natural dying, and weaving. Weavers built looms with scrap materials. In contrast to initial expectations, many of the weavers are men. They produce wool quilts in traditional and contemporary designs. Customers are interested in hearing stories about the product, which adds value to the quilts. As business grew, Mora's weavers have started specializing in alpaca wool and now work with alpaca breeders to spin 2,000 to 4,000 pounds of wool per day. Other spin-offs include an art center, a pottery studio, and a community-based mill, and there are plans to expand into a theater and a rural development center. By focusing on local assets, Mora has built a thriving cottage industry and improved the quality of life and hope for its people (Gomez 2005).

The asset-based approach fosters a "can do" attitude because a community realizes that it has a range of assets over which they have some influence.

Hawarden, Iowa, was ignored by its cable company in Denver when it wanted to expand the local telecommunications network in 1994. The community didn't take "no" for an answer.

Instead, they discovered their own assets by passing a $4.5 million revenue bond and building a hybrid fiber/coaxial framework. It kept one of the current employers in town and led to other economic opportunities (Schultz 2004).

## STRATEGY 6. BUILD A SHARED
## VISION ABOUT ENTREPRENEURSHIP

A community-based vision is the *big picture* about where the community or region is headed. A community vision about entrepreneurship cannot stand alone; it must be fully integrated with other aspects of a broader vision about community directions. Ideally, the process involves the key strategies mentioned earlier such as creating opportunities to learn, question, and think differently about entrepreneurship and focusing on community and regional assets.

In many cases, the visioning effort is a work in progress. For example, Owen County, Kentucky, has involved more than one-fourth of its residents in developing a community-based vision (RUPRI 2006). The entrepreneurship component is still being integrated into the broader community vision. Teams visit the county's innovative entrepreneurs and learn more about youth entrepreneurship as their dream matures.

In the case of Littleton, Colorado, several thousand people lost their jobs from the closure of a manufacturing firm. Rather than focus on recruiting jobs through industrial recruitment, a community vision emerged to grow entrepreneurs from the inside—a concept called *economic gardening* (RUPRI 2006).

The Littleton vision for entrepreneurship focuses on high-growth firms. Littleton provides free information such as marketing trends and Geographic Information Systems (GIS) software to map clients' addresses. They invest in an intellectual infrastructure such as great schools, training programs, and linking higher education with aspiring entrepreneurs to sharpen the skills of entrepreneurs and to keep their businesses competitive.

Littleton is also creating opportunities for trade organizations to emerge and for think tanks, including entrepreneurs and universities, to network and pursue other forms of innovation. The payoff has been that from 1998 to the present, jobs in the city have increased from 14,000 to 29,000 (RUPRI 2006). During that time, the city has not offered incentives or tax breaks to recruit businesses. The concepts behind economic gardening can be applied toward a rural vision for entrepreneurship: grow your own targeted group of entrepreneurs then provide them with information and technical assistance, infrastructure, and connections.

St. Lawrence County in upstate New York began a visioning process by focusing on economic leaks in which goods and services were being imported from outside the county. County leaders are working on opportunities to train leak-plugging entrepreneurs in almost every sector of the economy, including hydroponics, restaurants, alternative energy, uniforms, and stationery (Shuman 2006).

Regions can also develop a shared vision. Western North Carolina realized that it had an *invisible industry* of craftspeople who work in shops and galleries along back roads and highways in the Blue Ridge Mountains. This led to the creation of a *HandMade in America* initiative, which leads visitors to 500 sites along several road trails. It generates $120 million annually to the economy—four times more than burley tobacco contributed when it was the dominant crop (Shultz 2004).

Shared visions about entrepreneurship must be integrated within the context of a community's uniqueness, its values, and its people. It should involve opportunities to learn, to question, and to think differently about entrepreneurship. Fresh and diverse voices must be welcomed. The vision should pay attention to the creation of more resources for entrepreneurs and networks that will allow entrepreneurs to thrive. Typically, the visions focus on assets rather than deficits. Increasingly, rural communities combine their efforts to develop a shared vision for their region. The shared vision must also nurture leaders who can advocate for entrepreneurs and can stimulate collective action and policy changes.

## STRATEGY 7. FOSTER ENTREPRENEURIAL LEADERS AND ADVOCATES

The seventh strategy for fostering an entrepreneurial culture involves leadership. Low population density in rural areas suggests a lack of a critical mass of leaders for concerted action. So, entrepreneurial leaders and advocates must be nurtured through organizations such as the Cooperative Extension Service, the Chamber of Commerce, or civic organizations in order to fill the human capital gap (Hustedde 1991).

An entrepreneurial culture is not characterized by decentralized or centralized leadership but by many interrelated centers of leadership—*polycentric* leadership (Morse 1998). That is, an entrepreneurial community will have a series of circles which represent elements in the community such as finance, local government, social services, the arts, youth, and other groups. Leaders from these groups will be able to make decisions that are guided by shared visions.

The circles of leadership overlap when they are dealing with shared visions about entrepreneurship. For example, in Carter County, Kentucky, social services work hand in hand with educators who nurture and teach entrepreneurship to women with limited incomes. A youth entrepreneurship initiative in Grant County, Kentucky, involves a polycentric leadership of teachers, entrepreneurs, business leaders, and technical assistance and external groups such as the Kauffman Foundation and several universities.

Polycentric leadership works well if it moves beyond the superficial elements of team building (e.g., communications, courteous behavior, and strong relationships) to team learning. Leaders can learn to collectively think together about entrepreneurship and to move in a coordinated way, just as a flock of birds moves in coordinated patterns.

Opportunities must be created for team learning about entrepreneurship in which questions are asked about systems and assets as well as reflecting on some of the tough questions: What do we know about entrepreneurship? What do we need to know? How does entrepreneurship complement or challenge our values? Do we have a shared vision about entrepreneurship, and how should we act on that vision? and What kinds of policies need to be changed to foster entrepreneurship?

Venues such as conferences, workshops, roundtables, and think tank settings can create a climate for entrepreneurial leaders to emerge. The Georgia Department of Economic Development (2006) has created an initiative that provides a structure for grooming community-based entrepreneurial leaders. In order for a Georgia community to be officially designated as entrepreneurial-friendly, a community must take several key steps: (1) identifying a local organization and champion to lead a community-based entrepreneurship strategy; (2) increasing community awareness about the needs, resources, and benefits of home-grown businesses; (3) enhancing relationships with state and federal resource providers and others in educational sessions to help local leaders learn how entrepreneurs can be supported; (4) identifying potential, existing, and growth-oriented entrepreneurs; (5) identifying unique local assets that can support and foster entrepreneurship such as historic features, nature-based venues, and educational strengths; and (6) visiting and interviewing local entrepreneurs.

Communities that meet these and other criteria become members of the state of Georgia's entrepreneur-friendly team and are provided opportunities such as professional development, conferences, and a sharing of best practices (Georgia Department of Economic Development 2006). Although the Georgia Entrepreneur Friendly Initiative is not advertised as a formal leadership program, one can argue that the process itself fosters overlapping circles of community leaders who listen to entrepreneurs, understand local assets and entrepreneurial resources, and become involved in network building.

Another example of *polycentric* leadership for building an entrepreneurial culture is found in the Kentucky Entrepreneurial Coaches Institute. This unique leadership program was designed to foster a strong entrepreneurial culture by building a regional network of entrepreneurial leaders, advocates, and entrepreneurial coaches in tobacco dependent counties. The $1.28 million leadership program was funded by the Kentucky Agricultural Development Board and is being implemented by the University of Kentucky Cooperative Extension Service as the region makes the painful transition from a tobacco dependent economy.

Those chosen for the institute's competitive fellowships reflect the gender, age, ethnic, geographical, and career backgrounds in the region. They meet with entrepreneurial leaders and scholars, and visit entrepreneurs and entrepreneurial-friendly communities in nine seminars over a 15-month period. The seminars teach leadership and coaching skills, broaden creativity, and actively engage participants in the community and the region.

One institute goal is to form a regional identity by putting fellows together in cross-county teams to develop and carry out mini-grant proposals. Team projects have included technical and high school entrepreneurial initiatives, an entrepreneurial contest for ways to use a wood waste product, a seven-county agritourism initiative, and an entrepreneurial awareness program. A seminar in rural Scotland included visits with isolated entrepreneurs who linked into global markets and meetings with those involved in youth entrepreneurship programs and rural entrepreneurship policies. While there were many educational benefits from this trip, the shared experience built an incredibly strong support network among this diverse group of leaders (Hustedde 2006).

The first-year evaluation report showed that the 28 fellows in the 2005 class had more than a 1,000 contacts with entrepreneurs and service providers; they actually coached 115 entrepreneurs. They also made 416 informal presentations and 88 formal presentations. Five fellows ran for political office on pro-entrepreneurship platforms (Markley et al. 2006). In their campaigns, they asked difficult questions about investments in industrial parks and industrial recruitment: "Are we putting too many eggs in one basket (industrial recruitment)?" and "Do we need to balance our community's economic development portfolio?" These questions and other challenges raised entrepreneurship on the community's and region's radar screen.

The Georgia and Kentucky examples of *polycentric* leadership are likely to have significant impact; however, it may take five years or more to see a significant payoff or to measure their impact appropriately.

## CONCLUSION

Rural communities can be viewed as entrepreneurial ventures. They may display a wide spectrum of cultures that can be antagonistic, tolerant, or welcoming for entrepreneurs. Culture is more than an attitude. It is about a collective mind-set that influences behavior and actions; it shapes what is acceptable and what is not.

An entrepreneurial culture is rooted in two premises: (1) shared learning and (2) systems thinking. Shared learning is the ability to learn new knowledge and insights and how to share this knowledge with the community to influence change. Systems thinking is a way of viewing the community as a type of ecosystem in which entrepreneurship is linked to other aspects of community life. This living system perpetuates itself by adapting to the changing context of entrepreneurship.

The concepts of shared learning and systems thinking are embedded within seven major strategies for building an entrepreneurial culture: (1) create opportunities to learn, question, and think differently about entrepreneurship; (2) welcome fresh voices and embrace diversity; (3) mobilize resources for entrepreneurs; (4) cultivate networks for entrepreneurs to thrive; (5) focus on assets instead of deficits or problems; (6) build a shared vision for entrepreneurship; and (7) foster entrepreneurial leaders.

These seven strategies are ways to transform a community's culture into something that reflects the strengths of social and business entrepreneurs. The strategies should not be viewed as mechanical but as living and flexible approaches in which social and business entrepreneurs can prosper.

## REFERENCES

Averett, Wayne. 2005. Report 5: The IDEA center incubator in Tupelo, Mississippi. *Entrepreneurial Rural Communities National Case Studies.* www.farmfoundation.org/ruralcommunity.htm (October 12, 2006).

Chojnowski, Burt. 2005. Report 8: Fairfield, Iowa: The Emergence of a Serial Entrepreneurial Community. Entrepreneurial Rural Communities National Case Studies. http://www.farmfoundation.org/projects/documents/Report8Fairfield.pdf (October 12, 2006).

Dabson, Brian. 2003. Strengthening local economies through entrepreneurship. In *The American Midwest: Managing Change in Rural Transition.* ed., Norman Walzer, 177–96. Armonk, NY: M. E. Sharpe, Inc.

Dodd, Sara Drakopoulou. 2002. Metaphors and meaning: A grounded cultural model of U.S. entrepreneurship. *Journal of Business Venturing* 17(5): 519–35.

Flora, Cornelia Butler, and Jan L. Flora. 1993. Entrepreneurial social infrastructure: A necessary ingredient. *Annals of the American Academy of Political and Social Science* 529(September): 48–58.

Florida, Richard. 2002.*The Rise of the Creative Class.* New York: Basic Books.

Georgia Department of Economic Development's Small Business and Innovation Division. 2006. *Entrepreneur friendly initiative.* www.georgia.org/Business/Small Business/Entrepreneur+Friendly+Communities.htm (October 14, 2006).

Gomez, Carla. 2005. Report 3: *Tapetes de Lana* Weaving Center in Mora, New Mexico. *Entrepreneurial Rural Communities National Case Studies.* www.farmfoundation.org/ruralcommunity.htm (October 12, 2006).

Greenway, Lidell. 2005. Report 4: Douglas-Coffee County—One of Georgia's most entrepreneur-friendly communities. *Entrepreneurial Rural Communities National Case Studies.* www.farmfoundation.org/ruralcommunity.htm (October 12, 2006).

Grisham, Vaughn, L., Jr. 1999. *Tupelo: The Evolution of a Community,* Dayton, OH: Kettering Foundation.

Gruidl, John J., and Ronald J. Hustedde. 2003. Key practices in creating a learning community. In *The American Midwest: Managing Change in Rural Transition.* ed. Norman Walzer, 246–64. Armonk, NY: M. E. Sharpe, Inc.

Headd, Brian, Charles Ou, and Major Clark. 2004. Chapter One: Small business trends. In *The Small Business Economy: A Report to the President.* ed. Kathryn J. Tobias, 5–53. Washington, DC: U.S. Government Printing Office.

Hofstede, Geert H., and Gert Jan Hofstede. 2005. *Culture and organizations: Software of the mind.* New York: McGraw Hill Books.

Hustedde, Ronald J. 1991. Developing leadership to address rural problems. In *Rural community economic development.* ed. Norman Walzer, 111–23. New York: Praeger,

Hustedde, Ronald J. 2006. Kentucky leadership program coaches entrepreneurs. *Economic Development America* (Winter): 28–29.

Kretzmann, John P., and John L. McKnight. 1993. *Building communities from the inside out: A path toward finding and mobilizing a community's assets.* Chicago: ACTA Publications.

Krueger, Norris F. 2003. *Nurturing local economic resilience: How communities can develop entrepreneurial potential,* paper presented at Babson Kauffman Research Conference, Boston, MA.

Levitte, Yael. 2004. Bonding social capital in entrepreneurial communities—Survival networks or barriers. *Journal of the Community Development Society (Special Issue on Entrepreneurship in Community Development)* 35(1): 44–64.

Lichtenstein, Gregg A., Thomas S. Lyons, and Nailya Kutzhanova. 2004. Building entrepreneurial communities: The appropriate role of enterprise development activities. *Journal of the Community Development Society (Special Issue on Entrepreneurship in Community Development)* 35(1): 5–24.

Lounsbury, Michael, and Mary Ann Glynn. 2001. Cultural entrepreneurship: Stories, legitimacy, and the acquisition of resources. *Strategic Management Journal* 22: 545–64.

Markley, Deborah, John Gruidl, Ted Bradshaw, and James Calvin. 2006. *An evaluation of the Kentucky Entrepreneurial Coaches Institute: Insights and recommendations.* Chapel Hill, NC: RUPRI Center for Rural Entrepreneurship.

Markley, Deborah, and Don Macke. 2003. *Civic entrepreneurship, Monograph 3.* www.ruraleship.org/content/content/pdf/CivicEship.pdf (August 30, 2006).

McGranahan, D. A., and T. R. Wojan. "Recasting the Creative Class To Examine Growth Processes in Rural and Urban Counties." *Regional Studies,* forthcoming in 2006.

Moffitt, Leonard Caum. 1999. A complex system named community. *Journal of the Community Development Society* 30(2): 232–42.

Morse, Suzanne W. 1998. Five building blocks for successful communities. In *The community of the future.* eds. Frances Hesselbein, Marshall Goldsmith, Richard Beckhard, and Richard F. Schubert, 229–36. San Francisco, CA: Jossey-Bass.

Palestine Artist Relocation Project. Palestine, Illinois. www.artistrelocationproject
.com/ (September 5, 2006).
RUPRI Center for Rural Entrepreneurship. n.d. *Energizing Entrepreneurs, Chapter 6* www
.energizingentrepreneurs.org/. (September 5, 2006).
Rural Enterprise Assistance Project. 2006. *REAP business update* 15(7) www.cfra.org/
reap/newsletter/2006_07/hispanic_center.htm (October 14, 2006).
Schultz, Jack. 2004. *Boomtown USA: The 7-1/2 keys to big success in small towns.* Herndon, VA: National Association of Industrial and Office Properties.
Shaffer, Ron, Steve Deller, and Dave Marcouiller. 2004. *Community economics: Link-
ing theory and practice.* Ames, IA: Blackwell Publishing Professional.
Shuman, Michael. 2006. *The small-mart revolution: How local businesses are beating the
global competition.* San Francisco, CA: Berrett-Koehler Books.
Taylor, Melissa, Greg Dees, and Mark Swanson. 2003. *Promoting entrepreneurship in
central Appalachia: From research to action.* Berea, KY: Mountain Association for
Community Economic Development.
Thornton, Patricia H. 1999. The sociology of entrepreneurship. *Annual Review of So-
ciology* 25: 19–45.
U.S. Small Business Administration, Office of Advocacy. 2005. *Putting it together: The
role of entrepreneurship in economic development.* Conference Proceedings, March 7.
Washington, DC.
Wade, Jerry. 1989. Felt needs and anticipatory needs: Reformulation of a basic com-
munity development principle. *Journal of the Community Development Society* 20:
116–23.
Williams, Raymond. 1983. *Culture and Society, 1780–1950.* New York: Columbia
University Press.
Zanios, Jamie T. 2005. Report 6: North Iowa area community college entrepreneur
and capital networks. *Entrepreneurial Rural Communities National Case Studies.* www
.farmfoundation.org/ruralcommunity.htm (October 12, 2006).

# 4

# Entrepreneurship and Small Business Growth

*Norman Walzer, Adee Athiyaman, and Gisele F. Hamm*

The importance of small businesses in generating local employment, especially in rural areas has been recognized by policymakers and many programs are available to help start and promote these businesses. However the specific roles of entrepreneurship in fostering business start-ups, and therefore expanding regional growth, have not always been recognized.

While new firms can be any size, business start-ups in rural areas often are small with relatively few employees. Nevertheless, these businesses frequently are the fastest growing and may account for much of the job creation in rural areas. This chapter examines the importance of small businesses in regional economic growth and presents a conceptual model to understand factors affecting both the formation and growth in number of microenterprises in midwestern counties. Specifically, the relevance of local economic climate, business structure, natural amenities, and potential entrepreneurs in the region in explaining changes in the number of microenterprises in the county is examined.

## BACKGROUND

Entrepreneurship was not a major factor in neo-classical economics (Baumol 1968; Kirzner 1997). While production functions enable managers to optimize outputs given a set of inputs, the theory of the firm does not recognize the *gap-filling* and *input-completing* functions of entrepreneurs that lead to organizational efficiency, and more importantly, new firm starts (Leibenstein 1968; Beugelsdijk and Noorderhaven 2004). In practice, an entrepreneur recognizes gaps for goods/services in the market place, assembles necessary resources to complete the inputs needed in the production process(s), and optimizes the production process(s).

Thus, an entrepreneur's role includes more than managing an operation; it also involves recognizing and taking advantage of business opportunities. The new firm creation role of entrepreneurs has been studied from a variety of disciplines including social psychology and economics (Labriandis 2006) to identify common characteristics of entrepreneurs and to find ways to promote entrepreneurial behavior.

An endogenous growth theory is often used to justify the inclusion of entrepreneurial concepts in regional development (Pack 1994; Audretsch and Keilbach 2005). This theory uses two concepts to link entrepreneurship and economic growth: *diversity* and *selection*. Diversity is defined as knowledge created by firms' investments in research and development (R&D). Selection refers to the entrepreneurial activity of creating economic value from the knowledge created by R&D activities. According to Audretsch and Keilbach (2004a, 607):

> (individuals) placing a high value on knowledge that is not valued as highly by the hierarchical decision making organizations in incumbent firms will face an incentive to become entrepreneurs and start a new firm in order to appropriate the value of that knowledge.

Empirical tests show that statistically significant variations in economic growth among nations can be attributed to these entrepreneurial concepts (Beugelsdijk 2006).

At least two implications flow from discussions of the two entrepreneurship concepts. First, new firm starts indicate entrepreneurship. Second, environmental factors such as the socioeconomic-spatial characteristics of a community (e.g., population density, unemployment rate, distance from major cities, etc.) can facilitate or hinder entrepreneurship (Labrianidis 2006).

Four categories of environmental factors are examined in this chapter: (1) economic climate; (2) business structure; (3) natural amenities; and (4) potential for entrepreneurship in the county. A structural equation that permits the modeling of complex sequences of causal relationships, assessment of errors in measurement, and the identification of both direct and indirect effects within a system of equations is then applied to data on microenterprises in six midwestern states.

Microenterprises are important in the overall rural midwestern economy. The Association for Enterprise Opportunity (AEO) provides county-level data for two business groupings: (1) owner-operated businesses with no employees and (2) those with one to four employees. These businesses are a subset of rural businesses and include other enterprises besides start-ups or entrepreneurs. In the six midwestern states (Illinois, Indiana, Iowa, Kentucky, Missouri, and Wisconsin), 82 rural counties (17.8 percent) had 30 percent or more of their employment in these businesses, and 187 counties (40.7 percent) had 25 percent (AEO 2006).

Microenterprises in these states grew during the early 2000s with 85.2 percent of the counties reporting increases in number of establishments and 77.8 percent of the counties reporting increases in employment in these businesses. Rural counties adjacent to urban areas differed very little from remote counties in increases in numbers of businesses (86.3 percent versus 84.2 percent), but fewer remote counties reported employment growth in microenterprises (81.1 percent versus 75.0 percent).

## CONCEPTUAL FRAMEWORK

Successful entrepreneurship strategies lead to small business growth and determinants of small business employment patterns in the United States and other countries have been studied many times (Bruce et al. 2007). An extensive review of the literature on microenterprise business growth was reported by Doub and Edgcomb (2005) with some studies examining business start-ups and others focusing on established businesses. Three empirical studies summarized next provide a basis for formulating hypotheses about business formation rates at the microlevel and employment changes in a region.

### Acs and Armington

In 2005, Acs and Armington provided an extensive examination of new firm formation rates using Business Information Tracking Series (BITS) data for 384 labor market areas from 1991 to 1998 (2006). Differences in firm formation are associated with regional differences in human capital, growth in local population and income, and industry specialization. The researchers studied formation rates in six industry sectors, including business services, distribution, extractive, local marketing, manufacturing, and retail industries by year during the period of examination.

The findings differ by industry sector and year, but, in general, significant relationships were reported between formation rates and human capital measures such as proportion of college graduates and share of high school dropouts compared with the noncollege adult population.

The researchers also report significant relationships between intensity of service businesses and all establishments in the labor market area. Areas strong in service businesses had higher formation rates, and average size of establishment in the region was statistically related to formation rates. The unemployment rate was statistically significant in specific years, but seems to vary with the business cycle.

The analyses by Acs and Armington (2005) further demonstrated that firm birth rate is important in five industry sectors but not in manufacturing. The share of proprietors' income in a Labor Market Area (LMA) is positively related to overall firm formation rates showing that those areas with a strong presence of proprietors usually have a more favorable climate for entrepreneurs. This relationship, however, does not hold for all industry sectors.

The authors also report a positive relationship between percent of adults with a secondary school degree and firm formation rates; however, the proportion of adults with college degrees is not significantly related to formation rates. These results suggest that broad-based educational levels in the region may lead to more entrepreneurship than a high percentage of residents with higher education degrees.

Finally, Acs and Armington report a strong positive relationship between entrepreneurship and overall economic development. This finding is not unexpected and may be even more important in rural areas that lost large manufacturing industries and, thus, now rely more heavily on small businesses serving local as well as regional markets.

## Innovation and Information Consultants, Inc. (IIC, Inc.) Study

The Small Business Administration (SBA), Office of Advocacy, commissioned the Innovation and Information Consultants (2006) to examine factors affecting the growth and profitability of small businesses. This project studied changes in business employment at the national level using pooled data for 1997–1999 and 2000–2002, followed by verification with case studies in Kentucky, Maine, Nebraska, Nevada, North Carolina, and Utah, to identify important characteristics and policies leading to small business growth and profitability. Explanatory variables vary in their relationship to births compared with deaths and between periods of expansion and recession.

Results from an analysis of rural establishment growth show that rural population growth and urban-rural wage gap are positively related. The rural amenity index, urban small business growth, and a Rocky Mountain regional variable were also positively related but only during the recessionary period, while the urban amenity index, urban population, urban jobs, and Southeast regional variable were negatively related. During a period of economic expansion (1997–1999), rural small business profitability (measured by average nonfarm proprietors' income) and urban small business growth were negatively correlated with rural establishment growth.

Since one aim of the IIC, Inc. project was to determine the importance of local economic development for rural business prosperity, the authors examined small business performance from several angles. Changes in number of rural small businesses were related to population, per capita income, diploma recipients per 1,000 residents, real wages, share of nonfarm proprietors' income, density of urban establishments, urban jobs per 1,000 residents, and region of the country.

Profitability of rural small businesses was related to number of firm births adjusted for population, real farm proprietors' income, per capita income, average urban nonfarm proprietors' income, real wages in urban areas, real Gross State Product, and two regional variables (Great Lakes and Southeast).

## Papadaki and Chami

A somewhat related study of determinants of microbusiness growth patterns in Canada, using Micro-Enterprises 2000 Survey data, examined owner-founders of microbusinesses involving females, people employed in agriculture, and Hispanics in seven nonmanufacturing industries with between one and four employees in 1995 and still operating in 1999 (Papadaki and Chami 2002). The study divides determinants of business growth into three main factors: (1) owner-manager characteristics, (2) growth motivation, and (3) management know-how.

Several results have implications for the present study even though the Canadian study is a microstudy of businesses rather than a county-level analysis. Businesses whose owners had not completed high school reported slower growth. Gender, age, and immigrant status of owners did not affect business growth significantly.

Propensity of an owner to take risks was significantly related to growth, while the rate of growth in the businesses was less when the owner was currently employed outside of the business venture. This situation may reflect a lifestyle entrepreneur status and a relative shortage of time to devote to the business venture. Expressed desire or commitment to being one's own boss did not seem related to rate of growth.

Significant variables in the management know-how category included use of informal networks and the fact that the business venture was co-owned with a partner. The partnership relationship was important in business formation or later stages. Willingness of a business owner to share control and incorporate the specific talents and abilities of the partner may be especially important in small business success.

A business having been started by a family member or the owner having previous experience with the business was not associated with growth. Also surprising was that neither previous ownership nor prior involvement with a business of the same type was associated with business growth.

## Christofides, Behr, and Neelakantan

The importance of creating an entrepreneurial climate including the role of public agencies has been discussed extensively in the academic and

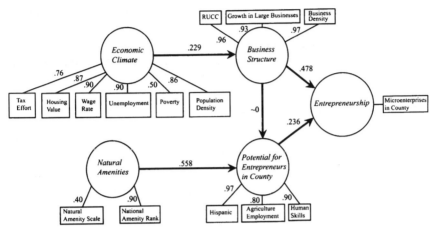

Notes: $\chi^2 = 19.32$; d.f. = 105; $p \geq .5$
**The model's error parameters can be obtained from Athiyaman and Walzer (2007).

**Figure 4.1.   The Effects of Contextual Factors on Entrepreneurship: Parameter Estimates**

professional literature as well as in this volume (Dabson, et al. 2003; Hustedde [chapter 3]; National Commission on Entrepreneurship 2002). Christofides, Behr, and Neelakantan (2001), using 1987–1999 data, identified determinants of county employment levels. This study did not focus directly on small business creation or success; rather, it examined the types of state programs contributing to gains in employment, income, and number of business establishments in urban and rural Pennsylvania. The results are interesting since they offer insights into the types of programs, as measured by state spending, associated with various countywide economic indices. Since the project does not examine small business growth patterns directly, it is not discussed in detail here.

In summary, the existing literature on entrepreneurship suggests the following causal sequence among variables. Entrepreneurship is affected by business structure in a region and the potential for entrepreneurship in the region (Acs and Armington 2005; IIC 2006). Business structure, however, results largely from the overall economic condition of the region (Christofides, Behr, and Neelakantan 2001). Similarly, the potential for entrepreneurship is determined by the natural amenities in the region (IIC 2006). Figure 4.1 is a schematic representation of the hypotheses and shows the strength of the relationship.

*The Hypotheses*

The link between *economic climate* and *business structure* is based on the following:

1. Prosperous economic conditions have a direct positive influence on business structure.
2. The link between *natural amenities in the county* and *potential entrepreneurship* suggests natural amenities are positively related to potential entrepreneurship.
3. The direct positive influence of economic conditions on business structure means that enhancements or improvements in business structure result in increases in microbusinesses.
4. County business structure results in significant increases in potential for entrepreneurship in a region.
5. The direct positive influence of natural amenities on entrepreneurship potential in the region suggests that increases in amenities bring increases in microbusinesses.

The measures associated with the conceptual framework are defined in table 4.1 and their relevance to the analyses described in subsequent pages.

## ECONOMIC CONDITIONS

Six measures describe economic conditions in a county and where possible, the relevance of each measure to the study of entrepreneurship is highlighted.

### Unemployment Rate

Residents in counties with higher unemployment are pressured to seek alternative employment opportunities and, in some cases, may start a business. Likewise, small counties that have lost manufacturing or another large industry are expected to have a higher proportion of their nonfarm employment in small businesses. Information on the average age of unemployed is not readily available however. Age of residents can also play an important role in business formation when older displaced workers have wealth to invest in a business venture.

### Poverty Rate

Median family income and per capita income are proxies for wealth. Percentage in poverty has been used in other studies and is included here, arguing that relatively high percentages of residents in poverty are unlikely to have access to wealth and conventional loans.

**Table 4.1.** Definitions of Variables Used in Analysis

| Name | Description |
|---|---|
| *Economic Climate* | The theoretical construct is represented by six observable indicators (see Figure 1 and descriptions about variables below). |
| Tax Effort | Per capita taxes paid as a proportion of income per capita |
| Housing Value | Median housing value in the county |
| Wage rate | Average wages in the county |
| Unemployment | Percentage unemployed in the county |
| Poverty | Poverty rate in the county |
| Population Density | Population per square mile in the county |
| *Natural Amenities* | Latent variable: Natural amenities. The construct relates to quality of life perceptions. It is captured by two indicators (see descriptions about variables V7 and V8 below). |
| Natural Amenity Scale | Natural Amenity Scale: A linear composite based on six indices such as winter sun (see www.sba.gov/advo/research/rs270tot.pdf) |
| Natural Amenity Rank | A rank ordering of the counties based on quality of life index. |
| *Business Structure* | This theoretical factor denotes business activities in the county. The construct is measured using three observable variables (V9 to V11). |
| RUCC | Rural-Urban Continuum Codes. Assesses the county's proximity to metro areas. |
| Growth in Large Businesses | Growth rate of enterprises with between five and 15 employees. |
| Business Density | Number of enterprises per 10,000 residents. |
| *Potential for Entrepreneurs in County* | Potential for entrepreneurship in the county. Three observable variables capture the construct (see V12 to V14 below). |
| Hispanic | Percentage of Hispanic residents in the county |
| Agriculture Employment | Percentage of county residents employed in agriculture |
| Human Skills | Percentage males, ages 25-34, with bachelor's degrees |
| *Entrepreneurship* | Defined as new firm starts in a region |
| Microenterprises in County | Changes to number of microenterprises in the county |

## Population Density

With limited resources for marketing, small businesses often serve mainly local areas and may be more successful in areas with higher population density as noted by Audretsch and Keilbach (2004b). More densely populated areas may also involve greater interactions among small business owners and operators. Business density is included separate from population density to distinguish these effects (see the discussions pertaining to the business structure factor).

## Median Housing Values

Persons interested in starting businesses or in expanding existing ventures require access to capital. By definition, microenterprises in this study did not have access to traditional lending sources, a common phenomenon in rural areas with a limited number of banks or financial institutions. Previous research has documented that personal savings and family resources often provide much of the start-up capital for small businesses (Blade Consulting Corporation 2003). Median housing value is included as a proxy for wealth or access to capital recognizing that housing may be protected in bankruptcy proceedings.

## Tax Effort

The local economic climate for business development and prosperity is also measured by tax effort defined as per capita taxes paid relative to income per capita. While taxes are usually not a deciding factor in selecting a business location for a small business (Area Development Online 2005), when not passed on to consumers, they can reduce the overall profitability of a business.

## Average Wages

Personnel costs are likely to be a more serious cost consideration in larger businesses, but these costs may still be important in microenterprises with employees. Thus, the average wage in a county was included to capture differences in personnel costs.

## NATURAL AMENITIES

Since the work of Johnson and Beale (2002) showing that retirement and tourism opportunities differentiated counties with respect to growth during the 1990s, there has been increased interest in amenities and quality of life considerations in potential economic development (Johnson and Beale

2002; Florida 2002; IIC 2006). Thus, we included two natural amenities variables to capture the *scenic* factor in counties. The theory is that entrepreneurs or those interested in starting businesses will be lured to these areas. The measures are composites of objective indicators such as: (1) warm winter, (2) winter sun, (3) temperate summer, (4) low summer humidity, (5) topographic variation, and (6) water area.

## BUSINESS STRUCTURE

Microbusinesses are often linked to larger businesses and, in some instances, are offshoots of these organizations, so business structure in a county can affect or determine prosperity. Note that this approach supports arguments in the endogenous growth theory that the concepts of diversity and selection determine entrepreneurship. Thus, three measures of business structure are included in subsequent analyses.

### Business Density

The density of businesses not only signifies markets available but also indicates opportunities for microbusiness owners to interact and share knowledge and/or expertise. The number of microenterprises per 10,000 residents is included to reflect business structure in a county.

### Rural-Urban Continuum Codes (RUCC)

Proximity to population (markets) and businesses is important to most enterprises serving a local or regional market but especially to microenterprises with limited marketing budgets. The Rural-Urban Continuum Codes (RUCC), also known as Beale Codes, are included to capture proximity to metro areas (Butler and Beale 1994).

### Growth in Larger Businesses

As noted previously, a limitation of the microenterprise data is that businesses can expand and grow into the next larger size category. To adjust for these experiences, the growth rate of enterprises with between 5 and 15 employees is included in the business structure category.

## POTENTIAL ENTREPRENEURSHIP FACTORS

Papadaki and Chami (2002) argue that specific population subgroups in rural areas more often engage in entrepreneurship. Three groups—(1) agriculture-based, (2) young male with bachelor degrees, and (3) immigrants—are included to reflect potential entrepreneurs.

### Employed in Agriculture

Businesses often start on a part-time basis and a flexible schedule can provide the time to manage and/or operate a new venture. In some cases, lifestyle entrepreneurs may include farm owners-operators or their families who start a business to maintain a lifestyle or perhaps even to survive economically. Two or more farm families may join in an operation; previous research identified partnerships as influencing success (Blade Consulting Corporation 2003). Agricultural employment in the Midwest is seasonal which can permit farm operators and employees to pursue off-farm employment or other business activities.

Likewise, farm owners and operators may have access to resources such as land and capital important in business formation. Farm owners-operators are already in business, so they may have skills and experiences needed to manage an operation. Some of their skills and knowledge are not directly transferable to new ventures; however, they are still familiar with basic management practices. In any event, the percentage of county residents employed in agriculture is included as a proxy for potential entrepreneurship.

### Percent Hispanic

Hispanics are one of the most rapidly growing segments of the population in the Midwest, even though the population base is still relatively small. In some counties, the main population growth during the past decade has involved Hispanics and, without this growth, these counties would have declined in population (Lasley and Hanson 2003).

Immigrants offer several advantages for starting and expanding businesses. First, they have access to established markets in other locations because they represent cultures and societies with perspectives and consumption habits different from the locale in which they relocated.

Second, arrival in a new location may create substantial pressure to generate incomes, which could mean starting a small business. Thus, percentage of Hispanic residents in a county is included to indicate potential entrepreneurship.

### Percent Males, Ages 25–34, with Bachelor's Degrees

Previous studies have debated the importance of young, educated males in entrepreneurial efforts (Autio 2005). This group is launching their careers, and an economy that focuses on information technology and computers offers many opportunities. Thus, microenterprises might be expected to be higher in counties with concentrations of these residents.

## Entrepreneurship Factor

As noted previously, entrepreneurship is a dynamic concept. It involves innovations in meeting new markets (e.g., new products), and managing or optimizing the production process. This all-inclusive concept is measured using microenterprises as a general proxy for entrepreneurship. Specifically, changes in the number of microenterprises in the counties are included in the empirical model.

## EMPIRICAL FINDINGS

As previously mentioned, the Midwest is an especially appropriate region in which to study the importance of the relationship of entrepreneurship, small business development, and employment growth because it offers a variety of urban and rural settings with a diversified economy, including agriculture, manufacturing, and service jobs, many of which have undergone a major transition in the past decade or more (Walzer 2003).

Regions in the Midwest also differ widely in socioeconomic conditions such as income, age, and educational attainment. The fact that large metro centers are surrounded by rural counties offers opportunities to test propositions about the interrelationships between microenterprises located in rural counties and large businesses in adjoining urban centers.

The six midwestern states included in this study have a strong agricultural sector and a large rural population base. At the same time, each state has numerous relatively small rural communities that have undergone population shifts in recent years. The sample states have a total of 460 rural counties with a combined population of 10.7 million residents and an age distribution not unlike the United States (table 4.2). In 2000, the unemployment rate in the sample rural midwestern counties was 5.3 percent, slightly less than the 5.8 percent for the nation. Agriculture and related industries in the counties represent 5.3 percent of employment compared with 1.9 percent for the United States, and manufacturing represented 21.8 percent compared with 14.1 percent nationally. Per capita income in the sample counties averaged $17,198—substantially below the $21,587 for the United States. No difference is found in the percentage of residents in poverty, however (12.4 percent for both the sample and the United States).

The results of the model estimated to quantify relationships among the various factors contributing to entrepreneurship and regional development are shown in figure 4.1. Five theoretical constructs—Economic

**Table 4.2.  Socioeconomic Characteristics, 2000**

| Characteristic | Sample* | Percent of Sample | United States | Percent of U.S. |
|---|---|---|---|---|
| **Population** | 10,737,998 | | 281,421,906 | |
| **Gender** | | | | |
| Males | 5,309,493 | 49.4% | 137,916,186 | 49.0% |
| Females | 5,428,505 | 50.6% | 143,505,720 | 51.0% |
| **Hispanic** | 186,612 | 1.7% | 35,238,481 | 12.5% |
| **Age Structure** | | | | |
| 0-17 | 2,659,996 | 24.8% | 72,142,757 | 25.6% |
| 18-24 | 999,662 | 9.3% | 27,067,510 | 9.6% |
| 25-34 | 1,297,482 | 12.1% | 39,577,357 | 14.1% |
| 35-44 | 1,656,416 | 15.4% | 45,905,471 | 16.3% |
| 45-64 | 2,483,901 | 23.1% | 61,749,839 | 21.9% |
| 65 and Over | 1,640,541 | 15.3% | 34,978,972 | 12.4% |
| **Civilian Labor Force** | | | | |
| (Population 16 Years and Over) | | | | |
| Employed | 4,938,393 | | 129,721,512 | |
| Unemployed | 275,869 | | 7,947,286 | |
| Unemployment Rate | 5.3% | | 5.8% | |
| **Industry Employment** | | | | |
| Agriculture, Forestry, Fishing, Hunting, and Mining | 264,094 | 5.3% | 2,426,053 | 1.9% |
| Manufacturing | 1,078,002 | 21.8% | 18,286,005 | 14.1% |
| Wholesale and Retail Trade | 733,165 | 14.8% | 19,888,473 | 15.3% |
| Finance, Insurance, Real Estate | 205,606 | 4.2% | 8,934,972 | 6.9% |
| Services | 1,756,242 | 35.6% | 54,435,821 | 42.0% |
| Public Administration | 213,710 | 4.3% | 6,212,015 | 4.8% |
| Other** | 687,574 | 13.9% | 19,538,173 | 15.1% |
| **Per Capita Income** | $17,198 | | $21,587 | |
| **Poverty Status** | | | | |
| Percent Total Persons in Poverty | 12.4% | | 12.4% | |

*Sample includes rural counties in Illinois, Iowa, Kentucky, Missouri, Indiana, and Wisconsin.
**Other consists of construction, transportation and warehousing, utilities, and information.

*Source*: U.S. Bureau of the Census 1990 and 2000

Climate, Business Structure, Natural Amenities, Potential for Entrepreneurs in a County, and Entrepreneurship—affect individual observed variables such as Tax Effort, Housing Value, and other factors. The observed variables cannot be measured precisely and therefore are also affected by other factors not included in the estimated model. Choosing the right number of measures for each theoretical variable is an art rather than a precise process (Bentler 1993). While theory was used as a basis for developing the model, we readily acknowledge that other indicators might work as well.

Of main interest to the current discussions are the paths or linkages among the theoretical constructs such as between Economic Climate and Business Structure or between Natural Amenities and Potential for Entrepreneurs in a County. Four of the five hypothesized relationships outlined earlier in this chapter were verified in the causal analysis.[1] The only insignificant causal path was the Business Structure to Potential for Entrepreneurs in a County linkage.

Thus, simply stated, the empirical analysis shows that Economic Climate is related to Business Structure in a county as shown by a path coefficient of .229. Likewise, Natural Amenities affect the Potential for Entrepreneurs in a County (.558). The Business Structure then influences the level of Entrepreneurship (.478) as does the Potential for Entrepreneurs in a County (.236). The outcome then is an increase in the number of Microenterprises in a County.

An individual- or firm-level analysis would be required to fully assess the selection concept discussed earlier. In other words, in light of the theory that individual employees in large firms also engage in start-ups, the intention of those employees to start businesses would need to be assessed. Since the current analysis was limited to aggregate data (for instance, Business Density), a relatively weak relationship between the aggregate indicators of Business Structure and potential Entrepreneurship can be expected.

Also important to note is that county Business Structure has approximately twice the impact on growth in Entrepreneurship (.478 versus .236) as Potential for Entrepreneurs in a County. Each of the four significant causal linkages is discussed next in terms of ways to promote local entrepreneurship.

### Economic Conditions to Business Structure

Economic base theory (Richardson 1969) categorizes business activities in a region into basic or nonbasic. Conceptually, basic activities promote growth and development in a region by generating income from outside the region whereas nonbasic activities mainly serve the domestic population. Since nonbasic activities reflect the level of income and demand in the region (economic conditions), it is logical to expect economic conditions to influence business structure.

The statistical analysis in this chapter supports the economic base theory in that the economic conditions in a county positively influence a region's business structure. Wealthier counties, measured by median value of owner-occupied housing, had higher business density. In addition, a significant increase in business activity occurred in counties with lower tax rates. In all, approximately 60 percent of the variability in county business structure is attributed to sound economic conditions.

Of the six variables used to measure economic climate, percentage unemployed in the county is the most accurate indicator according to the statistical analysis. Population density had the worst performance. Similarly, business density is the least error-prone indicator of business structure in the county.

## Natural Amenities to Potential Entrepreneurship

Rural lifestyles are perceived as offering beneficial aspects of well-being such as clean air, open spaces, gardens, and nature-based recreational opportunities (Cloke 1995). The causal model in this chapter shows that changes in natural amenities are positively related to changes in the potential pool of entrepreneurs. Put another way, one unit increase in quality of life perceptions about a county results in a .56 standard deviation increase in the potential pool of entrepreneurs. This relationship is significant in the sense that perceptions about quality of life predict the potential pool of entrepreneurship in a majority of instances ($R^2$ = 70 percent). Specific strategies to enhance quality of life perceptions at the county level are available in Athiyaman (2007).

## Business Structure to Entrepreneurship

Business structure in a county affects local entrepreneurship in several ways. For instance, denser economic activity leads to specialization (agglomeration effect) and thus firm starts. In addition, when for technologies with constant returns, proximity to markets often brings higher returns because of lower transportation costs. This situation, in turn, can attract entrepreneurial ventures. Finally, the higher density of human and physical capital could bring knowledge spillovers and hence entrepreneurship.

Business structure has a positive influence on local entrepreneurship with a standardized path coefficient of .478 indicating that business structure enhancements increase entrepreneurship. In fact, of all the variables used to analyze the causes of entrepreneurship, business structure has the most positive influence on new firm starts.

## Potential Entrepreneurs to Entrepreneurship

How do start-ups arise? According to Schumpeter (Baldwin 1954; te Velde 2001), the economy starts at a stationary state as posited by neo-classical theorists. Potentially profitable opportunities exist but these opportunities are recognized by only a few individuals with foresight (entrepreneurs). The entrepreneurs secure the necessary productive means through financial institutions and other sources. The entrepreneurs are soon followed by others who want to take a share of the market and the ensuing profits. Soon, the market becomes saturated with little or no room for potential new entrants. The market then returns to equilibrium conditions.

This explanation supports the concepts of diversity and selection outlined previously but what makes it especially interesting is the implicit assumption that a conducive business structure spawns entrepreneurs such as when financial institutions support entrepreneurial ventures. Without this support, the potential pool of entrepreneurs is only a weak predictor of new firm starts (the path coefficient is .23). However, when combined with business structure, the potential pool of entrepreneurs variable accounts for as much as 80 percent of the variability in entrepreneurship.

## SUMMARY AND CONCLUSION

Natural amenities are positively associated with potential entrepreneurship indicating that more attractive living environments attract entrepreneurs as suggested by Florida (2004) and others. Wealthier counties, measured by median value of owner-occupied housing, had higher business density and growth rates. Not surprisingly, counties with a positive business climate, such as those with growth in establishments of 5 to 19 employees, reported higher growth in microenterprises. These findings add validity to the claim that knowledge spillovers are a necessary condition for entrepreneurship.

Rural midwestern counties vary widely in the relative importance of microenterprises, with some counties having as much as one-third of the employment in these businesses. The analyses in this chapter offer several findings that can be useful in designing local development strategies involving entrepreneurship.

Specifically, the number of microenterprises grew more rapidly in counties with higher median housing value, natural amenities, lower average wages, and growth in enterprises with 5 to 19 employees.

To the extent that entrepreneurs start small with microenterprises, practitioners might target certain groups for special training and technical assistance efforts. Even if not all such groups are true entrepreneurs in the innovation sense, they are associated with microenterprise growth in the counties and, for this reason, can add to rural economic development.

There have been major changes in approaches to local economic development with much more attention now paid to seeking out local businesses with the potential to expand with technical support. Identifying new markets or helping small businesses stay current on technological advances is at the heart of the widely recognized Economic Gardening concept pioneered by Christian Gibbons in Littleton, Colorado, for example (City of Littleton 2006). This shift away from an industrial attraction focus and more focus on assessing the potential for local firms to prosper with management or marketing assistance will probably increase in the future. The analysis suggest that business structure is important for successful entrepreneurship activity although it may not be widely recognized by incoming entrepreneurs before they a start a business.

In the past, microenterprises have been an important component in the economies of many, if not most, small rural counties. There is every indication that these businesses will become even more important in the future, and more research is needed regarding factors that create the most suitable climate for these businesses to prosper. Identifying potential entrepreneurs interested in starting microenterprises and creating a supportive environment may well be one of those elements.

## APPENDIX: THE STRUCTURAL EQUATION MODEL

Structural equation models enable one to specify theoretical frameworks and test causal relationships. Consider the construct economic climate of a region. It can be measured using a variety of indicators such as per capita income, unemployment rate, etc. Since these indicators are often measured with error, linking these indicators with other variables such as new firm starts is bound to yield statistical estimates of association that involve measurement error. Structural equation models can overcome this limitation because relationships among variables can be estimated after adjusting for measurement errors.

The causal model in figure 4.1 uses two sets of equations: (1) measurement equations, and (2) structural equations. The first set of equation specifies the observed variables used to measure concepts. Specifically, it describes the reliabilities of the observed variables—the degree of correspondence between the theoretical constructs and their indicators of measurement. If reliability is less than one in magnitude, then the indicator contains measurement errors.

The second set of equations—the structural equations, highlights the hypothesized causal relationships among the theoretical concepts. In matrix notation, the structural equations for the model can be represented as

**Structural Equations**

$$
\begin{bmatrix} F3 \\ F4 \\ F5 \end{bmatrix} =
\begin{bmatrix} r1 & 0 & 0 & 0 \\ 0 & r2 & r3 & 0 \\ 0 & 0 & r4 & r5 \end{bmatrix}
\begin{bmatrix} F1 \\ F2 \\ F3 \end{bmatrix} +
\begin{bmatrix} D3 \\ D4 \\ 0 \end{bmatrix}
$$

Similarly, the measurement model is written as:

**Measurement Equations**

$$
\begin{bmatrix} V1 \\ V2 \\ V3 \\ V4 \\ V5 \\ V6 \\ V7 \\ V8 \\ V9 \\ V10 \\ V11 \\ V12 \\ V13 \\ V14 \\ V15 \end{bmatrix} =
\begin{bmatrix}
\lambda 1 & 0 & 0 & 0 & 0 \\
\lambda 2 & 0 & 0 & 0 & 0 \\
\lambda 3 & 0 & 0 & 0 & 0 \\
\lambda 4 & 0 & 0 & 0 & 0 \\
\lambda 5 & 0 & 0 & 0 & 0 \\
\lambda 6 & 0 & 0 & 0 & 0 \\
0 & \lambda 7 & 0 & 0 & 0 \\
0 & \lambda 8 & 0 & 0 & 0 \\
0 & 0 & \lambda 9 & 0 & 0 \\
0 & 0 & \lambda 10 & 0 & 0 \\
0 & 0 & \lambda 11 & 0 & 0 \\
0 & 0 & 0 & \lambda 12 & 0 \\
0 & 0 & 0 & \lambda 13 & 0 \\
0 & 0 & 0 & \lambda 14 & 0 \\
0 & 0 & 0 & 0 & \lambda 15
\end{bmatrix} *
\begin{bmatrix} F1 \\ F2 \\ F3 \\ F4 \\ F5 \end{bmatrix} +
\begin{bmatrix} E1 \\ E2 \\ E3 \\ E4 \\ E5 \\ E6 \\ E7 \\ E8 \\ E9 \\ E10 \\ E11 \\ E12 \\ E13 \\ E14 \\ E15 \end{bmatrix}
$$

In order to estimate the model, 15 measured variables are used. In all, these 15 variables contain 120 measured variances and covariances. In line with Bentler (1993), one path is fixed from each theoretical contruct to a measured variable. This provides ten unknown factor weights. In addition, 15 error variances ($E_i$), two residual error of prediction variances (Di), three variances/covariances of the independent latent variables (F1, and F2), and five direct latent variable effects were estimated: that is the paths from F1 to F3, F2 to F4, F3 to F4, F3 to F5, and F4 to F5. With 35 parameters to be estimated, there are 85 degrees of freedom. Finally, since the model contains variables measured in different units, for instance, percentages, and monetary values, standardized values are reported to facilitate comparison of the effects of the variables included in the model.

Figure 4.1 shows the parameter estimates of the model. The structural equation programs developed by Bentler (1993) were employed to calibrate the model. Further information about the model is available in Athiyaman and Walzer (2007).

## NOTE

1. Bentler's (1993) structural equation algorithm was applied to the data in Appendix 1. More information about this model can be found in Athiyaman and Walzer (2007).

## REFERENCES

Acs, Zoltan C., and Catherine Armington. 2005. *Using census BITS to explore entrepreneurship, geography, and economic growth.* (Small Business Research Summary. No. 248). Washington, DC: SBA, Office of Advocacy.

Area Development Online. 2005. *20th annual corporate survey.* www.area-development .com/FrameCorpSurvey4.html (January 7, 2006).

Association for Enterprise Opportunity (AEO). 2006. *About microenterprises.* www .microenterpriseworks.org/about/whatis.htm (January 7, 2006).

Athiyaman, Adee. 2007. *Perceptions about community services in rural Illinois: Implications for marketing communication strategies.* Working Paper, Illinois Institute for Rural Affairs, Western Illinois University, Macomb.

Athiyaman, Adee, and Norman Walzer. 2007. Entrepreneurship growth in a cross section of midwestern counties. Working Paper, Illinois Institute for Rural Affairs, Western Illinois University, Macomb.

Audretsch, David B., and Max Keilbach. 2004a. Entrepreneurship and regional growth: An evolutionary interpretation. *Journal of Evolutionary Economics* 14: 605–16.

Audretsch, David B., and Max Keilbach. 2004b. *Entrepreneurship capital and economic performance* (Discussion Papers on Entrepreneurship, Growth and Public Policy 2004-01). Jena, Germany: Max Planck Institute of Economics, Group for Entrepreneurship, Growth and Public Policy.

Audretsch, David B., and Max Keilbach. 2005. Entrepreneurship capital and regional growth. *The Annals of Regional Science* 39: 457–69.

Autio, Erkko. 2005. *Global Entrepreneurship Monitor 2005 report on high-expectation entrepreneurship*. Babson Park, MA and London: Babson College and London Business School.

Baldwin, Robert. 1954. Some theoretical aspects of economic development. *Journal of Economic History* 14(4): 333–45.

Baumol, William. 1968. Entrepreneurship in economic theory. *American Economic Review* 58(2): 64–71.

Bentler, Peter M. 1993. *Structural Equations Program*, BMDP, California: Los Angeles.

Beugelsdijk, Sjoerd. 2006. Entrepreneurial culture, regional innovativeness and economic growth. *Journal of Evolutionary Economics* 15: 6–29.

Beugelsdijk, Sjoerd, and Niels Noorderhaven. 2004. Entrepreneurial attitude and economic growth: A cross-section of 54 regions. *Annals of Regional Science* 38: 199–218.

Blade Consulting Corporation. 2003. *Expected costs of startup ventures*. Prepared for the SBA, Office of Advocacy. Vienna, VA: Blade Consulting Corporation.

Bruce, Donald, John A. Deskins, Brian C. Hill, and Jonathan C. Rork 2007. *Small business and state growth: An econometric investigation* (Report #292). Washington, DC: Small Business Administration.

Butler, Margaret A., and Calvin L. Beale. 1994. *Rural-Urban Continuum Codes for metro and nonmetro counties, 1993*. (Staff Report No. 9425). Beltsville, MD: Agriculture and Rural Economy Division, Economic Research Service, U.S. Department of Agriculture.

Christofides, C. A., Todd Behr, and Pats Neelakantan. 2001. *A retrospective of Pennsylvania's economic development programs*. Harrisburg: Center for Rural Pennsylvania.

City of Littleton: Business and Industry Affairs. 2006. *Economic Gardening*. www.littletongov.org/bia/economicgardening/default.asp (March 26, 2007).

Cloke, Paul. 1995. Rural lifestyles: material opportunity, cultural experience, and how theory can undermine policy. *Economic Geography* 72(4): 433–49.

Dabson, Brian, Jennifer Malkin, Amy Mathews, Kimberly Pate, and Sean Stickle. 2003. *Mapping rural entrepreneurship*. Washington, DC: Corporation for Enterprise Development.

Doub, Marian, and Elain L. Edgcomb. 2005. *Bridges to success: Promising strategies for microenterprise business growth in the United States*. Washington, DC: FIELD, Aspen Institute.

Florida, Richard. 2004. *The rise of the creative class and how it's transforming work, leisure, community and everyday life*. New York: Basic Books.

Innovation and Information Consultants (IIC), Inc. 2006. *An empirical approach to characterize rural small business growth and profitability*. Prepared for the SBA, Office of Advocacy. Concord, MA: IIC, Inc.

Johnson, Kenneth M., and Calvin L. Beale. 2002. Nonmetro recreation counties: Their identification and rapid growth. *Rural America* 17(4): 17–19.

Kirzner, Israel. 1997. Entrepreneurial discovery and the competitive market process: An Austrian approach. *Journal of Economic Literature* 35: 60–85.

Labriandis, Lois. 2006. Fostering entrepreneurship as a means to overcome barriers to development of rural peripheral areas in Europe. *European Planning Studies* 14(1): 3–8.

Lasley, Paul, and Margaret Hanson. 2003. The changing population of the Midwest: A reflection on opportunities. In *The American Midwest: Managing change in a rural transition*, ed. Norman Walzer, 16–39. Armonk, NY: M. E. Sharpe.

Leibenstein, Harvey. 1968. Entrepreneurship and development. *American Economic Review* 58(2): 72–78.

Montgomery, Mar, Terry Johnson, and Syed Faisal. 2000. Who succeeds at starting a business? Evidence from the Washington self-employment demonstration. Grinnell, IA: Grinnell College, Department of Economics.

National Commission on Entrepreneurship. 2002. *Entrepreneurship: A candidate's guide: Creating good jobs in your community*. Washington, DC: National Commission on Entrepreneurship.

Pack, Howard. 1994. Endogenous growth theory: Intellectual appeal and empirical shortcomings. *Journal of Economic Perspectives* 8(1): 55–72.

Papadaki, Evangelia, and Bassima Chami. 2002. Growth determinants of microbusinesses in Canada. *Small Business Policy Branch* (July): 1–50.

Richardson, H. W. 1969. The Economic Significance of the depression in Britain. *Journal of Contemporary History* 4(4): 3–19.

te Velde, R. A. 2001. *Schumpeter's theory of economic development revised*, paper presented at the Future of Innovation Studies Conference, The Netherlands, 20–23 September.

U.S. Bureau of the Census. 2000. *Various files by state*. www2.census.gov/census_2000/datasets/100_and_sample_profile/ (July 3, 2002).

U.S. Bureau of the Census. 1990. *1990 Summary Tape File 1 (STF 1)*. http://factfinder.census.gov/servlet/DTGeoSearchByListServlet?ds_name=DEC_1990_STF1_&_lang=en&_ts=44204506671 (July 10, 2002).

Walzer, Norman, ed. 2003. The American Midwest: Managing change in rural transition. Armonk, NY: M. E. Sharpe.

# 5

# The Drivers of Regional Entrepreneurship in Rural and Metro Areas

*Jason Henderson, Sarah A. Low, and Stephan Weiler[1]*

In a rapidly globalizing economy, traditional rural assets such as cheap land and labor can no longer ensure regional prosperity. New mixes of assets, such as those leveraging local strengths in workforce, innovation, lifestyle, finance, and information, will shape economic prospects for both rural and metro areas in this globalizing environment. Entrepreneurship in particular is already an important component of rural prosperity, with its role in rural economic success becoming even more essential in the new millennium.

Entrepreneurs have been shown to be a critical mechanism for new ideas and innovations to take root in the marketplace (Small Business Administration 2005). Entrepreneurs create local jobs, wealth and growth, and are themselves innovative users of other assets and resources. Research has found a strong correlation between entrepreneurship and long-term employment growth at the regional level (Acs and Armington 2003). Fostering local entrepreneurship and innovation is becoming a favorite strategy in aiding economic development (Pages 2004). Yet few measures exist for rural regions to gauge their entrepreneurial assets.

This chapter outlines new indicators of entrepreneurship and uses these metrics to understand the reasons for the wide spatial variation in entrepreneurship. The first section explores why entrepreneurs are vital components of regional economic development. The second section constructs measures of the local quantity of entrepreneurs and the value they generate. The third section compares trends between metropolitan and nonmetropolitan counties to provide insight into rural America's entrepreneurial base. The fourth section examines the county characteristics that drive spatial variations in entrepreneurship quantity and value. In particular, the analysis seeks to understand whether differences exist between rural and metropolitan entrepreneurship, and which regional drivers are affected by such differences. The final section sketches potential policy implications of the findings.

## IDENTIFYING AN ENTREPRENEUR

The first fundamental challenge in building an entrepreneurship indicator is defining an entrepreneur. Despite decades of research focused on defining entrepreneurship, a commonly accepted definition has failed to emerge (Gartner 1988); however, the role of entrepreneurs as owners-managers does differentiate them from other economic participants. As owners, entrepreneurs are risk-bearers. They reap the rewards for innovative, entrepreneurial success and bear the consequences of innovative, entrepreneurial failure. While the prospect for huge profits from a successful firm motivates entrepreneurs, the risk of bankruptcy can make the leap into entrepreneurship daunting.

In addition to their role as owners, entrepreneurs are also managers. As managers, entrepreneurs are decisionmakers with management control over the firm. Entrepreneurs decide when to be innovative, what innovations to adopt, and how far to push the innovative changes in the firm. A further key element of entrepreneurs' management role is the resource decisions they make. Each must decide how to acquire and bundle resources together to build competitive advantages in the marketplace.

Entrepreneurs are indeed unique economic players (figure 5.1). Entrepreneurs are distinguished from corporate managers and career professionals because while the latter have decisionmaking roles in the organization, career managers in general are not the risk-bearers or owners of the company. While stockholders are corporate owners, they are not entrepreneurs because they, in general, transfer decisionmaking responsibilities to corporate management.[2] Entrepreneurs develop from many sources—the unemployed, private workers, and corporate managers. Many begin as part-time entrepreneurs.

Self-employment is the simplest type of entrepreneurship (Blanchflower and Oswald 1998). Entrepreneurs in this study are defined as those people who are self-employed because they satisfy the basic characteristic of entrepreneurs: owner-management. By owning their business, they exert management control in the business and they have the right to extract business profits.[3] They also assume the risks associated with the loss of their business.

Not all entrepreneurs are alike in their impact on local economies (Henderson 2002). Some entrepreneurs start their business to fulfill a dream or

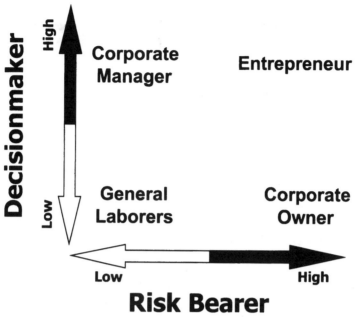

**Figure 5.1    Owner-Manager Matrix of Entrepreneurs**

to follow a chosen lifestyle. They may open a coffee shop near a lake or teach piano lessons in a small town. Many such lifestyle entrepreneurs benefit their community by enhancing the local quality of life. These firms indirectly boost regional growth by enhancing the area's mix of stores and other businesses. Lifestyle entrepreneurs mainly contribute to a region's measure of entrepreneurial breadth by adding numbers of entrepreneurs to a region.

Other firms generate more direct economic value for their region. By focusing on creating wealth, income, and jobs, such high-value entrepreneurs enhance economic growth while identifying and exploiting assets in their region. Some entrepreneurs start new businesses and sell them to finance new ventures. These serial entrepreneurs repeatedly search for new avenues to create wealth, income, and jobs.

## MEASURING RURAL AMERICA'S ENTREPRENEURIAL SEEDBED

The contrast between lifestyle and high value entrepreneurs is one indication of the tremendous diversity of entrepreneurship. To effectively capture this diversity, various measures of entrepreneurial activity are needed. First, an entrepreneurial breadth measure is created to analyze the quantity of entrepreneurs across regions. Second, an entrepreneurial depth measure is created to analyze the value these entrepreneurs generate in the regional economy.

## Entrepreneurial Breadth

How many entrepreneurs does a region have? A region rich in entrepreneurs is expected to contain the seeds to grow an entrepreneurial economy and achieve economic prosperity. While no indicator can determine perfectly the quantity or breadth of entrepreneurship in a local community, the percentage of workers who are proprietors sheds light on the breadth of regional entrepreneurial seedbeds in America. In particular, the entrepreneurial breadth indicator shows that the concentration of entrepreneurs indeed varies spatially at the county level.

Entrepreneurial breadth is calculated as the number of nonfarm proprietors divided by total nonfarm employment in a county. This ratio allows us to compare concentrations of entrepreneurs across vastly different areas, from sparsely populated rural towns to major metropolitan areas, on an equivalent basis. Nonfarm proprietor and employment data are obtained from Bureau of Economic Analysis–Regional Economic Information System (BEA–REIS 2004).

The entrepreneurial breadth measure indicates that there is wide spatial variation in the concentration of entrepreneurs across the country. Entrepreneurship is especially broad in the Great Plains. Some counties have 70 percent of their workers owning and managing their own businesses (figure 5.2). In other counties, the self-employed account for as little as 1.5 percent of workers.

Entrepreneurial breadth is greater in more rural counties, counties with small towns, and no large cities. Counties are divided into three groups, based on the size of their core cities. The Census Bureau identifies metropolitan counties as those having at least one city with a population of 50,000 or more, while micropolitan counties are nonmetropolitan counties that are based around a core city of between 10,000 to 50,000 people. We classify the remaining counties with no cities larger than 10,000 as town counties.

The entrepreneurship breadth measure indicates that the quantity of entrepreneurs is higher in less populated, more insular counties. Town counties had the highest level of entrepreneurial breadth, where proprietors accounted for 22.4 percent of nonfarm employment and a location quotient (LQ) of 1.402.[4] Micropolitan counties also had above average entrepre-

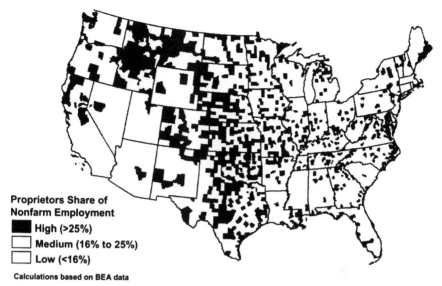

**Proprietors Share of
Nonfarm Employment**

■ High (>25%)

□ Medium (16% to 25%)

□ Low (<16%)

Calculations based on BEA data

Figure 5.2.   Entrepreneurial Breadth, 2001

neurial breadth, with proprietors accounting for 17.6 percent of nonfarm employment and a LQ of 1.101.[5] In contrast, metropolitan proprietors made up only 15.4 percent of nonfarm employment, leading to a below-average metro LQ of 0.96.

Rural places may have high levels of entrepreneurial breadth for various reasons. First, the small size of rural economies naturally leads to smaller firms serving smaller populations. In 2002, the average employment in rural establishments was 12.0 people compared to 16.2 people in metro establishments.[6] A smaller firm size implies a higher ratio of owners to workers and, thus, higher entrepreneurial breadth.

Second, the industry structure of rural economies also results in higher breadth levels. Rural (nonmetropolitan) self-employment is more concentrated in construction and retail trade industries (figure 5.3). Retail firms tend to be smaller than firms in other industries, reinforcing the impacts associated with smaller firm size. In the construction industry, persons may be considered independent contractors instead of employees. Consequently, they would be identified as proprietors instead of wage earners.

## Entrepreneurial Depth

Some regions may have more entrepreneurs, but how much income and value do they create? High concentrations of entrepreneurship enhance the

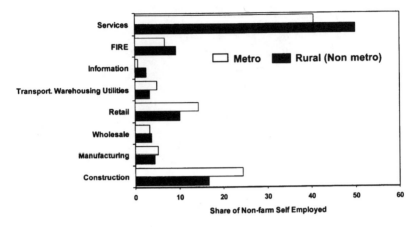

*Source*: U.S. Bureau of the Census 2003

**Figure 5.3.   Self-Employed in Major Industry by Metropolitan Status**

quality of life in a region, but economic growth is driven by the value that entrepreneurial activity generates. Some entrepreneurs earn more income, add more value, and enhance regional growth and prosperity more than other entrepreneurs. Depth of entrepreneurship differs from breadth in that it examines the value of entrepreneurial activities rather than the number of entrepreneurs. Income and value-added measures are used to measure entrepreneurial depth across regions.

*Entrepreneurial Income*

The goal of entrepreneurial depth measures is to better understand the economic value entrepreneurs generate. One basic measure of prosperity is to analyze the incomes associated with entrepreneurs, under the assumption that entrepreneurs with higher incomes are operating profitable firms which add more monetary value to the community. As average proprietor income rises, the region as a whole becomes more prosperous.

A useful income-based measure of entrepreneurship depth is the ratio of proprietor income to proprietor employment in a county. Proprietor income and employment data was obtained from Bureau of Economic Analysis–Regional Economic Information System (BEA–REIS 2004) data. Nonfarm proprietor income was divided by the number employed as nonfarm proprietors in 2001.

The entrepreneurial income metric indicates a wide distribution in the income that entrepreneurs are creating in their communities (figure 5.4). On average, proprietors earned $28,900 in 2001; however, average proprietor income at the county level ranged widely from less than $2,500 in Hayes

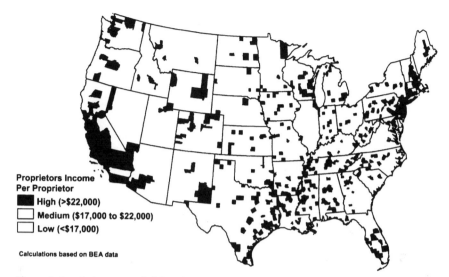

**Figure 5.4.   Entrepreneurial Depth: Income**

County, Nebraska, to $152,000 in New York County, New York. The limitation of the income measure is that these data include both part-time and full-time proprietors, so the metric may be skewed by the ratio of proprietors whose income only partially supports their lifestyle.

The geographic pattern of proprietor income suggests that entrepreneurial depth is strongest in densely populated areas. Proprietors in metropolitan counties had higher annual income than their rural peers. With an average proprietor income of $19,056, metropolitan counties had an above-average LQ of 1.09. The LQs for micropolitan and town counties were 0.59 and 0.53, respectively, and were well below the national average as average proprietor income was $15,956 and $14,256. Average proprietor income was lower than average wage and salary income in all county types, underscoring the fact that some entrepreneurs pursue their craft on a part-time basis. The higher metropolitan proprietor incomes reflect both the higher costs of living in urbanized areas along with the higher opportunity cost of forgoing traditional wage and salary employment to pursue entrepreneurial activities. In this sense, the "hurdle rate" for metropolitan entrepreneurs is higher than that of their rural counterparts.

*Entrepreneurial Value-Added*

An alternative measure of entrepreneurial depth is the value the entrepreneur contributes to their product or service. This value-added metric can be estimated by the ratio of proprietor income to the total sales of their products and services.[7] This indicator is a better measure of entrepreneurial depth for two reasons. First, value-added is a direct measure of the proprietor's contribution to the product or service provided to the market. The metric reflects the proportion of the overall value of the good that is due directly to the entrepreneur's ideas and skills. Second, value-added is a better measure of depth than average income because the ratio is not skewed by varying mixes of part-time versus full-time entrepreneurs.

The value-added measure indicates that the value entrepreneurs add to their communities varies widely across the nation (figure 5.5). The value-added measure provides a slightly different picture of entrepreneurial depth than the income measure, although the two are still highly correlated (0.81). Counties with a high value-added measure are less clustered than counties with a high income measure, and they are also less concentrated along the east and west coasts.

Analysis across metropolitan, micropolitan, and town counties reveals that metropolitan proprietors contribute and capture more value from their products and services than micropolitan and town county proprietors, thus generating more income per sales dollar. Metropolitan counties had the highest ratio of proprietor income to nonemployer receipts (0.703). Town counties had the lowest income-to-receipts ratio (0.461), with the ratio for micropolitan counties marginally higher at 0.483. As a result, the location

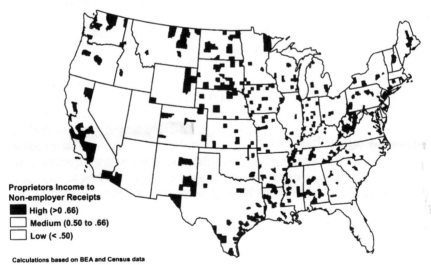

Proprietors Income to
Non-employer Receipts
■ High (>0 .66)
□ Medium (0.50 to .66)
□ Low (< .50)

Calculations based on BEA and Census data

**Figure 5.5.    Entrepreneurial Depth: Value-Added**

quotients were the highest for metropolitan counties (1.037), followed by micropolitan (1.005) and town counties (0.976). These results are similar to those from income depth, but all the value-added LQs were closer to the average of one, indicating the value-added is less spatially dependent than either the breadth or income metrics.

Rural areas lag metropolitan places in capturing high income or value-added associated with entrepreneurial activity. The lack of access to larger markets is one reason for the lack of entrepreneurial depth in rural areas. These locations simply contain smaller economies and fewer market opportunities, which are limited by the size and remoteness of rural communities (Dabson 2001). Entrepreneurs that operate in such limited markets will have fewer income generating opportunities and lower depth measures, especially in terms of income.

Lack of access to larger markets also constrains the value-added measure because more remote firms pay higher costs to access a more distant market. In comparing two firms selling the same product in the same market, the more remote firms will have higher transportation costs, limiting income and reducing the value-added measure.

The value entrepreneurs generate is also affected by the types of industries in which regions specialize (Malecki 1994). Entrepreneurs working in industries that take advantage of greater worker skills are likely to generate more value for themselves and their local economy; however, in both goods and service-producing sectors, rural entrepreneurs are highly concentrated in lower-skilled industries. Only 21 percent of the self-employed in rural manufacturing specialized in high-tech industries compared to 27.8 percent of the self-employed in metropolitan areas.[8]

In service sectors, half of the rural self-employed operate in consumer service industries, which tend to utilize lower-skilled workers. Moreover, only 28 percent of the rural self-employed operate in service producing industries that tend to employ high-skilled workers, well below the 45 percent of metropolitan self-employed involved in producer services.[9]

The skill differences are also reflected in the occupations of the entrepreneurs. Rural entrepreneurs tend to work in more blue-collar occupations than their metropolitan counterparts. Compared with the metropolitan self-employed, higher shares of rural self-employed work in production, natural resource, and construction occupations (figure 5.6). These occupations tend to have lower levels of educational attainment. The share of rural self-employed in professional, management, business, and financial occupations is much lower than the share of metropolitan self-employed in these fields. According to Census Bureau data (2004), professional, management, business, and financial occupations tend to have higher levels of educational attainment.

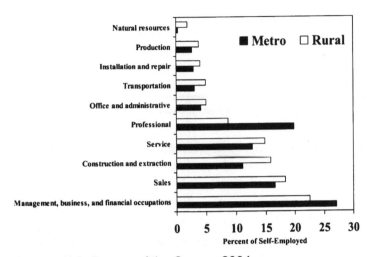

*Source*: U.S. Bureau of the Census 2004

**Figure 5.6.   Self-Employment by Occupation by Metropolitan Status**

## WHAT REGIONAL FACTORS DRIVE ENTREPRENEURIAL BREADTH AND DEPTH?

The mapping and statistics analyzed thus far reveal substantial variation in the quantity and economic value of entrepreneurs across U.S. counties. The contrasting patterns of entrepreneurial breadth and depth measures by metropolitan and nonmetropolitan counties in particular suggest the forces associated with entrepreneurial quantity and value are different. Regression analysis at the county level is therefore used to identify the regional factors that are related to entrepreneurial breadth and depth measures, focusing on those related to human capital, natural amenities, financial capital, infrastructure, and local economy size. Table 5.1 in the appendix shows variable definitions and sources.

### Human Capital

One of the most unique and important features of entrepreneurs is the set of skills and ideas, or human capital, they bring to their enterprises. In entrepreneurial research literature, the distinction between entrepreneurs and nonentrepreneurs is often based on their traits and/or behaviors (Gartner 1988), which in turn are shaped by their human capital. Various measures of human capital have in fact been found to be highly related to entrepreneurship. Educational attainment is one measure of human capital that is expected to be related to entrepreneurship, as both knowledge and critical thinking skills are invaluable to an entrepreneur. Prior research in-

**Table 5.1.   Data Description and Source**

| Variable | Source | Variable Description |
|---|---|---|
| **Dependent Variable** | | |
| Breadth | BEA-REIS | (Proprietor employment/total nonfarm employment), 2001 |
| Depth-Income | BEA-REIS | (Proprietor income over proprietor employment)* 100, 2001 |
| Depth-Revenue | BEA-REIS & Census | Average proprietor income (BEA) over average non-employer receipts (Census), 2001 |
| **Independent Variables** | | |
| *Human Capital* | | |
| College | Census | Percent of population age 25+ with BS degree or higher, 2000 |
| Foreign | Census | Percent of population foreign born, 2000 |
| Info/Arts | BEA-REIS | Location quotient of NAICS 52 & 71 (Information & Arts, Entertainment Employment) over total nonfarm employment |
| *Amenities* | | |
| Topography | ERS | Scale, 20 being the highest mountain; 0 being the flattest plains |
| *Financial Capital* | | |
| Deposit/Pop | FDIC & Census | Total deposits ($1,000) over population |
| *Infrastructure* | | |
| Interstate | Census | Dummy variable: counties containing a portion of interstate highway |
| Broadband | FCC | Counties with >3 high-speed internet providers, 1999 |
| *Local Economy* | | |
| Metro* | ERS | Metropolitan counties, 2003 |
| Micro* | ERS | Micropolitan counties, 2003 |
| West** | Census | AK, AZ, CA, CO, HI, ID, MT, NM, NV,OR, UT, WA, WY |
| Midwest** | Census | CT, IA, IL, IN, KS, MA, ME, MI, MN, MO, |
| Northeast** | Census | MY, ND, NE, NH, NJ OH, PA, RI, SD, VT, WI |

*Nonmetro and nonmicro counties are the omitted conditions.
**Southern states are the omitted condition.

dicates that proprietors who create the most value are more likely to have a college education (Acs and Armington 2004).

Knowledge can be obtained from formal education but also from leveraging the knowledge from other places, especially foreign countries. Many immigrants engage in entrepreneurial activity after coming to the United

States. Research has found the percentage of foreign born in a region to positively affect both entrepreneurship and firm formation (Lee, Florida, and Acs 2004); we test that proposition directly as well.

Entrepreneurship is not only about knowledge but also about creativity. While all regions have some creative endowment, some regions' entrepreneurs seem better able to tap their own and nearby pools of creativity. Florida (2002) created a "Bohemian Index," to measure creativity, which is an LQ of the local concentration of authors, designers, musicians, performers, artists, and other similarly creative occupations. Florida and others find this Bohemian Index to have a positive and significant relationship with high-tech industry formation (Florida 2002) and entrepreneurship (Lee, Florida, and Acs 2004). In a simple application of this concept, an Information/Arts variable was constructed to summarize the regional concentration of information and entertainment employment.

The results show that *human capital* is significantly related to the value that entrepreneurs create and capture, but not related to the quantity of entrepreneurs in a community. College education rates, percent of foreign born residents and creative sector employment are positively associated with both income and value-added measures of entrepreneurship depth. Counties with higher levels of educational attainment, a larger foreign-born community, and a greater concentration of creative activity contained entrepreneurs that were able to generate large incomes and value from entrepreneurial activity. Human capital, however, was not found to be associated with the entrepreneurship breadth metric measuring the quantity of entrepreneurs in a local county. While positive, college education rates and creative sector employment are insignificantly related to breadth. In fact, breadth was found to be significantly lower when the percent of foreign born in a region increases. A possible explanation for this finding is the successful entrepreneurs that create high levels of value tend to grow larger firms, which lowers the entrepreneurial breadth measure.

## Amenities

Recent research also suggests that regions with higher levels of natural amenities have higher levels of economic activity. As economic opportunities move from goods-producing activities which are often tied to the locations of physical resources to more service-based activity, people have more flexibility in deciding where to live and work (Rappaport 2003). The small scale of their firms makes proprietors especially free to locate where they please. Many locate in areas with attractive topography, abundant water area, and comfortable temperature and humidity levels. In the 1990s, proprietor growth was stronger in rural places with higher levels of natural amenities (Henderson 2002). The analysis here focuses on the widely accepted measure of topography, indicating the ruggedness and altitude of the regional terrain.

*Natural amenities* have a strong relationship to both entrepreneurial breadth and depth. Regions with more topographical variation appear to be places of high self-employment. This finding may result from people wanting to live a certain lifestyle in scenic, mountainous locations; self-employment may provide the best opportunities for them to live that lifestyle. While entrepreneurs may be drawn to high amenity regions for lifestyle opportunities, they have been able to create businesses that produce high value-added for their communities.

### Financial Capital

Access to financial capital is widely seen as a critical factor in developing a region's entrepreneurship potential (Barkley 2003). Entrepreneurs in rural areas are often at a particular disadvantage in gaining such access as their small size and often novel ideas do not mesh well with established information gathering and loan scoring systems. Yet substantial local pools of available capital can be invaluable in generating a self-reinforcing cycle of entrepreneurial lending. Recent research indicates that extensive regional asset ownership has a significant and positive effect on firm formation rates (Garofoli 1994; Sutaria and Hicks 2004). Therefore, the regressions use a county's average bank deposits per capita to approximate the pool of local assets potentially available for lending.

Access to *financial capital* also appears essential to regional entrepreneurial success. Average bank deposits per capita are positively associated with the value-added entrepreneurial depth metric. Bank deposits and high value entrepreneurship simultaneously contribute to each other. Bank deposits allow entrepreneurs to grow, who can in turn generate higher local bank deposits.

### Infrastructure

Regional infrastructure, such as roads and telecommunications, allows entrepreneurs to access resources and markets more easily. These factors are likely to be especially important for entrepreneurs who are further away from key markets and suppliers. In terms of roads, interstate highways are perhaps the best indicator of the connectedness of the region to the nation's car- and truck-oriented commerce network. The existence of an interstate in a county is likely to promote high value entrepreneurship. The role of the Internet in business transactions has now also become a necessary condition for success, so access to broadband Internet access is likely to positively influence entrepreneurship as well. Broadband access may be especially important in allowing entrepreneurial income and value to flourish.

Entrepreneurship has a strong relationship with *infrastructure,* especially in terms of interstate highway and high-speed broadband Internet access. Entrepreneurship depth measures have a positive relationship with both access measures, indicating that such infrastructure raises the average income and value-added of entrepreneurship. Entrepreneurship breadth has a negative relationship with interstate and Internet access, however. Small entrepreneurs, those who contribute most to the breadth measure, may be hindered by the lack of infrastructure access, forcing them to start and stay smaller than their more networked counterparts. Interstate highways and high speed broadband Internet access and are most common in urban regions and provide vital transportation, communication, and information networks for existing and potential growth businesses.

## Local Economy

Entrepreneurship is expected to be stronger in locations with large, vibrant economies. Regional researchers have found that agglomeration is key to stimulating economic growth (Krugman 1991). Density and size tend to create substantial advantages in labor and product markets for both workers and firms. Who are often attracted to metro places and locations because there is a larger local market to test a wider range of their offerings while also providing a much greater range of resource, financial, and labor inputs. By contrast, smaller and more remote local economies limit the ability of entrepreneurs to build economies of scale (Dabson 2001). Lack of economies of scale limits the local demand for products and makes resource acquisition more difficult.

Even after accounting for human capital, natural amenities, financial capital, and infrastructure assets, the *local economy* metropolitan and micropolitan dichotomous variables are still significantly related to entrepreneurial depth and breadth. Relative to town counties, metropolitan counties are characterized by higher levels of entrepreneurial depth, both in terms of income and value added, and by lower levels of entrepreneurial breadth.

Micropolitan counties also have higher levels of entrepreneurial depth and lower levels of breadth compared to town counties, although the relative differences are not as strong as the metropolitan differences. The results suggest that regions with larger levels of agglomeration are better able to support the creation of high-value entrepreneurs compared to regions with low agglomeration levels.

## Differences in Rural versus Metro Impacts

The initial analysis assumes that the impacts of human capital, natural amenities, financial capital, and infrastructure assets would be similar across rural and metropolitan counties; however, this assumption may not hold true as suggested by the significance of the metro/micro local economy variables even after controlling for the four other categories of entrepreneurial drivers. In fact, the differences in the level of agglomeration in rural and metropolitan areas may enhance the marginal impacts of the various county assets. For example, human capital may have a greater impact on entrepreneurial development in highly agglomerated metro areas. Additional analysis was performed to test if the impacts of human capital, natural amenities, financial capital, and infrastructure on entrepreneurship varied across rural and metropolitan counties.[10] The results are presented in table 5.3 in the appendix.

**Table 5.2.  Regression Results with Interaction Variables**

|  | Breadth | Depth-Income | Depth-Revenue |
|---|---|---|---|
| *Human Capital* | | | |
| College*Metro | -0.266* | 2991.7* | 0.497* |
| | (0.045) | (362.70) | (0.094) |
| Foreign*Metro | -0.191* | 4732.74* | 0.863* |
| | (0.073) | (581.90) | (0.150) |
| Info/Arts*Metro | -0.018** | 323.68* | 0.054* |
| | (0. 007) | (58.94) | (0.015) |
| *Amenities* | | | |
| Topography *Metro | -.006** | -4.66 | -0.0003 |
| | (.003) | (24.37) | (.006) |
| *Financial Capital* | | | |
| Deposits *Metro | -2.22e-06 | 0.03* | 2.78e-06 |
| | (1.66e-06) | (0.01) | (3.41e-06) |
| *Infrastructure* | | | |
| Interstate *Metro | -0.025* | 269.87* | 0.044* |
| | (.007) | (53.86) | (0.014) |
| Broadband *Metro | -0.007 | 399.10* | 0.090* |
| | (0.017) | (133.08) | (0.034) |
| Adjusted R-square | 0.156 | 0.340 | 0.062 |
| F-stat | 47.61 | 130.9 | 21.3 |
| Observations | 3,020 | 3,020 | 3,020 |

*Significant at 0.01 level
**Significant at 0.05 level

The results suggest that human capital and infrastructure may have stronger impacts on the value of entrepreneurship in metro counties than in other counties. In general, the impact of human capital and infrastructure variables on entrepreneurship varies significantly across metropolitan and nonmetropolitan regions.[11] Initial results revealed that counties with high levels of human capital supported entrepreneurs that created and capture more value from entrepreneurial activity. It appears that larger, more agglomerated metropolitan areas are able to reap even larger benefits in terms of entrepreneurial income and value-added impacts associated with high levels of educational attainment, foreign-born population, and information and arts employment. Moreover, it appears that metro areas also receive larger marginal benefits from infrastructure as marginal income and value-added of entrepreneurship is higher in metropolitan areas as well.

In terms of breadth or the quantity of entrepreneurial activity, a contrasting tale emerges.[12] In terms of quantity, it is nonmetropolitan or rural counties, not metropolitan counties, that are enjoying larger benefits associated with human capital, topographic variation, and infrastructure. Nonmetropolitan or rural counties with higher levels of human capital, topographic variation, and interstates are found to support higher quantities of entrepreneurial activity. Thus, human capital, topography, and interstates may be stimulating more entrepreneurial activity in rural places compared to their metro counterparts—yet, the challenge of producing high-value entrepreneurial activity still remains.

## POLICY IMPLICATIONS AND CONCLUSION

Entrepreneurship will be crucial in shaping the future of regional economic development, especially in smaller and more remote rural areas that depend heavily on entrepreneurial activity. Entrepreneurship creates jobs and wealth within a region, ultimately leading to prosperity. While proprietorship is prevalent in rural areas, high value entrepreneurship, which creates the most economic benefit, is stronger in metropolitan areas.

Still, rural regions seem to be a natural seedbed for entrepreneurship. The breadth measure shows that a high proportion of rural workers are self-employed. Seedbeds seem to occur easily in areas with sparse economic activity, creating opportunities to fill local needs with small establishments, leading to many entrepreneurs who contribute greatly to the quality of life in rural areas. The challenge is to create entrepreneurs who have higher income, create more value, and provide greater contributions to regional prosperity.

Education matters when it comes to creating high-value entrepreneurs. Counties with higher levels of educational attainment have more entrepreneurs who produce higher incomes and more value-added. While the relationships between educational attainment and high-value entrepreneurial activity are stronger in metropolitan areas, educational attainment is more positively correlated with the quantity of entrepreneurs in rural places.

Communities may want to focus on educational training and development as a mechanism to promote entrepreneurship while noting that it is not necessary to generate a mass of doctorate holders to build entrepreneurial regions. In comparing the educational attainment of the self-employed to government and private sector workers, the self-employed have moderate levels of educational attainment. They have more educational attainment than private sector workers but less education than government workers (Henderson 2004a). The self-employed are not necessarily people with graduate or professional degrees, but they are more likely to be people with some college or technical education.

Educational institutions are quickly becoming more engaged in entrepreneurial education. More colleges and universities are offering more courses and supporting new entrepreneurship centers. According to Inc.com, more than 1,600 colleges and universities offer courses and programs in entrepreneurship, up 533 percent since the 1980s (Adkins 2006a). The Rural Community College Initiative has identified entrepreneurship and small business development as a key economic development role for community colleges (Rubin 2001) Entrepreneurship education is also moving into K–12 education. The National Federation of Independent Business has created the Youth Entrepreneur Foundation, which has spurred the creation of curriculum for teachers (Adkins 2006b). Youth entrepreneurship is also receiving strong support from foundations such as the Kauffman Foundation (Blumberg 2006).

The findings also suggest that regional quality of life is related to high-value entrepreneurship, as is the proportion of the foreign-born population. Counties with higher levels of natural or scenic amenities, creativity, and diversity had more entrepreneurs who produced more income and added more value. Counties may want to focus on boosting the quality of life in their communities to spur entrepreneurs. By being known as an amenity-rich, creative place open to the diversity of people and ideas, communities can help foster local entrepreneurs and attract those that are footloose. In rural places, natural amenities seem to have an especially large impact on entrepreneurial development.

Yet, even accounting for these features, high-depth entrepreneurship still appears concentrated in metropolitan counties. The value-added indicator reveals that rural entrepreneurs generate less value from their activities than their urban counterparts. Entrepreneurs in urban centers may especially benefit from proximity to the variety of high-value marketplaces in urban areas, high population density, and transportation nodes. This generation of high-value entrepreneurs in urban areas is reinforced by the greater impacts of human capital and infrastructure in such regions relative to rural places.

The lack of large concentrations of local economic activity makes it essential for rural places to develop networks and links to nodes of economic activity. These places are often city-based nodes that feature broader and deeper market and supplier possibilities for entrepreneurs. Furthermore, the larger amount of business activity itself generates valuable information on market prospects for probing entrepreneurs, who in turn can use the information to sharpen their own business plans.

Network development and partnerships across sector and place are keys to the success of boosting entrepreneurship in Appalachian Ohio (Emery, Fisher, and Macke 2003). With support from the Appalachian Regional Commission (ARC), six regional economic, community, arts, and nature development organizations partnered to create the Appalachian Ohio Regional Investment Coalition (AORIC). This coalition is helping facilitate entrepreneurial development by helping entrepreneurs in Appalachian Ohio tap funding, facilities, and other resources to spur business growth.

Infrastructure development may be especially important in developing these networks. Transportation infrastructure allows entrepreneurs to connect to other locations, both in terms of their markets and their suppliers. In rural areas, interstates have a strong correlation with entrepreneurial development. Furthermore, high-quality telecommunications allows rural entrepreneurs to connect with resources, assets, and information in other regions to overcome limited local capacities. For example, the Small Business Administration has an E-Business Institute (www.sba.gov/training) that offers free online courses and national training events to assist entrepreneurs. Such cross-regional flows can help both types of region, as more urbanized areas can tap the often cheaper assets of rural places while rural areas can take advantage of denser urban marketplaces.

High-value entrepreneurs contribute to regional prosperity through the jobs and income they add to a regional economy. Entrepreneurs are true assets to their region, as well as innovative users of other regional assets. Regional leaders can use these breadth and depth indicators to gauge how high-value entrepreneurs could become part of a regional development strategy. These strategies could usefully include productive partnering with other regions to take advantage of mutual complementarities such as those sketched between rural and urban places.

## NOTES

1. The views expressed in this chapter are those of the authors and do not necessarily reflect the positions of the Federal Reserve Bank of Kansas City or the Federal Reserve System.

2. McGrath, McMillan, and Scheinberg (1992) find that entrepreneurs are more risk tolerant than corporate professionals.

3. It is important to remember that the self-employed are *not* the only entrepreneurs, however. Aspiring entrepreneurs would not be identified as self-employed because they have not started a business to employ themselves. In some cases, entrepreneurs start by doing a part-time business before becoming fully self-employed. Thus, the self-employed are best recognized as a subset of entrepreneurs in the United States.

4. Location quotients (LQs) are an economic analysis tool which compares a local measure to a reference measure. In this case, county proprietor breadth is compared to national proprietor breadth: if the county's breadth is the same as the national average, the LQ equals one.

5. The LQ for all nonmetropolitan counties was 1.213. Proprietors accounted for 19.4 percent of nonfarm employment in nonmetropolitan counties.

6. Calculations were based on County Business Patterns data.

7. The value-added measure is constructed as the ratio of nonfarm proprietor income over the nonemployer receipt data. Nonfarm proprietor income data for 2001 was obtained from BEA–REIS. Proprietor receipt data were obtained from U.S. Census Nonemployer Receipts, 2001, which stems from the receipts reported by proprietors to the Internal Revenue Service on Schedule C.

8. The U.S. Department of Agriculture categorizes manufacturing industries into high-tech, value-added, and routine categories. In high-tech industries, almost 27 percent of the jobs were in skilled occupations compared to 9.3 percent in value-added industries and 10.3 percent in routine industries (Henderson 2004b).

9. The U.S. Department of Agriculture categorizes service producing industries into consumer, producer, recreation, and transportation, utilities, and wholesale categories. In producer industries, almost 37 percent of the jobs were in skilled occupations compared to 25 percent in other service-producing industries (Henderson 2004b).

10. To test for differences in the marginal impacts of human capital, amenities, financial capital, and infrastructure across rural and metropolitan counties, regression models that included an interaction term created from a metropolitan dummy variable and the four drivers are estimated.

11. The human capital and metropolitan interaction variables are positively associated with entrepreneurial depth, suggesting that the marginal income and value-added impacts associated with high levels of educational attainment, foreign population, and information and arts employment are larger in the more agglomerated metropolitan areas. The infrastructure and metro interaction variables are also positive and significantly associated with entrepreneurial depth.

12. The regressions show that the human capital, topography, and the interstate interaction terms are negative and significant, indicating that these factors' impacts are lower in metropolitan areas and stronger in nonmetropolitan or rural areas.

## REFERENCES

Acs, Zoltan, and Catherine Armington. 2004. Employment growth and entrepreneurial activity in cities. Discussion Paper on Entrepreneurship, Growth and Public Policy, Max Planck Institute for Research into Economic Systems, Group Entrepreneurship, Growth and Public Policy, Jena, Germany.

Acs, Zoltan, and Catherine Armington. 2003. *Endogenous growth and entrepreneurial activities in cities.* U.S. Bureau of the Census.

Adkins, Jasmine. 2006a. Study: Entrepreneurship programs continue to expand. *Inc.com* www.inc.com/criticalnews/articles/200606/colleges.html (June 2, 2006).

Adkins, Jasmine. 2006b. New curriculum focuses on high-school entrepreneurs. *Inc.com* www.inc.com/criticalnews/articles/200606/courses.html (June 1, 2006).

Barkley, David. 2003.Policy options for equity financing for rural entrepreneurs. *Main Streets of Tomorrow: Growing and Financing Rural Entrepreneurs,* 107–25. Conference Proceedings. Center for the Study of Rural America, Federal Reserve Bank of Kansas City.

Blanchflower, David, and Andrew Oswald. 1998. What makes an entrepreneur? *Journal of Labor Economics* 1(January): 26–60.

Blumberg, Jess. 2006. Kauffman Foundation pledges $35 million for college programs. *Inc.com* www.inc.com/criticalnews/articles/200606/kauffman.html (June 27, 2006).

Dabson, Brian. 2001. Supporting rural entrepreneurship. *Exploring Policy Options for a New Rural America,* 35–48. Conference Proceedings. Center for the Study of Rural America, Federal Reserve Bank of Kansas City.

Emery, Brenda, Larry Fischer, and Don Macke. 2003. Boosting entrepreneurship in Appalachian Ohio. Main Streets of tomorrow: Growing and financing rural entrepreneurs. Conference Proceedings. Federal Reserve Bank of Kansas City. (April 28–29).

Florida, Richard. 2002. *The Rise of the Creative Class.* New York: Basic Books.

Garofolli, Gioacchino. 1994. New firm formation and regional development: The Italian case. *Regional Studies* 28(4): 381–93.

Gartner, William B. 1988. Who is an entrepreneur? Is the wrong question. *American Journal of Small Business* 12(4): 11–32.

Henderson, Jason. 2002. Building the rural economy with high growth entrepreneurs. *Economic Review* (3rd Quarter): 45–70. Federal Reserve Bank of Kansas City.

Henderson, Jason. 2004a. Who are the rural entrepreneurs? Paper presented to the North American Regional Science Association International meetings. Seattle, WA.

Henderson, Jason. 2004b. Will the farm rebound lead a rural recovery? *Economic Review* (First Quarter): 65–80.

Krugman, Paul. 1991. *Geography and trade.* Cambridge, MA: MIT Press.

Lee, Sam Youl, Richard Florida, and Zoltan Acs. 2004. Creativity and entrepreneurship: A regional analysis of new firm formation. Jena, Germany: Discussion Papers of Entrepreneurship, Growth and Public Policy, Max Planck Institute for Research into Economic Systems, Group Entrepreneurship, Growth and Public Policy.

Malecki, Edward. 1994. Entrepreneurship in regional and local development. *International Regional Science Review* 16(1&2): 119–53.

McGrath, Rita Gunther, Ian C. MacMillan, and Sara Scheinberg. 1992. Elitists, risk-takers, and rugged individualists? An explanatory analysis of cultural differences between entrepreneurs and non-entrepreneurs. *Journal of Business Venturing* 7: 115–35.

Pages, Erik. 2004. What's so new about new entrepreneurship policies? State government initiatives to foster new venture creation. Paper presented at the Knowledge Clusters and Entrepreneurship in Regional Economic Development Conference. Minneapolis, Minnesota.

Rappaport, Jordan. 2003. Moving to nice weather. *Federal Reserve Bank of Kansas City Research Working Paper,* 03–07.

Bureau of Economic Analysis–Regional Economic Information System (BEA–REIS), 1969–2004. U.S. Department of Commerce. CD.

Rubin, Sarah. 2001 Rural colleges as catalysts for community change, the RCCI experience. *Rural America* 16(2): 12–19.

Small Business Administration. 2005. *The innovation-entrepreneurship NEXUS: A national assessment of entrepreneurship and regional economic growth and development* www.sba.gov/advo/research/rs256tot.pdf (February 20, 2007).

Sutaria, Vinod, and Donald Hicks. 2004. New firm formation: Dynamics and determinants. *Annals of Regional Science* 38: 241–62.

U.S. Bureau of the Census, Department of Commerce. 2004. *Educational attainment in the United States: 2003.* www.census.gov/prod/2004pubs/p20-550.pdf (February 20, 2007).

# APPENDIX: EMPIRICAL ANALYSIS

An empirical model of entrepreneurial breadth and depth was estimated to analyze the relationship of various community characteristics and the quantity and value of entrepreneurial activity at the county level. Based on the five core categories of hypothesized entrepreneurial drivers suggested by existing research, an empirical model was estimated where the entrepreneurial breadth and depth measures were included as dependent variables and independent variables were included to measure human capital, amenities, financial capital, infrastructure, and other features of the local economic landscape.

The empirical model was estimated in linear form, with results of the three regressions reported in table 5.3. Variance inflation factors were less than 2 suggesting that multicollinearity is not a significant issue in estimation. Adjusted R-squares range from 0.09 to 0.32, satisfactory levels for cross-sectional analyses, and F-statistics for all equations are significant at the 0.05 percent level. The Hausman Specification Tests on the results from initial ordinary least squares regressions detects a simultaneity problem between the dependent variables and the explanatory variables. A two-stage least squares (2SLS) estimation method was implemented to reduce the effects of simultaneity and resulted in coefficient similar in sign and significance to OLS results. The White Test does not indicate heteroskedasticity in the data and residual plots show few outlying observations. Nevertheless, we still tried weighting the 2SLS equations by population, resulting in coefficients of similar sign and significance to their unweighted equivalents. Given these findings, we focus on the unweighted results.

**Table 5.3.  Regression Results**

| | Breadth | Depth-Income | Depth-Value |
|---|---|---|---|
| *Human Capital* | | | |
| College | -33.10 | 963.23* | -0.0574 |
| | (254.12) | (204.80) | (0.0518) |
| Foreign | -1,516.41* | 3,522.39* | 0.4493* |
| | (343.99) | (277.23) | (0.0701) |
| Info/Arts | -18.89 | 182.50* | 0.0221* |
| | (40.21) | (32.40) | (0.0082) |
| *Amenities* | | | |
| Topography | 72.39* | 15.72 | 0.0065* |
| | (16.17) | (13.03) | (0.0033) |
| *Financial Capital* | | | |
| Deposit | 0.52 | 11.62* | 0.0020* |
| | (1.33) | (1.07) | (0.0003) |
| *Infrastructure* | | | |
| Interstate | -286.61* | 131.90* | 0.0238* |
| | (31.61) | (25.47) | (0.0064) |
| Broadband | -316.42* | 444.27* | 0.0638* |
| | (57.53) | (46.37) | (0.0117) |
| *Local Economy* | | | |
| Metro | -160.92* | 118.80* | 0.0046* |
| | (38.87) | (31.32) | (0.0079) |
| Micro | -457.64* | 43.68 | 0.0044 |
| | (37.70) | (30.39) | (0.0077) |
| *Regional* | | | |
| West | 329.50* | -253.08* | -0.0225* |
| | (51.19) | (41.25) | (0.0104) |
| Midwest | 104.54* | -135.94* | 0.0293* |
| | (33.04) | (26.63) | (0.0067) |
| Northwest | 47.83 | 125.18* | 0.0280* |
| | (60.49) | (48.75) | (0.0123) |
| *Constant* | 2,447.26* | 1,090.12* | 0.4219* |
| | (39.86) | (32.12) | (0.0081) |
| Adjusted R-square | 0.158 | 0.317 | 0.089 |
| F-stat | 48.2 | 117.9 | 25.5 |
| Observations | 3,020 | 3,020 | 3,020 |

* Significant at 0.01 level

# 6

# What Makes a Successful Entrepreneur?

*Thomas S. Lyons, Gregg A. Lichtenstein,*
*and Nailya Kutzhanova*

This chapter argues that success in entrepreneurship is contingent on the mastery of a skill set, and it discusses why and how entrepreneurship skills can be developed. In doing so, the myth that entrepreneurs are "born" to success is debunked, and we question the ability of other theories to fully explain why entrepreneurs fail or succeed. Then, the skills necessary for successful entrepreneurship are identified, how these skills can be measured and their development tracked is examined, and the transformational process of entrepreneurship skills development is explored.

## THE MEANING AND IMPORTANCE OF
## ENTREPRENEURSHIP SUCCESS

In order to understand how one approaches helping entrepreneurs become more successful, what is meant by "success" in entrepreneurship must be defined. A successful entrepreneur is one who is able to generate individual and community wealth by developing a business asset, and can do this repeatedly under a variety of circumstances. This requires that an entrepreneur consistently overcome the obstacles faced in obtaining and using the resources required to start, grow, and sustain a business (Lichtenstein and Lyons 1996). Doing so entails acquisition of a set of skills.

The importance of entrepreneurship to local and regional economies is well-established elsewhere in this book, but what about the importance of an entrepreneur's ability to develop a business asset? It is widely acknowledged that assets are the building blocks of wealth creation (Sherraden 1991). Assets come in a variety of forms—homeownership, stock and bond portfolios, savings, and so on. Owning a business is also an asset, not just because the income it produces can lead to savings and investment, but because it can be passed along intergenerationally. In this light, it becomes clear that the ability to develop a business asset, when taken collectively across many individuals, can contribute to community economic development in significant ways.

Yet, much of what is done in the realm of entrepreneurship assistance for economic development purposes focuses on providing resources, financial or technical (e.g., providing financial capital, handing off information or knowledge, and related issues). These are transactional exchanges that do little to build an entrepreneur's capacity to develop and sustain a business asset in the long run. What is required is a set of long-term, highly interactive relationships capable of transforming an entrepreneur's skills. In this way, the probability of success, as has been defined, is greatly enhanced.

## WHY "OLD SCHOOL" THINKING ON ENTREPRENEURSHIP SUCCESS IS LIMITED

For many years, it was widely accepted that entrepreneurs who enjoyed success were people with innate characteristics or traits that permitted them to function effectively in the world of business creation (Greenberg and Sexton 1988; Huefner and Hunt 1994; Kassicieh, Padosevich, and Banbury 1997; Schumpeter 1991). This personality or trait perspective on entrepreneurship probably has been the most recognized theory of entrepreneurship success. Though it has received a fair amount of criticism, it still influences the entrepreneurship research agenda and policymaking in this arena. Because these characteristics are inherited, it is believed, entrepreneurship research can only observe and study this special type of people but do nothing to increase their supply.

The research agenda of the personality perspective scholars is guided by attempts to find and describe the unique characteristics that distinguish entrepreneurs as part of a special talent group; however, the large number of studies on entrepreneurial attributes has failed to produce a consistent description of an entrepreneur's personal characteristics (Bhide 2000; Shaver and Scott 1991). While some traits described seemed to be typical for most entrepreneurs (e.g., a need for achievement), the other characteristics can only be applied to a specific study group or to very few individuals.

The personality trait research has yielded diverse results. Some authors have argued that a high need for achievement is a distinct characteristic of entrepreneurs (Begley and Boyd 1986; Hornaday and Aboud 1971; McClelland et al. 1953; Rauch and Frese 2000). Others suggest that the most important quality is an internal locus of control (Brockhaus 1982), while still others suggest that it is the risk-taking propensity of entrepreneurs that makes them who they are (Brockhaus and Horwitz 1986; Hull, Bosley, and Udell 1980; Timmons, Smollen, and Dingee 1985). While several researchers have identified factors that distinguish entrepreneurs, few of these factors, if any, have been validated by more than a single study.

Cooper and Dunkelberg (1987) studied a sample of 890 entrepreneurs and found that these individuals tended to be better educated, came from families where the parent owned a business, started firms related to their previous experience, and located their businesses where they are already living and working. These entrepreneurs did not have any outstanding innate characteristics, and the diversity found in this sample was, perhaps, its most distinguishing feature.

Kassicieh, Padosevich, and Banbury (1997) attempted to find attitudinal, situational, and personal characteristics that would predict future entrepreneurs among a sample of inventors at federal laboratories. The authors compared nonentrepreneur inventors who, at the time of the study, worked at the laboratories and entrepreneurs who left the laboratories within the previous five years to start their own ventures.

The nonentrepreneur inventors were divided into two groups, using discriminant factors from previous studies: (1) those who were predicted to become and (2) those who were not predicted to become entrepreneurs. The study found that both the entrepreneurs and those predicted to be entrepreneurs differed from the nonentrepreneur group in that they were more likely to take into account ownership of intellectual property, had attempted more spin-offs in the past, had provided consulting services, were more willing to take risks, and often had relatives who were entrepreneurs.

The entrepreneurs and inventors predicted to be entrepreneurs also demonstrated an inclination to be entrepreneurs; a positive perception of support, resources, and incidence of entrepreneurship in their laboratories; a feeling of more control over their destinies; a perceived value in their achievements; and a greater belief in themselves. Yet, the observed differences among the study groups still do not explain how some inventors become entrepreneurs.

As Low and MacMillan (1988) note, the problem with the commonly noted "need for achievement" characteristic among entrepreneurs is that this trait can also be found within groups of salespeople, managers, and other professionals. Other characteristics found to be relevant to entrepreneurs can be applied to the general population as well (Gartner 1989; Greenberg and Sexton 1988). The attempts to test for these factors as potential predictors of entrepreneurial success have not been positive. A problem with the set of personality research studies is that they use different, and often incompatible, population samples and the generalizability of the findings is questionable (Gartner 1989). In general, personality traits research can be said to have failed to produce any consistent evidence as to the existence of unique entrepreneurial characteristics that differentiate entrepreneurs from the general population.

Another critical weakness of personality research is that an entrepreneur is portrayed as a person with inherited talents that can be easily expressed within an entrepreneurial venture. The dynamics of entrepreneurial processes and the unevenness of entrepreneurs' career paths are not accounted for in the personality perspective frame.

The inability of the personality perspective on entrepreneurship to produce a consistent profile of an entrepreneur is not the only shortcoming of this perspective. Perhaps an even more important consideration involves the policy decisions that follow from this personality perspective. The assumption that entrepreneurs are born makes attempts to encourage and develop entrepreneurs virtually meaningless. This has manifested itself in a variety of ineffective policies for fostering entrepreneurship that range from "hands off," free market approaches to government and nonprofit interventions that assume entrepreneurs know where to find the help offered when they need it. Conversations with a wide variety of entrepreneurs have revealed that one of their biggest challenges is knowing where to go for relevant help when they need it, which suggests that entrepreneurs are not merely "naturals" who always "figure it out" on their own.

The personality perspective on entrepreneurship offers a very stagnant approach to entrepreneurship. Business performance is viewed as a function of some set of innate psychological characteristics. Yet, why do some entrepreneurs improve over the course of their lives and their entrepreneurial experience? The whole system of social environments, with family history, social background, networks, and different experiences throughout a lifetime that seem important to an entrepreneur, is not included in the personality perspective on entrepreneurship. These relevant factors are simply ignored.

The personality perspective has also fallen short in accounting for the different stages of business development that actually translate into the diverse roles entrepreneurs play in their businesses (Cope 2005). It has failed not only because it was not able to find consistent characteristics that would describe an entrepreneur, but also because of its inability to incorporate other important factors into the analysis, to explain the dynamic nature of entrepreneurship, and to step beyond personal characteristics as explanatory variables.

At its essence, this argument is yet another manifestation of the endless debate that pits nature vs. nurture. Are entrepreneurs born or are they made? Some champions of the "entrepreneurs are born that way" paradigm, in an effort to perpetuate their beliefs under intensifying scrutiny, have sought to couch their argument in an acknowledgment of the role of environment in determining entrepreneurial success by holding that innate traits of entrepreneurs permit them to act on the opportunities and challenges presented by the context in which they operate (Pendergast 2006). If no innate characteristics, consistently attributable to entrepreneurs, have been proven to exist, however, there must be another explanation.

The unsuccessful search for the special entrepreneurial personality profile has led to attempts to find other explanations. Researchers in this field have been looking for something more tangible to study, which has resulted in a behavioral perspective on entrepreneurship. Instead of searching for the entrepreneur's traits (Low and MacMillan 1988), the behavioral perspective turns to studying entrepreneurial behaviors. Gartner (1989) called on researchers to move their attention into the arena of entrepreneurial behavior because the personality characteristics of entrepreneurs are secondary to their behavior.

While the individual entrepreneur was the focus of analysis in the personality perspective, the behavioral perspective views entrepreneurs through the roles, functions, and activities in which they engage in the process of finding business opportunities and creating new ventures. Thus, the focal point of the behavioral perspective is the process of organization creation. According to Carter, Gartner, and Reynolds (1996), the creation of an organization involves several activities, and the focus of entrepreneurial research should be on studying what these activities are, how many of them have to be accomplished in the business start-up period, and when these activities start and end.

Some of the studies within this behavioral tradition propose that there is a special order to different entrepreneurial activities: discovering a problem, developing a solution, accumulating resources, marketing products, creating an organization, producing, and selling. These activities represent milestones in a process (Block and MacMillan 1985). During the entrepreneurial process, entrepreneurs experiment with different hypotheses about products, markets, and competition and test them through experience.

Carter et al. (1996) compared three groups of entrepreneurs—(1) entrepreneurs who started a business, (2) entrepreneurs who gave up on starting a business, and (3) entrepreneurs who are still trying—and then identified different profiles of activities undertaken by each group.

The entrepreneurs who started a business were more aggressive and active. They quickly engaged in "tangible" activities such as buying equipment and facilities, taking a loan, and generating sales. The entrepreneurs who gave up a business start-up found that their business ideas were not successful, and as a result, ceased their activities. Interestingly, this group undertook mostly the same activities as the successful group.

The "still trying" entrepreneurs had undertaken fewer activities that make business real to others, like buying equipment and setting up operations, but spent more time on saving money and preparing a business plan. Carter, Gartner, and Reynolds (1996) recommended that potential entrepreneurs act quickly and aggressively in pursuing business opportunities and day-to-day business activities.

While Carter, Garnter, and Reynolds (1996) identify the activities relevant to different levels of success in starting a business, they do not provide an explanation for the difference between the aggressive and fast actions by successful entrepreneurs and the sluggish behavior of less successful entrepreneurs. How can one explain the different performance of similar actions by the three groups of entrepreneurs? Can the same differences among the study groups be observed over a longer period of time? These questions remain unanswered.

The goal of entrepreneurial behavior has been viewed as the creation of an organization. Once the business has started, the entrepreneurial activities are considered to be accomplished. Consequently, behavioral perspective studies have focused on the start-up stage, despite the fact that Robinson and Pearce (1986) have demonstrated that venture performance is different at the various stages of business development and that the activities undertaken by the entrepreneur vary with changes in each business stage as well.

One of the examples of behavioral perspective-influenced studies is a model proposed by Greenberg and Sexton (1988) that incorporates several dimensions as explanatory factors. This model hypothesizes that the decision to initiate a new venture is a function of the interactions among several factors, including an individual's entrepreneurial vision, desire for personal control, situational factors, social supports, and perceptions about him or herself as an entrepreneur and about venture success.

Van de Ven, Hudson, and Schroeder (1984) studied the start-up of 14 educational software companies. The sample was split into two categories: (1) high and (2) low performance. The authors found the following individual characteristics related to success: education and experience, internal locus of control and risk reduction, a broad and clear business idea, and personal investment.

At the organizational level, success was positively related to planning activities (although paradoxically, spending more time on a detailed business plan seemed to result in lower performance), small-scale start-up, incremental expansion, single person command, and active involvement of top management and board members in decisionmaking. The study also suggested that assistance in the form of equity capital, training, or guaranteed contracts was actually maladaptive, and that firms competing for contracts on an independent basis advanced more quickly, at least during the short run.

The behavioral perspective has produced a new wave of studies examining the actions of entrepreneurs to bring new organizations to life. One important achievement of the behavioral perspective is its utilization of a field research methodology in which behavioral researchers investigate the complicated process of organization creation and look for answers in the realm of everyday business activities.

Although the behavioral perspective on entrepreneurship has moved entrepreneurial research a step forward by researching entrepreneurial actions, it is limited in its explanatory power of entrepreneurship success. Focusing on the functions that entrepreneurs perform provides some important insights into the entrepreneurial process, but it does not add more to an understanding of entrepreneurial performance.

There is a certain parallel between the trait and behavioral perspectives on entrepreneurship. In the personality trait paradigm, the methodological search targets universal personal characteristics, while the behavioral perspective looks for generic entrepreneurial actions/functions/behaviors. If one can demonstrate a set of common actions performed by successful entrepreneurs, then one also must provide an explanation of what makes the performance of these functions successful. As Cope (2005) rightfully points out, the ability of entrepreneurs to learn and adapt is missing from the behavioral perspective.

The personality perspective claims that personal characteristics contribute to business success, although it fails to prove it. The behavioral perspective has largely overlooked the question of business success factors; instead, it has moved the research into looking for the important components of the business creation process. In other words, the behavioral perspective studies various important components of business creation but has left the question of how the process begins, develops, and grows without an answer. In its attempt to avoid a focus on entrepreneurial personal traits, the behavioral perspective has lost touch with the individual entrepreneur. It has become mechanistic.

While we acknowledge that proper motivation is an essential prerequisite to successful entrepreneurship—a "fire in the belly" (Fackler 2001)—we are not prepared to ascribe any other innate traits (and whether or not motivation is innate is open to debate) to this phenomenon. Furthermore, we would argue that behaviors are little more than manifestations of the skill set possessed by the entrepreneur.

Another emergent and distinctive domain of entrepreneurship research involves a cognitive approach which has moved the focus of analysis to the thinking, or cognitive, processes of entrepreneurs. The main assumption is that various cognitive processes underlie the behavior of an entrepreneur. Researchers study the processes that explain how entrepreneurs receive, manage, and act upon available information. In this regard, the cognitive approach has advanced research beyond behavior analysis by attempting to explain the causes of entrepreneurial behavior. For example, Shane and Venkataraman (2000) assert that there are two categories of factors influencing the probability that particular people will discover business opportunities: (1) the possession of the information necessary to identify an opportunity and (2) the cognitive properties required to utilize it.

Studies in the field of human cognition have found a limitation on the information-processing capability that people have and use and that entrepreneurs face a shortage of information on possible market outcomes on a regular basis. The cognitive school of thought suggests that entrepreneurs have mental visions, scripts, and maps of desirable outcomes that guide them through the process. People making a decision use various kinds of mental maps or scripts, using scripts, schema, and heuristics based on previous experience to deal with uncertainty.

Siegel, Siegel, and MacMillan (1993) explored characteristics separating high- and low-growth companies. They found that substantial industry experience is an important characteristic of high-growth companies. High-growth companies also focused more than low-growth companies on attempts to generate higher revenue with a single product; as a result, the high-growth companies demonstrated a higher level of expertise in market and product diversification. High-growth companies operate with fewer managerial resources and are more efficient and effective. They also develop close contacts with customers. The authors argue that these capabilities can serve as objective, measurable criteria and can be used in predicting business performance when studied in a more quantifiable way.

Several studies provide insights into the decisionmaking processes of entrepreneurs. For example, Minniti and Bygrave (2001) maintain that entrepreneurs make decisions based on two different types of knowledge. One is the specific knowledge of the market in which they operate. This type of knowledge can be described as technical expertise regarding products and a specific market.

Another type of knowledge is a more general expertise on "how to be entrepreneurial," which is acquired by doing or observing. The entrepreneurial process is described as a learning process where entrepreneurs filter the signals from competing hypotheses, and, as a result of learning in action, receive support from positive outcomes. Negative outcomes teach entrepreneurs to avoid other types of actions. The positive actions eventually compose the knowledge base upon which entrepreneurs make decisions (Minniti and Bygrave 2001).

Mitchell and Chesteen (1995) suggest that entrepreneurial expertise is presented in the form of an "expert script," and this script can be used to improve entrepreneurial expertise. The expert script is advanced and structured knowledge in a specific area. The expert script, or schemata, can be developed through experience in the field, and it improves the information processing capability of individuals (Glaser 1984). An individual in an appropriate situational context recognizes specific cues that activate a specific expert script.

Mitchell and Chesteen (1995) attempted an educational application of the expert script concept. The results demonstrate that experiential treatment can enhance a novice's venture expertise through different learning activities involving contact with experts. This study provides important insight into ways to improve entrepreneurial expertise. It also offers an important implication for entrepreneurship education because the authors demonstrate that the cognition-based instructional pedagogy is more effective than traditional methods of teaching entrepreneurial expertise such as only teaching business planning.

Much of the cognition-based literature argues that an entrepreneur's decision to initiate a venture is based on his or her intentions to proceed while the entrepreneurial intentions are generated by an entrepreneur's perceptions of how realistic and attractive his or her actions can be. As Krueger (2000) points out, opportunities are in the eyes of the beholder. He proposes that the cognitive intangible infrastructure facilitates the perception of opportunities by an entrepreneurial organization. The perception of desirability (personal and social) and perceptions of feasibility (personal and organizational) are critical factors in the intentions that guide entrepreneurial behavior.

In a study on perceptions, Simon and Houghton (2002) explore how the decision context may affect the decision to introduce a pioneering product. These authors study biases and their influence on the entrepreneurial decisionmaking process. They found that entrepreneurs in smaller, younger companies that offer pioneering products are more likely to exhibit the illusion of control, the law of small numbers (making a conclusion based on a small number of cases), and reasoning by analogy. These biases contribute to underestimating competition, overestimating demand, and overlooking requisite assets.

The cognitive approach suggests that the perception of opportunity is in fact a cognitive phenomenon. Keh, Foo, and Lim (2002) examine the opportunity evaluation process and its relation to perception biases and risk perception. These authors find that illusions of control and belief in the law of small numbers are related to how entrepreneurs evaluate opportunities and that risk perception mediates opportunity evaluation.

Markman, Balkin, and Baron (2002) assessed general self-efficacy and regretful thinking in the context of technological innovation. Results, obtained from a random sample of 217 patent inventors, showed the difference in the general self-efficacy and regretful thinking among the inventors who started a business and those who did not start a business. The first group of technological entrepreneurs tended to have significantly higher self-efficacy. The technological entrepreneurs tended to have stronger regrets about business opportunities while technological nonentrepreneurs tended to have stronger regrets regarding career and education decisions. The two groups did not differ in terms of the quantity of these regrets.

The importance of feedback to the cognitive process is demonstrated in a study by Gatewood et al. (2002). Groups of students were given positive or negative feedback about their entrepreneurial abilities (regardless of actual abilities). Results showed that the group receiving positive feedback had higher entrepreneurial expectancies than the group receiving negative feedback. The type of feedback, however, did not affect the task effort or quality of performance. The study also found that males had higher expectancies about entrepreneurial ventures than did females.

Politis (2005) brings attention to the role of experience in the entrepreneurial process. The process of entrepreneurial learning is suggested to consist of three main components: (1) entrepreneurs' career experiences, (2) the transformation process, and (3) entrepreneurial knowledge in terms of increased effectiveness in opportunity recognition and in coping with the liabilities of newness.

An important entrepreneurship policy consideration emanating from this research is that the incremental and slow character of entrepreneurial learning does not prove the effectiveness of formal training and education. Stimulating activities should be based on developing creativity, critical thinking, and reflection that will enhance the motivation and ability to develop entrepreneurial knowledge (Politis 2005).

The cognitive approach represents a wide variety of studies uncovering the internal thinking processes of the entrepreneur. There are many useful cognitive concepts such as perceptions, biases, or intentions, and theoretical models have been adopted and applied to explain the entrepreneurial process, as in the studies described above. The cognitive approach's main contribution to the field is its reorientation of entrepreneurial theory toward the entrepreneur or, in other words, "the people side of entrepreneurship research" (Mitchell et al. 2002, 100).

In contrast to the personality trait approach, the cognitive perspective endeavors to explain variations among entrepreneurs. The cognitive approach also incorporates the dynamics of the entrepreneurial process. It explains that entrepreneurs do not come to entrepreneurship fully ready to succeed, but, instead, learn and develop throughout their career. The entrepreneurs in the cognitive perspective are not significantly different from the general population and can gain or lose from the processing of limited information. They acquire and adapt their knowledge and overcome obstacles and problems as any other person would.

Cope (2005) calls for a model of dynamic learning that would combine the interactive relationship between an entrepreneur, his or her business, and the environment. The learning perspective on entrepreneurship maintains that each individual comes to entrepreneurship with unique experiences, skills, and abilities that would define learning tasks, and the learning process is characterized by constant change. Learning involves different modes such as learning by doing, from peers and mentors, from customers, and through critical events. The entrepreneurial learning perspective can integrate different approaches in the field to help explain how entrepreneurs learn and develop.

Thus, differing perspectives have been pursued on the path to an emerging entrepreneurship theory. This theory has evolved well beyond "old school" thinking that relates entrepreneurial success to the possession of innate traits. Yet, in its current state, this body of theory is still not actionable in that it does not give clear direction to enterprise development policymakers as to how to successfully foster entrepreneurship in a sustainable way. It is time to take the next step by shifting the focus to the systemic and systematic development of entrepreneurial skills.

## A Focus on Entrepreneurial Skills

In recent years, evidence from research has mounted in support of the conclusion that entrepreneurs are made and not born (Fiet 2002; Shefsky 1994). These studies tend to show that entrepreneurs learn from others— that opportunity recognition is a systematic process that can be learned. From a practical perspective, this is positive news for those who seek to assist entrepreneurs because it may offer ways to proactively work to build their capacity for success. The following assertions constitute the foundation for this argument:

- Success in entrepreneurship hinges on the mastery of an identifiable skill set.
- These skills can be developed.
- Entrepreneurs do not all operate at the same skill level.

The term *skills* is defined broadly. Entrepreneurs require specific skills if they are to make full use of the financial and technical assistance resources they need. This necessary skill set can be categorized into four main dimensions: (1) technical skills, (2) managerial skills, (3) entrepreneurial skills, and (4) personal maturity skills (Gerber 1995; Lichtenstein and Lyons 1996). *Technical skills* are the "tools of the trade"—the skills required to engage in business in a given industry. An entrepreneur whose company is in the home healthcare industry, for example, must master a different set of technical skills than those needed by an entrepreneur in the plastic injection molding industry. *Managerial skills* are those necessary for the daily operation of a business such as administrative, management, financial, and legal skills. *Entrepreneurial skills* involve the ability to recognize viable business opportunities and act on them through innovation.

Finally, *personal maturity skills* include self-awareness, accountability, emotional, and creativity skills; these are related to those skills that make up what Daniel Goleman (1995) refers to as "emotional intelligence" (43). All of these skills are entirely developable. Some may take longer than others to develop; however, given the necessary time commitment and intensity of relationship, individuals can be transformed from being would-be entrepreneurs to successful entrepreneurs.

The third assertion is that entrepreneurs do not all come to the activities of entrepreneurship at the same skill level. Instead, there is a range of skill levels found in any population of entrepreneurs. In a sense, this might be thought of as a hierarchy of skills, ranging from very low to very high. A simple illustration can be drawn from the realm of entrepreneurship itself.

At one end of the entrepreneurial spectrum is the so-called nascent entrepreneur—someone who has never started a business before and, therefore, has few, if any, of these skills. At the other end of this spectrum are the "serial" entrepreneurs, who have started and grown several businesses, both failures and successes, and have acquired numerous skills along the way. Between these two extremes lie numerous other entrepreneurial skill set combinations.

## The Entrepreneurial League System (ELS) as a Ladder of Skill Development

Because, as asserted above, entrepreneurs operate at different levels of skill, it does not make sense to address their skill development in a one-size-fits-all fashion. Yet, that is precisely the way that most assistance providers approach supplying financial and technical help. Their motivation is efficiency, but this is usually achieved at the expense of effectiveness. Categorizing entrepreneurs according to skill level and matching assistance appropriately can avoid this dilemma.

The ELS is a conceptual framework and a functioning operating system for developing entrepreneurs' skills by providing them with individual and group coaching and access to the most appropriate technical and/or financial assistance at the appropriate stage in their development and at the appropriate price (Lichtenstein and Lyons 2001). At its heart is the idea that entrepreneurs can be categorized by their level of skill, as measured on the

**Table 6.1.   The Entrepreneurial Levels of Degree of Skill**

| Skills:<br>Level: | Technical | Managerial | Entrepreneurial | Personal<br>Maturity |
|---|---|---|---|---|
| **Majors** | Outstanding | Outstanding | Outstanding | Outstanding |
| **AAA** | High | High | High | High |
| **AA** | High | Medium | Medium | Medium |
| **A** | High/<br>Medium | Low | Low | Low |
| **Rookie** | Low/No | Low/No | Low/No | Low/No |

*Source*: Lichtenstein and Lyons 2001

dimensions of technical, managerial, entrepreneurial, and personal maturity noted in the previous section of this chapter. The ELS utilizes the baseball farm system as a metaphor for the resulting hierarchy, or ladder, of skills (see table 6.1). The idea is to develop entrepreneurs by moving them up the skills ladder from wherever on the ladder they begin their developmental journey.

Table 6.1 is simplistic in the sense that it suggests that skills are uniform across skill dimensions for each league level in the system. In reality, an entrepreneur who might be classified as having Single A skills, on average, may actually have varying skill levels across the dimensions.

The ELS operates on the principle that in order to ensure that an entrepreneur is able to advance up the ladder of skill development a system must be in place that connects all of the rungs of the ladder and makes sure all rungs (skill levels) are served. Numerous communities, for example, provide strong assistance at the Rookie and Single A levels and have been effective at serving Triple A entrepreneurs as well, but they do not serve Double A entrepreneurs. This situation amounts to a missing rung in the ladder that precludes the development of local entrepreneurs above the Single A level and, in some cases, results in the loss of those effected entrepreneurs to the community.

## The Measurement of Entrepreneurship Skills

To be able to effectively assign entrepreneurs to appropriate skill levels and track their development requires a tool for assessing, or measuring, entrepreneurship skills. The ELS utilizes such a tool, which permits the measurement of individual skills, allows scoring by skill dimension, and provides an overall score. The ability to provide entrepreneurs with the right technical and financial assistance at the right stage of their development and that of their company, and at the appropriate price rests with the capability to classify both entrepreneurs and entrepreneurship assistance providers by skill level. In this way, skills measurement lies at the heart of the ELS.

The skills assessment tool was developed with the help of a behavioral psychologist from Northwestern University, John S. Lyons. It is a clinimetric tool, with a measurement design strategy that is based on communication theory as opposed to psychometric theory, which underlies such tools. Psychometric tools are research based and focus on precision of measurement at the expense of relevance to practice (Feinstein 1999; Lyons, Weiner, and Lyons 2002).

Rather than relying on pencil and paper (or Web-based) assessments or a battery of tests, a clinimetric tool involves face-to-face interaction between a trained diagnostician and entrepreneurs. It is designed to be simple to use and score, requiring minimal training. Its focus of measurement is on the observable, not on subjective states, and internal consistency is irrelevant to its effective functioning. Incorporation of communications theory into this model adds these characteristics:

- Each rating level has immediate implications for action.
- There is minimal redundancy in the items covered but desired redundancy in the information collected.
- The language used in the process is clearly understood by all involved.
- The chief purpose of measurement is effective communication of needs and strengths to the entrepreneurs and the coaches (e.g., the process, itself, facilitates learning and reflection) (Feinstein 1999; Lyons, Weiner, and Lyons 2002).

Thus, the ELS entrepreneurial skills assessment tool is action oriented, not research oriented; it is clinical (Lyons and Lyons 2002).

Using this clinimetric/communications model, the tool measures a variety of specific skills within the four skill dimensions previously noted: (1) technical, (2) managerial, (3) entrepreneurial, and (4) personal maturity. For each skill, a set of questions can be asked of an entrepreneur (or entrepreneurial team) to elicit behavior that reflects skill level: Rookie, Single A, Double A, or Triple A.

A simple scoring system corresponds to an entrepreneur's level of skill for each skill measured (a higher score indicates a higher level of skill). Scores can be totaled across a skill dimension and across all four dimensions to provide an overall skill-level. Thus, an entrepreneur might be a Double A player on the technical dimension, a Single A player on the managerial dimension, a Rookie on the entrepreneurial dimension, a Single A player on the personal maturity dimension, and a Single A player overall. This assessment permits agencies to provide assistance that is skill level appropriate. It facilitates the creation of a "game plan" for developing skills, and it allows the tracking of an entrepreneur's progress toward developing those skills over time.

## Developing Entrepreneurship Skills

How can entrepreneurship skills be developed in a systemic, systematic, and strategic way? The ELS does this by designing a system whose architecture separates the function of developing entrepreneurs from the function of addressing their needs for technical and financial assistance. The activities of these two complementary subsystems—referred to as the Entrepreneur Development Sub-System and the Service Provision Sub-System—are then coordinated to allow entrepreneurs to successfully advance up the ladder of skill development in a transformational way.

While many individuals and organizations in the classroom and the field impart knowledge, deliver training, dispense information, and engage in short-term coaching, no one is actually *developing* entrepreneurs' skills in the pure sense of that term. Current programs in enterprise development only deal with half of the equation for economic success; they address the needs that firms have for technical and financial assistance but do little to build a pipeline of highly skilled entrepreneurs capable of using that assistance effectively to build companies.

It is commonly assumed that entrepreneurs are ready for this assistance when it is offered. In fact, they often are not ready to effectively and fully utilize the help provided. This is because being able to appropriately use technical and financial resources is a function of the entrepreneur's skill level. If skill level and resource are not properly matched, the desired outcome will not be achieved. The missing function in most communities or regions is one that is responsible for creating a supply of highly skilled entrepreneurs capable of building successful companies—the Entrepreneur Development Sub-System.

The development of skills requires transformational change—that is, fundamental change and a leap to a higher level of performance (Lichtenstein and Lyons 2001). It is not achieved through the individual, short-term, transactional exchanges that are the norm in our society and that characterize enterprise development, in particular. Transactions, taken alone, can never produce a transformation. Individual courses, training programs, idea exchanges, consulting, and similar activities, while helpful, will not *develop* an entrepreneur's skills. To develop these skills requires coordinated, long-term, sustained interactions. Since service provider operations and their funding are not designed for these purposes, it is not, and should not be, the responsibility of individual service provider organizations to *develop* entrepreneurs. This requires the establishment of a new, complementary function whose exclusive purpose is to create a pipeline of highly skilled entrepreneurs.

The Entrepreneur Development Sub-System of the ELS brings together three major sets of activities in support of developing entrepreneurs' skills so that they can move their companies through the stages of the business life-cycle more efficiently and effectively:

1. Talent scouting
2. Opportunity scouting
3. Performance coaching

Using a variety of tools and techniques tailored to the specific context, the ELS provides a talent scouting function. Both aspiring and current entrepreneurs are identified and brought into the system. The chief prerequisites are proper motivation and a goal of growing one's business. The entrepreneurs are oriented to entrepreneurship, especially if they are just starting, and to the ELS. Those who are in the pre-venture stage are helped with identifying a market opportunity, developing an offering, and preparing to launch their venture.

The opportunity scouting function of the Entrepreneur Development Sub-System of the ELS involves the use of "scouts" responsible for identifying market opportunities. These scouts scour the community, looking everywhere, including shop floors; hospitals; university, private, and government laboratories; and unused patents, among other sources. These opportunities are then assembled into an "opportunity register," which can be used to match opportunities and potential entrepreneurs.

Care is taken to ensure that each entrepreneur has a skill set appropriate to the identified opportunity. This is essential to the long-term success of the new enterprise. As an example, it takes a more sophisticated skill set to run a chain of restaurants than it does to operate a single restaurant. An entrepreneur in the ELS who is a restaurateur will not be rushed into running a chain of restaurants until such time as his or her skills are up to the task. Another part of the opportunity scouting function is the pursuit of opportunities for strategic alliances among companies in the system to capture new business as a group.

Performance coaching involves classifying entrepreneurs by skill level, using the assessment tool discussed above. Entrepreneurs are then clustered by skill level into "Success Teams"; thus, there is a Rookie Success Team, a Single A Success Team, and so forth. Assembling entrepreneurs at like skill levels for coaching purposes is crucial as we have found that they interact better when they are in true peer groups.

Each success team is assigned a "performance coach." This individual helps each entrepreneur in the team prepare a "game plan" for developing his or her skills going forward. The performance coach works with the entrepreneurs on both a one-on-one and group basis. The purpose of the coaching is to help entrepreneurs focus on the execution of their game plans and the operation of their businesses.

The Service Provision Sub-System is developed by first articulating, or mapping, the extent and level of assistance available to entrepreneurs in the community. This involves identifying all service providers, then assessing them according to how their services help their client entrepreneurs meet the latter's needs and at what entrepreneurship skill level they are working (see table 6.2 for a general depiction of this latter concept).

This mapping exercise makes it possible to then identify gaps in service delivery that can subsequently be filled. It also makes it possible to more strategically address the issue of offering services at the "right price." An entrepreneur with Rookie-level skills whose business is in the start-up stage is able to pay little or nothing for technical or financial help, while a Triple A entrepreneur operating a company in the growth stage is very capable of paying for assistance at market prices.

A perusal of table 6.2 shows that the service providers who work with entrepreneurs at lower skill levels tend to be publics and nonprofits. These

**Table 6.2. Development Level Targeted by Service Providers**

| Entrepreneurial Development Level | Type of Enterprise Development Assistance Providers |
| --- | --- |
| Majors | Venture capitalists, professional consulting practices, investment bankers, etc. |
| AAA | Angel investors, emerging business consulting practices, university tech transfer offices |
| AA | Manufacturing extension programs, small business development centers, small specialized venture funds, high technology incubation programs, etc |
| A | Microenterprise programs, small business development centers, business incubation programs, etc. |
| Rookie | Microenterprise programs, youth entrepreneurship programs, etc. |

organizations typically offer assistance at no or low cost. At higher levels of entrepreneurship skill, the service providers are more likely to be private. When thought about in this way, service provision can be organized in a manner that ensures appropriate pricing.

Individual and group performance improvement on the part of the service providers that make up the system is made possible by the work of a neutral, third party facilitator. This individual builds trust among the members of the service provision team and facilitates their learning and growth. The ELS provides a lingua franca that makes communication and collaboration possible.

While each subsystem is developed independently, they must ultimately be brought together in a dynamic balance. The Entrepreneur Development Sub-System continuously prepares clients to effectively use technical and financial assistance by helping them to develop their skills. The Service Provision Sub-System provides that technical and financial assistance in a transparent, systematic, and strategic way.

## How Developing Skills in This Way Benefits an Entrepreneur

The approach to developing entrepreneurial skills described in this chapter benefits the entrepreneurs served in several ways. First, it causes participating entrepreneurs to *focus* on their businesses. Entrepreneurs participating in the ELS process uniformly cite this as its chief benefit. It is too easy for entrepreneurs to become distracted by things that are tangential to growing their companies. The ELS's coaching process keeps them on track, employing both individual attention and peer pressure.

Another benefit to entrepreneurs lies in the way in which the system prepares them to fully avail themselves of technical and financial assistance, not only helping them to build the skills they need to use these services but structuring the delivery of the services to ensure their maximum relevance. This approach provides an environment conducive to individual transformation.

Understanding their current skill level, creating a game plan for skill development, working with a coach, and interacting with peers help entrepreneurs establish reference points from which to work. They can use these reference points as a basis for expanding the vision for their companies. For example, an entrepreneur in an ELS project in West Virginia entered the system operating a limousine service. Over the course of his skill development process, he realized that he was not simply in the limousine business; he was actually in the entertainment business. This led to the creation of unique experiences for his customers that have allowed him to substantially expand his enterprise.

Lastly, but of considerable importance, a focus on the development of skills using this framework permits an entrepreneur to ascend a ladder of skill development in a systematic fashion. Entrepreneurs appreciate being able to know where they currently stand and what they need to do to get to the skill level to which they aspire. Some entrepreneurs have even expressed that this system gives them a feeling of "relief."

In one instance, an entrepreneur, whose business was located in an incubator, was frustrated by the fact that she had worked hard to build her business for more than a year and was still struggling while another entrepreneur, whose business was located adjacent to hers, was in and out of the incubator and operating on his own in a six-month time span. She wondered what was "wrong" until the ELS approach taught her that the other entrepreneur was operating at a higher skill level and that she could be just as successful by continuing to work to build her skills.

## CONCLUSION

At the beginning of this chapter, success in entrepreneurship was defined as the mastery of a skill set. This assertion is based on an analysis of the theoretical literature and our own field research. We do not find the school of thought that holds that entrepreneurs possess innate personality traits to be compelling. Even if these theorists were correct, their theory is not useful when looking at fostering entrepreneurship as an economic development strategy. There is nothing one can do about innate traits. We suspect that this theory has contributed significantly to the relatively poor quality of past enterprise development activities in general. If entrepreneurs are to succeed or fail on their own personalities, why does it matter what is done to assist them?

While the behavioral school of thought offers a systematic understanding of enterprise building and the entrepreneur's role in it and introduces the use of field research—both positive developments—it places too much emphasis on business start-up and fails to account for the place of learning in the entrepreneurship process. Entrepreneurship should, and does, take place throughout the business life cycle, and, as the cognitive school of thought tells us, there is a learning process in entrepreneurship.

It is the cognitive perspective, with a focus on the entrepreneur, on the learning process, and on learning through experience, that acts as a bridge between the personality and behavioral perspectives and the "theory of skill development" expounded in this chapter. This latter theory makes cognitive theory actionable. It provides a framework for systemically, systematically, and strategically developing entrepreneurs' skills and, in so doing, enhancing their chances of success.

# REFERENCES

Begley, T. M., and D. P. Boyd. 1986. Executive and corporate correlates of financial performance in smaller firms. *Journal of Small Business Management* 24: 8–15.

Bhide, A. V. 2000. *The origin and evolution of new businesses.* Oxford, UK: Oxford University Press.

Block, Z., and I. C. MacMillan. 1985. Milestones for successful venture planning, *Harvard Business Review* 85(5): 184–96.

Brockhaus, R. H., Sr. 1980. Risk taking propensity of entrepreneurs. *Academy of Management Journal* 23: 509–20.

Brockhaus, R. H., Sr. 1982. The psychology of the entrepreneur. In *Encyclopedia of entrepreneurship*, ed. C. L. Kent, D. L. Sexton, and K. N. Vesper, 39–57. (Englewood Cliffs, NJ: Prentice Hall.

Brockhaus, R. H., Sr., and P. S. Horwitz. 1986. The psychology of the entrepreneur. In *The art and science of entrepreneurship*, ed. D. L. Sexton and R. W. Smilor, 25–48. Cambridge, UK: Ballinger.

Carter N. M., W. B. Gartner, and P. D. Reynolds. 1996. Exploring start-up event sequences. *Journal of Business Venturing* 11: 151–66.

Cooper, A. C., and W. C. Dunkelberg. 1987. Entrepreneurial research: Old questions, new answers, and methodological issues. *American Journal of Small Business* 11(3): 1–20.

Cope, J. 2005. Toward a dynamic learning perspective of entrepreneurship. *Entrepreneurship Theory and Practice* 29(4): 373–97.

Fackler, Y. 2001. *Fire in the belly: An exploration of the entrepreneurial spirit.* Cork, Ireland: Oak Tree Press.

Feinstein, A. R. 1999. Multi-item Instruments vs. Virginia Apgar's principles of clinimetrics. *Archives of Internal Medicine* 159: 125–28.

Fiet, J. O. 2002. *The systematic search for entrepreneurial discoveries.* Westport, CT: Quorom Books.

Gartner, W. B. 1989. Some suggestions for research on entrepreneurial traits and characteristics. *Entrepreneurship Theory and Practice* 14(1): 27–38.

Gatewood, E. J., K. G. Shaver, J. B. Powers, and W. B. Gartner. 2002. Entrepreneurial expectancy, task performance. *Entrepreneurship Theory and Practice* 27(2): 187–207.

Gerber, M. E. 1995. *The e-myth revisited: Why most small businesses don't work and what to do about it.* New York: HarperCollins.

Glaser, R. 1984. Education and thinking: The role of knowledge. *American Psychology* 39(2): 93–104.

Goleman, D. 1995. *Emotional intelligence: Why it can matter more than IQ.* New York: Bantam.

Greenberg, D. B., and D. L. Sexton. 1988. An interactive model of new venture initiation. *Journal of Small Business Management* 26(3): 1–7.

Hornaday, J. A., and J. Aboud. 1971. Characteristics of successful entrepreneurs. *Personnel Psychology* 24: 141–53.

Huefner, J. C., and H. K. Hunt. 1994. Broadening the concept of entrepreneurship: Comparing business and consumer entrepreneurs. *Entrepreneurship Theory and Practice* 18(3): 61–75.

Hull, D. L., J. J. Bosley, and G. G. Udell. 1980. Renewing the hunt for the Heffalump: Identifying potential entrepreneurs by personality characteristics. *Journal of Small Business* 18(1): 11–18.

Kassicieh, S. K., H. R. Padosevich, and C. M. Banbury. 1997. Using attitudinal, situational, and personal characteristics variables to predict future entrepreneurs from national laboratory inventors. *IEEE Transactions on Engineering Management* 44: 248–57.

Keh, H. T., M. D. Foo, and B. C. Lim. 2002. Opportunity evaluation under risky conditions: The cognitive processes of entrepreneurs. *Entrepreneurship Theory and Practice* 26(2): 125–48.

Krueger, N. F., Jr. 2000. The cognitive infrastructure of opportunity emergence. *Entrepreneurship Theory and Practice* 24(3): 5–23.

Lichtenstein, G. A., and T. S. Lyons. 1996. *Incubating new enterprises: A guide to successful practice.* Washington, DC: Aspen Institute.

Lichtenstein, G. A., and T. S. Lyons. 2001. The entrepreneurial development system: Transforming business talent and community economies. *Economic Development Quarterly* 15(1): 3–20.

Low, M. B., and I. C. MacMillan. 1988. Entrepreneurship: Past research and future challenges. *Journal of Management* 14(2): 139–61.

Lyons, J. S., D. Weiner, and M. B. Lyons. 2002. *Measurement as communication: The child and adolescent needs and strengths.* Winnetka, IL: Buddin Praed Foundation.

Lyons, T. S., and J. S. Lyons. 2002. *Assessing entrepreneurship skills: The key to effective enterprise development planning?* Paper presented at the Annual Conference of the Association of Collegiate Schools of Planning, Baltimore, MD.

Markman, G. D., D. B. Balkin, and R. A. Baron. 2002. Inventors and new venture formation: The effects of general self-efficacy and regretful thinking. *Entrepreneurship Theory and Practice* 27(2): 149–66.

McClelland, D. C., J. W. Atkinson, R. A. Clark, and E. L. Lowell. 1953. *The achievement motive.* Princeton, NJ: Van Nostrand.

Minniti M., and W. Bygrave. 2001. A dynamic model of entrepreneurial learning. *Entrepreneurship Theory and Practice* 25(3): 5–16.

Mitchell R. K., L. Busenitz, T. Lant, P. P. McDougall, E. A. Morse, and J. B. Smith. 2002. Toward a theory of entrepreneurial cognition: Rethinking the people side of entrepreneurship research. *Entrepreneurship Theory and Practice* 27(2): 93–104.

Mitchell R. K., and S. A. Chesteen. 1995. Enhancing entrepreneurial expertise: Experiential pedagogy and the new venture expert script. *Simulation and Gaming* 26(3): 288–306.

Pendergast, W. R. 2006. Entrepreneurial contexts and traits of entrepreneurs. *The ICFAI Journal of Entrepreneurship Development* 3(1): 9–19.

Politis, D. 2005. The process of entrepreneurial learning: A conceptual framework. *Entrepreneurship Theory and Practice* 29(4): 399–424.

Rauch, A., and M. Frese. 2000. Psychological approaches to entrepreneurial success: A general model and an overview of findings. In *International review of industrial and organizational psychology,* ed. C. L. Cooper and I. T. Robertson, 101–42. New York: Wiley.

Robinson, R. B., Jr., and J. A. Pearce. 1986. Product life-cycle considerations and the nature of strategic activities in entrepreneurial firms. *Journal of Business Venturing* 3(1): 207-24.

Schumpeter, J. 1991. Comments on a plan for the study of entrepreneurship. In *Joseph A. Schumpeter: The economics and sociology of capitalism*, ed. R. Swedberg, 406-28. Princeton, NJ: Princeton University Press.

Shane, S., and S. Venkataraman. 2000. The promise of entrepreneurship as a field of research. *Academy of Management Review* 25(1): 217-26.

Shaver, K. G., and L. R. Scott. 1991. Person, process, choice: The psychology of new venture creation. *Entrepreneurship Theory and Practice* 15: 23-45.

Shefsky, L. E. 1994. *Entrepreneurs are made not born*. New York: McGraw-Hill.

Sherraden, M. 1991. *Assets and the poor*. Armonk, NY: M. E. Sharpe, Inc.

Siegel, R., E. Siegel, and I. C. MacMillan. 1993. Characteristics distinguishing high-growth ventures. *Journal of Business Venturing* 8: 169-80.

Simon, M., and S. M. Houghton. 2002. The relationship among biases, misperceptions and introducing pioneering products: Examining differences in venture decision contexts. *Entrepreneurship Theory and Practice* 26(2): 105-25.

Timmons, J. A., L. E. Smollen, and A. L. M. Dingee. 1985. *New venture creation* (2nd ed.) Homewood, IL: Irwin Publishing.

Van de Ven, A. H., R. Hudson, and D. Schroeder. 1984. Designing new business start-ups: Entrepreneurial, organizational, and ecological considerations. *Journal of Management* 10(1): 87-107.

# 7

# Building Communities through Entrepreneurship Development: Financing Entrepreneurs and Entrepreneurial Support Systems

*Deborah M. Markley*

Most local economies are built on the efforts and success of entrepreneurs—whether the local pharmacist on Main Street or the homegrown manufacturer on the edge of town. While nationally, small enterprises employ about half the private sector workforce and produce about half of private sector output (U.S. Small Business Administration, Office of Advocacy 2006), in a specific community, the importance of small entrepreneurial ventures may be even more significant.

Increasingly, local economic development practitioners and other community leaders recognize the importance of encouraging these small entrepreneurial ventures as a key part of their local economic development efforts, and they are building entrepreneurial support systems to encourage local entrepreneurs and to help transform the local economy. The overarching goal of an entrepreneurial support system is to transform a community or regional economy by encouraging the creation and development of entrepreneurs. It is a human development strategy in that the focus is on entrepreneurs and on providing a nurturing support environment that helps entrepreneurs create and grow businesses. The support infrastructure that entrepreneurs need includes many parts—technical assistance, training and education, networking with peers and mentors, and access to financial capital.

This chapter focuses on access to the full range of financial capital instruments—from micro loans to venture investments—for entrepreneurs starting and growing businesses in rural communities. The key to the effective use of financial capital is for an entrepreneur to have access to the right kind of capital at the right stage of enterprise development, combined with the appropriate entrepreneurial skills to use the capital to create and sustain the business. The first section of this chapter describes constraints on capital access by rural entrepreneurs and issues related to capital access as rural entrepreneurs start up, operate, and grow their businesses.

In addition, since entrepreneurship development is a long-term economic development strategy, the system of support for entrepreneurs must be sustainable over the long term as well. The second section of this chapter, therefore, describes how communities can access the financial resources to build and sustain an entrepreneurship development system. Specific attention is paid to discussing the challenges of accessing public funding for local economic development efforts and the opportunities provided by community philanthropy and foundations for supporting entrepreneurship development.

## FINANCING RURAL ENTREPRENEURS

In a study of Inc. 500 companies, Amar Bhide (2000) concluded that "the well-funded and carefully planned start-up represents the exception" (22) rather than the rule among entrepreneurial ventures. Indeed, most of the company founders interviewed bootstrapped their start-ups with modest amounts of capital—an average of only $25,000 in 1996. Almost three-quarters of this start-up capital came from personal savings, credit cards, family, and friends. Equally important, only 7 percent had financing from banking institutions, and only 7 percent received investments from formal venture capital institutions or angel investors.

Rural entrepreneurs face an even more challenging environment in terms of accessing capital to support their business enterprises because of three significant constraints. First, there are fewer capital providers in most rural communities, and the transaction costs associated with identifying and accessing capital outside the community are high. Consolidation in the banking industry has reduced the number of institutions serving rural markets and has changed the mix of institutions. While branches of larger banking institutions may bring more skilled lenders to rural communities, they often change the lending mix and decisionmaking locus in such a way that local entrepreneurs find it harder to acquire the capital they need. While a determined entrepreneur may locate sources of capital beyond the local market, the costs of that capital are likely to be higher.

Second, in many rural communities, entrepreneurs are not adequately prepared to access capital from available suppliers—a case of undeveloped deal flow. To obtain a loan from a bank or an investment from a venture capitalist, an entrepreneur must present a business plan and financial statements that provide adequate information to justify a lending or investment decision. In many cases, entrepreneurs are unprepared to access the capital that may exist in their communities, providing further justification for the creation of a system of support for entrepreneurs rather than simply creating more capital programs.

Third, as noted in the study by Bhide (2000), most entrepreneurial ventures start with little outside capital. The entrepreneurs' assets, and those of family and friends, are most often used to launch a venture. In rural communities, entrepreneurs often lack the assets to commit to the start-up process—accessing any source of capital may first require some focus on asset building especially among low- and moderate-income rural entrepreneurs. The increased promotion and use recently of the Individual Development Account (IDA) as a vehicle for saving for business development represents an important corollary strategy for accessing capital for some entrepreneurs in rural America (Ssewamala, Lombe, and Curley 2006).

In spite of these constraints, entrepreneurs are starting and growing businesses throughout rural America. In some cases, the entrepreneurs themselves have become adept at finding and tapping the capital needed to move their ventures forward. In other cases, public and private sector institutions have recognized capital gaps and created innovative solutions to meet the needs of rural entrepreneurs. In both cases, however, it is important to understand how the capital needs of entrepreneurs vary as a business develops and which forms of capital are best suited to meet those needs.

## THE CHANGING CAPITAL NEEDS
## OF RURAL ENTREPRENEURS

Each stage in the development of a business venture requires different amounts and forms of capital. To keep the focus of discussion on the entrepreneur, and not the business, this section identifies four distinct times during which entrepreneurs are likely to seek capital to support their dreams about the business:

1. *Financing Idea Generation and Testing.* This is the time when the entrepreneur is developing a marketable product or service. For example, an entrepreneur with an idea about the next generation of tax preparation software may be developing and testing the program. An entrepreneur with a dream of opening a wireless Internet cafe on main street may be doing customer surveys and beginning to identify suitable technology.
2. *Financing Enterprise Start-Up.* With testing complete, the entrepreneur begins the start-up process. This phase requires capital for building inventories, purchasing equipment, covering infrastructure costs, and other aspects of starting a business.

3. *Financing Enterprise Operations.* With the doors to the business open, an entrepreneur will likely begin looking for the capital to cover the ongoing operating costs of the business. While many small entrepreneurs operate with little or no debt—in 1998, 50 percent of businesses with less than five employees had no loans or lines of credit (RUPRI Rural Finance Task Force 1997)—most entrepreneurs have difficulty covering all of their operating costs from current income.

4. *Financing Enterprise Growth.* Finding the capital to grow a business is an important obstacle for many entrepreneurs. While it is possible to bootstrap a business start-up, it is difficult to finance active growth without the support of external sources of debt or equity capital.

The following sections discuss the sources of capital available to entrepreneurs in rural communities during each of these periods of business development. The institutional innovations to address capital gaps that arise are also described.

## Financing Idea Generation and Testing

With few exceptions, the capital required to generate and test entrepreneurial ideas comes from the entrepreneur's personal resources. In focus groups in rural communities across North Carolina, entrepreneurs identified a need for small amounts of capital, preferably in the form of grants, to help them develop a product or test a concept. At this stage, entrepreneurs have no revenue stream and, as a result, need access to capital that requires no initial payback and that is "patient" through the development process (i.e., the entrepreneur may make no or interest-only payments during the start-up phase, and the timing of future payments may be tied to performance milestones such as sales).

Most formal lending and investment institutions are unwilling or unable to provide this type of capital because of their need to generate a return for investors (venture capital funds) or because of regulatory restrictions (banking institutions). Lacking access to this type of capital, entrepreneurs turn instead to their savings, credit cards, and investments/loans from family and friends.

Access to pre-venture development funds is difficult in urban as well as rural communities. Entrepreneurs are in a typical catch-22 situation—they must develop a product or concept in order to convince investors of the marketability and potential profitability of the idea, yet they need capital to take the first steps toward product development. This dilemma explains the heavy reliance by most entrepreneurs on their own or local resources in this idea generation stage.

Given the nature of the capital requirements at the idea generation stage of enterprise development, the public sector may play a role in supporting the capital needs of rural entrepreneurs. The State of Kentucky has undertaken a multipart initiative to address the financial and business assistance needs of entrepreneurs in this stage of development.

The Kentucky Science and Technology Corporation (2006) is a private, nonprofit organization that manages the Kentucky Enterprise Fund (KEF)—pre-venture and seed venture funds established through state investment to address this early capital gap. One of the funds within KEF is the Rural Innovation Fund, specifically targeted to address the pre-venture capital needs of businesses in rural Kentucky. At the most basic level, the Rural Innovation Fund invests up to $25,000 in proof of concept or prototype development for rural Kentucky-based entrepreneurs. The one-time investment comes without the expectation of payback. It provides an initial pool of capital that, when supplemented by the entrepreneur's own financial and human capital, can launch a business concept into a marketable business opportunity.

Kentucky combines access to pre-venture capital with access to assistance for entrepreneurs through a series of Innovation and Commercialization Centers across the state. These centers provide assistance to entrepreneurs with growth potential and, through the statewide network, bring more advanced services to entrepreneurs even in remote rural locations.

Access to capital to support idea generation and testing is an important constraint for most entrepreneurs but especially for rural entrepreneurs. Few states or communities have targeted programs to provide grant or "patient" investment funds for rural entrepreneurs with good ideas; however, the long-term success of the efforts in Kentucky may provide encouragement and a model for other states to follow. Until then, rural entrepreneurs will continue to depend on their own resources and those of their personal networks to develop the ideas that may become the rural businesses of tomorrow.

### Financing Enterprise Start-Up

Once a product has been developed or a service concept proven, the entrepreneur begins the process of starting an enterprise. In the early stages of business development, entrepreneurs often face two challenges. First, they must gain access to capital at a time when they may have a limited sales history, be experiencing cash flow problems, have high upfront costs for activities like marketing, and demonstrate limited or no profitability. Institutional lenders, such as banks, engage in very limited lending to start-up ventures because of these characteristics. Consequently, entrepreneurs must turn to alternative types of financial institutions or programs.

Second, for some entrepreneurs, the cost of capital may prove to be a significant challenge. High-interest costs may be difficult for an entrepreneur to handle during a time of inconsistent sales and cash flow. Flexible loan terms and repayment schedules may be important to an entrepreneur, assuming there are sources of capital available in the community. For most entrepreneurs, however, the primary concern is capital access not cost.

At this stage, informal and nontraditional sources of capital continue to predominate—family, friends, and personal savings/borrowing; microenterprise programs; and community or state revolving loan funds. Consequently, for rural entrepreneurs, accessing capital to finance enterprise start-up depends on the personal and family assets available to the entrepreneur and the local availability of these types of alternative financing institutions. Building assets to promote economic development in rural America is as old as the original Homestead Act of 1862. Entrepreneurial spirits who saw the opportunity inherent in the open spaces of the west used this public policy intervention as a way to build assets that could, in turn, be used as the seed stock for future generations. Rural America in the twenty-first century presents new challenges to those trying to build assets in support of entrepreneurship, however.

As the economic base has shifted from agriculture and natural resource extraction to routine manufacturing and now to services, the ability to build assets has declined for many in rural America. Low-wage manufacturing and service jobs make it difficult for rural residents to save and grow the assets they might use for entrepreneurship, education and training, or home ownership. If personal assets are a primary source of start-up capital for entrepreneurs, then building assets that rural residents can use to support entrepreneurship should be an important component of any entrepreneurship development strategy.

One new policy intervention offers the potential to help entrepreneurs build assets to use for business start-up—IDAs. IDAs are matched savings accounts that allow low-wealth individuals to save for homeownership, education and training, and business ownership. According to CFED (2005), approximately 50,000 individuals, both rural and urban, are saving through IDAs. In 2004, about 75 percent of the IDA programs, nationally, permitted savings to be used for small business start-up.

An evaluation of the outcomes of IDA programs in 14 community-based sites, both rural and urban, included in a national demonstration project found that low-income individuals could save and that financial education was an important factor in higher savings outcomes (Grinstein-Weiss and Curley 2003); however, another study of IDAs in rural North Carolina identified important constraints on asset building in rural communities—isolation, and historical and cultural obstacles that, in turn, make it difficult to find funding, recruit participants, find qualified staff, and build trust in the IDA programs (Bailey et al. 2006).

These insights suggest that IDA programs alone may not provide the asset-building boost that rural entrepreneurs need to build the personal assets for business start-up; As part of an entrepreneurial support system, however, IDAs are an important tool that many communities and states currently use to help rural entrepreneurs gain the initial capital needed to launch a business enterprise.

Business start-up is often financed through alternative financing institutions, specifically microenterprise programs and community revolving loan funds. Microenterprise programs have grown dramatically throughout the United States during the past 20 years. These programs provide loans, and often technical assistance, to businesses with fewer than five employees and that require $35,000 or less in start-up capital. Most microenterprise programs have been funded through a combination of foundation and public sources. The industry has been well-documented through the efforts of the Aspen Institute's FIELD (The Microenterprise Fund for Innovation, Effectiveness, Learning and Dissemination) program (Edgcomb and Klein 2005). In 2000, microenterprise development programs served between 150,000 and 170,000 individuals.

Microenterprise development programs provide an important source of capital for rural entrepreneurs who are starting businesses. Of the 554 microenterprise programs documented in the United States in 2002, 60 percent (332) serve rural markets (AEO 2005). Many of these programs received funding from the U.S. Department of Agriculture's Rural Business Enterprise Grant (RBEG) program.

Microenterprise programs provide access to small loans that entrepreneurs would not receive from banking institutions. Borrowers often have limited or poor credit history, limited assets and collateral, and frequently limited experience with credit and financing. The microenterprise programs provide more than capital to entrepreneurs. They provide the support, training, and mentoring assistance vital to a small entrepreneur in the start-up phase.

One example of a successful rural microenterprise program is the Mountain Microenterprise Fund (MMF) which serves the 12 western-most counties in North Carolina. In addition to providing access to capital for microentrepreneurs, MMF offers an eight-week business plan course, Foundations, on a sliding fee scale. Graduates of the Foundations course can enroll in the Membership program, providing them with access to additional counseling and other resources. Participants in MMF programs become part of a network of microentrepreneurs who can offer support during the business start-up process. Graduates can also become an important resource for MMF by helping new entrepreneurs just getting into the program.

Community-based revolving loan funds also provide entrepreneurs who are starting businesses with access to capital that is unavailable from more traditional banking institutions. Revolving loan funds (RLFs) lend to entrepreneurs from a pool of capital and, as loans are repaid, the monies are loaned to other entrepreneurs in the region. Rural RLFs have been started by communities, utilities, community development organizations, and others, often using federal sources of funds such as USDA's RBEG program. Most RLFs are focused on addressing capital gaps in their market—making loans to entrepreneurs who do not have access to other sources of capital. While some entrepreneurs in the start-up phase can often qualify for these loans initially, many require access to business assistance and training programs in order to develop the business plan and financial statements/projections needed for a lending decision.

The Rural Enterprise Assistance Program of the Center for Rural Affairs in Nebraska makes loans from a revolving loan fund in addition to offering a peer lending program. The focus of these programs is on providing debt capital to rural-based entrepreneurs who are starting new or growing existing businesses in the state. To receive a direct loan, the entrepreneur must create one or retain one full-time job, thus allowing self-employed entrepreneurs to benefit from the program. Typically, entrepreneurs who use the program have been unable to get a loan from a bank or need an additional partner to qualify for a bank loan. The peer lending program provides an opportunity for rural entrepreneurs to borrow $1,000 initially and, upon repayment, qualify for additional loans of $2,000, $4,000, $8,000, and up to $10,000 (Center for Rural Affairs 2006).

Most rural entrepreneurs who are just starting businesses rely on their own or alternative sources of capital rather than institutional sources of capital such as banks and venture capital funds. The success of these entrepreneurs in gaining access to start-up capital depends in large part on the availability of these alternative programs in their communities or regions. The increased prevalence of both microenterprise programs and community-based revolving loan funds, either as part of a community development financial institution or another community-based organization, throughout rural America provides an opportunity for shared learning about how these sources of capital can be most effectively provided to entrepreneurs who are just starting in business.

## Financing Enterprise Operations

After the initial start-up phase, an entrepreneur's main capital challenge is to find the resources to finance the ongoing operations of the business. Depending on the size and capital needs of the entrepreneur's venture, the alternative financial institutions described above—microenterprise programs and community-based revolving loan funds—may still play an important role in meeting the capital needs of rural entrepreneurs.

Banks and nontraditional lenders, such as community development financial institutions, are playing an increasingly important role as the capital needs of entrepreneurs grow. In addition, some public sector programs, such as Small Business Administration (SBA) guaranteed loan programs and the U.S. Department of Agriculture's Intermediary Relending Program (IRP), may become important to rural entrepreneurs in regions served by banks and community institutions that deliver these programs locally.

Historically, community banks have played an important role in most rural communities. Community bankers made the loans to build the rural economy. The challenge, as articulated by Mark Drabenstott (2005) with the Center for the Study of Rural America, Federal Reserve Bank of Kansas City, is whether these community bankers will continue to adapt and accept a new role in rural America—one that requires them to lend to new economy businesses, to support locally grown entrepreneurs, and to think regionally.

Community banks have traditionally been important to local entrepreneurs and small businesses, lending proportionally more of their resources to small businesses and farms than their larger counterparts. With deregulation and consolidation in the banking industry has come increased concern about access to capital for small business borrowers, especially in rural communities. The evidence on the impact of deregulation on entrepreneurs is still out, however (Hanc 2006).

On one hand, rural entrepreneurs have benefited from the "relationship" lending of many community banks, where the local banker relies on local knowledge of the entrepreneur and the community to assess the potential risk associated with a loan. This type of lending is especially important for new entrepreneurs seeking capital to support their business operations.

On the other hand, larger banks may bring new services and sources of credit to a rural market and may be able to overcome through their use of standardized lending criteria the discriminatory lending practices that some minority entrepreneurs may experience in smaller communities. In both cases, an entrepreneur's access to capital may depend in large part on a local banker's attitude toward lending to small businesses in support of local economic development and the entrepreneur's ability to make the case for financing—specifically, having the collateral and assets needed to satisfy the local bank's requirements.

The ability to access bank capital may depend, in part, on the use of guaranty programs such as those offered through SBA. The SBA's primary loan guaranty program, 7(a), makes it easier for banks to lend to entrepreneurs who are unlikely to qualify for loans on reasonable terms. Up to 85 percent of loans under $100,000 may be guaranteed by SBA, reducing the risk to the local bank and, thus, increasing the bank's ability to lend to an entrepreneur.

Another innovation that can make access to capital from local banks easier for entrepreneurs is the Capital Access Program (CAP) concept. The North Carolina Rural Economic Development Center (2006) has established a CAP designed to expand the level of risk that participating banks can accept in making loans to rural entrepreneurs. The program creates a loan loss reserve that can be tapped by participating banks to cover losses associated with making loans with greater risk to entrepreneurs. The loan loss reserve is capitalized by fees charged to the borrower that are matched by the program. In North Carolina, these matching funds have been provided by a state foundation and the Appalachian Regional Commission.

Even with a well-documented business plan and clear financial statements, it is possible that a rural entrepreneur may still have difficulty obtaining a loan from a bank. Banking institutions are regulated and, as a result, are limited in terms of the risk they can accept on the loans that they make. In some rural areas, community development financial institutions (CDFIs) have been created to meet the capital needs of local entrepreneurs. CDFIs are private financial institutions whose mission is community development. These institutions focus on the "double bottom line"—economic returns and positive community impacts. CDFIs may take a variety of institutional forms, including community development banks, loan funds, credit unions, microenterprise programs, and venture funds (CDFI Coalition 2006). As such, these organizations may be important in meeting the capital needs of entrepreneurs at various stages in the development of an enterprise.

CDFIs and other community development organizations can also be important sources of capital for entrepreneurs through their use of public sources of funds such as the IRP. USDA's IRP provides community organizations, including CDFIs, with a pool of long-term, low-interest funds that can be reloaned to qualified borrowers in rural regions. This source of public sector funds can be important to capitalizing the CDFIs who, in turn, make the funds available to entrepreneurs for business development.

CDFIs are important sources of operating capital to entrepreneurs for two reasons. One, they can offer capital to entrepreneurs whose lack of collateral or credit history limits their access to bank loans. The CDFI evaluates both potential return from the loan and the value the entrepreneur's business brings to the community. For example, a CDFI may choose to lend to an entrepreneur who is bringing a grocery store to main street because the deal is judged based on the positive potential returns to the entrepreneur (and the CDFI) as well as the value the grocery store brings to the downtown area and its benefit to low-income residents who may now shop locally.

Two, CDFIs often couple technical or business assistance with lending, either in partnership with other support providers or through their own staff. For entrepreneurs in this stage of business development, having access to training and technical resources to help operate the business is often as critical, if not more so, than access to the capital itself.

In Appalachian southeastern Kentucky, the Kentucky Highlands Investment Corporation (KHIC) has operated for more than 30 years. This CDFI has a long track record of making capital and business assistance available to entrepreneurs in a very rural and distressed part of the country. In a case study of the organization, Markley and Barkley (2003) conclude that the "focus of Kentucky Highlands' activities is on the entrepreneur and his or her enterprise, not the capital used to support the entrepreneurs. KHIC works with individual entrepreneurs to put together a package of assistance that will increase the probability of the new business' success" (13–14).

The KHIC has succeeded in tapping many sources of funds to capitalize its programs, including SBA and IRP. These funds, in turn, have given this CDFI the flexibility to customize assistance to entrepreneurs to best meet their needs. In some cases, the need may be met with a working capital loan. In others, the loan might come with an agreement to have a member of KHIC's staff work side by side with the entrepreneur to overcome a business challenge and effectively use the capital provided. KHIC, like other CDFIs, has the flexibility and mission to provide support to rural entrepreneurs that more traditional, regulated financial institutions cannot.

As with the availability of capital to support business start-up, access to operating capital also depends to some extent on the availability of alternative financial institutions (e.g., CDFIs) or programs (e.g., CAP) to provide capital when bank lending is not feasible. While these programs are increasingly available in or already serve rural communities, access to nontraditional sources of capital in more isolated rural places is still difficult. Any entrepreneurial support system must address the availability and cost of capital for entrepreneurs once they have started business operations and require a source of working capital.

### Financing Enterprise Growth

Entrepreneurs who are actively growing an enterprise often seek outside sources of both debt and equity capital. While banking institutions are a primary source of debt capital for growing businesses, the most critical capital gap for rural entrepreneurs relates to access to equity or venture capital. There is often an information gap for rural entrepreneurs in understanding equity capital markets. Most rural entrepreneurs are familiar with the requirements of debt capital. Accepting a loan creates an obligation to repay the capital on a specific schedule and at a predetermined cost.

Equity capital, however, is often more mysterious to rural entrepreneurs. An equity investment conveys a share of ownership in the company to the investor, reducing to some extent the entrepreneur's control over his or her creation. The investor, in turn, gives up the certainty of repayment for a share in the future profits of the enterprise.

Venture capital institutions serve as a conduit between investors and entrepreneurs and provide the information entrepreneurs need to understand the equity transaction. These institutions pool the investment capital of private sector institutions or individuals and then invest in entrepreneurial ventures that offer the promise of significant rates of return. The experience of venture capital investing in the United States suggests, however, that entrepreneurs in more rural parts of the country are not well served by these traditional institutions (RUPRI Rural Equity Capital Initiative 2001).

Equity capital investing in the United States is concentrated both geographically, sectorally, and by stage of investment (PriceWaterhouseCooper 2006). In 2005, more than $21 billion in venture capital investments were made, with 60 percent going to four regions: (1) Silicon Valley, (2) New England, (3) the New York metro area, and (4) the Los Angeles metro area. More than 60 percent was invested in just four states: (1) California, (2) Massachusetts, (3) New York, and (4) Texas. Of this total venture investing, about half went to just three sectors: (1) software, (2) biotechnology, and (3) telecommunications; and 80 percent was in expansion or later stage investments rather than seed or early stage investments.

The concentration in this industry has been consistent over time, and it does not bode well for entrepreneurs in rural markets. Most venture capital firms are located in the regions in which investments are concentrated. Given the hands-on nature of venture investing, most deals are made close to the offices of the venture investors. If a rural entrepreneur is able to attract investment from a traditional venture capital fund, the capital investment often comes with a significant string attached—that the company be moved to the region in which the venture fund is located. While this requirement may bring much needed capital to a rural entrepreneur, it does not support the economic development goals of rural communities.

Two trends in equity capital investing have brought a glimmer of hope to rural entrepreneurs actively growing their businesses and who need an investment of equity capital to meet growth aspiration: (1) the increased number of community development venture capital institutions and (2) the rise in formal angel investing networks. Community development venture capital (CDVC) institutions, like CDFIs, make investment decisions based on a "double bottom line"—economic return on the investment and the community development return that is achieved.

In a 1995 report on nontraditional venture capital institutions in rural America (RUPRI Rural Equity Capital Initiative 2001), the authors found a diverse group of institutions organized to provide equity capital to rural entrepreneurs. Programs ranged from publicly funded and managed to privately funded and managed and included community-level as well as state-level programs. While not all of these programs have succeeded in achieving their double bottom line goals, the lessons learned from the early innovators have helped create a growing and robust CDVC industry.

According to an assessment by the Community Development Venture Capital Alliance, the trade association for the CDVC industry, in 2001, community development venture fund investments were distributed geographically in a pattern similar to the distribution of establishments across rural and urban areas (Schmitt 2003). While traditional venture funds made 98.4 percent of their investments in metro counties, CDVC funds made 76 percent of their investments in metro areas. This figure is slightly below the percent of establishments located in metro counties, 80.8 percent.

Traditional funds made no investments in completely rural counties, where 2.2 percent of establishments reside, but CDVC funds place 2.2 percent of investments in these same counties. The CDVC industry clearly has an important role to play in providing rural entrepreneurs with access to the equity capital they need to grow.

CEI Community Ventures, Inc. (2006) is a CDVC that was organized as a subsidiary of Coastal Enterprises, Inc. (CEI) in Maine. CEI had a long history of supporting business development in rural Maine when it created CEI Community Ventures. Community Ventures makes investments in businesses at all stages of development (early, development, and later) in amounts ranging from $250,000 to $750,000. While the investment criteria include traditional measures such as management and market, they are also trying to make deals in targeted rural communities and in companies that help them meet their financial, social, and environmental goals. This $10 million fund is sustainable in part because of its relationship with and support from CEI.

The other trend that bodes well for rural entrepreneurs seeking equity capital is the rise of angel investor networks throughout the country. Angel investors are high net worth individuals who invest directly in an entrepreneurial venture or who pool their investment capital in networks that invest in entrepreneurs. The Center for Venture Research at the University of New Hampshire estimates that, in 2004, angels invested $22 billion, an amount equal to that invested by traditional venture capital firms (Jossi 2005). Angel investors bring much more than their investment capital to entrepreneurs, however; they usually have entrepreneurial or managerial experience that can be critically important to a rural entrepreneur experiencing rapid growth.

In the past, angel investors were linked to entrepreneurs through relatively informal networks. A local banker might know an investor and put that person in touch with an entrepreneur whose idea or business might be of interest. This process, especially in rural communities, was relatively inefficient and depended on angel investors making their interests known in the community. Consequently, transaction costs were high.

Angel investor networks started in recent years help to formalize the matchmaking process between private investor and entrepreneur. Networks allow individual angels to pool their capital and provide a more formal structure for introducing entrepreneurs to investors. Some networks have managers who screen business plans and then invite entrepreneurs to make presentations to investors. The angels may decide to invest as a group or choose to invest as individuals. Networks have appeared even in relatively small rural regions, using a model set up first in Minnesota as Regional Angel Investment Networks (RAIN) (see www.rainsourcecapital.com/).

Wisconsin has taken the concept to a statewide level with the creation of the Wisconsin Angel Network (WAN), an effort to create new and support existing networks throughout the state. WAN is designed to provide information and resources to encourage the creation of angel networks and to increase deal flow by connecting networks to each other and to more traditional venture funds in the state.

In 2005, Wisconsin instituted a tax credit program to encourage investments in entrepreneurial ventures, providing a state income tax credit of 25 percent of investments made by individuals in qualified businesses over two years. This tax credit has, in turn, increased angel investing in the state, with the entire initial $3 million allocation of tax credits being claimed in 2005. Many of the angel investor networks created in the state serve rural or underserved populations, including those focused on making investments to women (Batog 2006).

In summary, rural entrepreneurs especially face challenges meeting their capital needs throughout the business development process. Unlike their urban counterparts, rural entrepreneurs often have limited options in terms of the financial market institutions available to meet their needs. Compounding these capital access challenges is more limited availability of the support services needed by entrepreneurs to make the most effective use of capital and other resources. For too many rural entrepreneurs, capital is just one of the support needs they face. Yet models do exist, even in rural regions, for providing access to the type of capital needed by entrepreneurs from start-up through growth and for creating the support systems to meet their other business assistance needs. As community leaders and economic development professionals develop strategies to address the capital needs of entrepreneurs, it is critically important to take a systems approach—viewing capital access as one part of a larger and more comprehensive system of support for entrepreneurs in rural and urban communities.

## FINDING CAPITAL TO BUILD THE SYSTEM

Meeting the capital needs of entrepreneurs in rural communities is an important component of any entrepreneurship development strategy; however, entrepreneurship development is a long-term process. To move an entrepreneur from developing a marketable idea to starting a viable business to growing a sustainable venture requires a support system that is long lived and sustainable over time. If one goal of an entrepreneurship development system is to create a more entrepreneurial culture in a rural community, efforts to change the culture will require an investment in youth entrepreneurship, leadership development, and other activities that take time and resources.

For an entrepreneurial support system to be transformative, it must first be sustainable. This section discusses the challenges of garnering public support for entrepreneurship development at the community level and then describes two potential sources of long-term support for entrepreneurship: (1) foundations and (2) community philanthropy.

### The Challenge of Local Support for Entrepreneurship Development

While rural entrepreneurs often serve regional, national, and even international markets, they are rooted in communities. Their ability to succeed has a direct impact on their communities, through job generation, sales and property taxes, and an indirect impact in terms of the quality of life and the environment of entrepreneurship that may be created by their presence. It makes sense, then, to consider how communities and local governments can support the creation of entrepreneurship development systems.

The reality in most communities, however, is one of limited resources and increasing demands placed on local units of government through devolution and policies enacted at the state and federal levels. The ability of local units of government to identify new sources of funds to support entrepreneurship development is limited. The question then becomes how to encourage a reallocation of economic development resources from more traditional activities (e.g., marketing, recruitment) to entrepreneurship development.

The success in reallocating local resources depends in large part on the ability to make a case for entrepreneurship development at the local level. Making the case requires two things: (1) sharing evaluation research describing the outcomes of investments in entrepreneurship development in other rural regions and (2) documenting the outcomes of investments already occurring in the local community. Both of these activities will help to build a case for local leaders to consider; however, to build long-term sustainability for entrepreneurship development, insulated from the political process, private sector resources are needed.

## Finding Other Partners—Foundations

The microenterprise field was advanced through the initial support of a few national foundations—the Charles Stewart Mott Foundation, the Ford Foundation, and the Levi Strauss Foundation. In entrepreneurship development, foundation support is important in two ways. One example is the W. K. Kellogg Foundation. Through its Entrepreneurship Development Systems for Rural America grant project, the foundation has invested in six laboratories for entrepreneurship development systems throughout the rural United States.

The significant investments made in six different models for creating an entrepreneurship development system should provide the lessons learned that can propel the field of rural entrepreneurship development forward in a significant way. Part of building a sustainable system is learning about and adapting what the early innovators have found to be successful. One specific aspect of each innovative system within the Kellogg project is a focus on building long-term sustainability. The models for sustainability developed in these laboratories will provide important guidance and insights for other rural regions as they create entrepreneurship strategies of their own.

Another important role for foundations is as a partner in the creation of regional entrepreneurship development systems. Regional foundations have played an important role in the creation of CDFIs and CDVCs in the past, and entrepreneurship development provides another opportunity for community engagement. For example, foundations in Minnesota, North Carolina, and Oregon have become partners in community- and state-level strategies to promote entrepreneurship development. This match between regional foundations and community-based or regional projects is important—it keeps the focus on achieving regional transformation through investment in entrepreneurship development. It also provides an opportunity to bring the nonfinancial resources of the regional foundation to the partnership, whether in terms of management experience or the persuasive powers of foundation leadership within the region. Most importantly, the private sector resources of regional foundations can be a powerful complement to public sector resources, adding potential stability to the system as a cushion against the capacity constraints often associated with local public sector resources.

## A Role for Community Philanthropy

One untapped resource in many rural communities is the charitable assets that exist in the community at present or as part of the intergenerational wealth transfer that will occur in most rural communities over the next 20 or more years. Most rural communities are familiar with charitable giving. It is what sustains youth athletic teams, church building campaigns, and efforts to expand libraries and recreational facilities across rural America. What is more unusual is to see charitable assets dedicated to supporting economic development activities.

Through the work of the Nebraska Community Foundation, rural communities throughout the state have created affiliated community funds to focus local fund-raising efforts (Anft 2003). Using a wealth-transfer analysis tool, the foundation completed a study that provided an estimate for each county of how much wealth will be passed between generations in the community in the next ten years. Local leaders were then asked to consider the impact of retaining just 5 percent of the wealth through a local community foundation. More than 100 affiliated funds have been created in the state since 2001, putting together endowments of almost $6 million, with pledges of almost $13 million. These local foundations have the capacity to generate locally controlled resources that can be used to support the goals of the local community.

A further innovation bringing community philanthropy together with entrepreneurship development is the Home Town Competitiveness (HTC) approach developed by the Nebraska Community Foundation, the RUPRI Center for Rural Entrepreneurship, and the Heartland Center for Leadership Development. HTC brings together leadership development, youth engagement, community philanthropy, and entrepreneurship development into a long-term sustainable strategy for community development. From the perspective of providing sustainable financial support for the creation of an entrepreneurship development system, the important innovation in this model is the connection between community philanthropy and entrepreneurship—a key goal of the local community funds is to create a source of funds for investing in entrepreneurship development.

For example, in the small rural community of Ord, Nebraska, economic development grants made by the local foundation have spurred the creation of an "investors group" to continue and strengthen the entrepreneurship development activities in the community (see chapter 8). This marriage of community philanthropy and entrepreneurship is an important lesson learned for building sustainable systems of support for entrepreneurs in rural America.

## CONCLUSION

A successful entrepreneurial venture is not built on financial capital alone. It takes a system of support to help a rural entrepreneur identify, develop, and realize the dream of building a business. Access to the right kind of capital at the right time can smooth the path to business creation, however. Rural entrepreneurs face important obstacles in accessing the full range of capital resources necessary to finance idea generation and development, business start-up, operations, and growth.

Part of the challenge for a community is to build an entrepreneurship support system that can create new sources of capital locally and help entrepreneurs tap into sources of capital outside the local region. Fortunately, innovative models for addressing the capital needs of entrepreneurs, even in rural markets, exist and can serve as a guide for rural communities and regions.

Meeting the capital needs of entrepreneurs, however, is only one part of the challenge for local leaders. The other challenge is to build sustainable systems of support for entrepreneurs that match the long-term needs of entrepreneurship development. While local and state public sector resources may continue to be limited, communities can look inward to their own charitable resources. The model of community philanthropy linked to entrepreneurship development described here offers hope for even small rural communities that are seeking the resources to create a more sustainable economic future.

# REFERENCES

Anft, Michael. 2003. Nebraska charities hope local wealth will help revive main street. *Chronicle of Philanthropy* (December 11).

Association for Enterprise Opportunity (AEO). 2005. *Microenterprise Fact Sheet: Microenterprise Development in Rural United States.* www.microenterpriseworks.org/microenterpriseworks/files/ccLibraryFiles/Filename/000000000288/Rural%20Microenterprise%20Fact%20Sheet.pdf. Arlington, VA.

Bailey, Jon, et al. 2006. Wealth building in rural America: Programs, policies, and research. St. Louis: Center for Social Development, Washington University at St. Louis.

Batog, Jennifer. 2006. Angel investments spurred by state tax credit program. *Business Journal of Milwaukee* (March 3). http://milwaukee.bizjournals.com/milwaukee/stories/2006/03/06/story6.html. (April 21, 2006).

Bhide, Amar V. 2000. *The origins and evolution of new businesses.* New York: Oxford University Press.

CDFI Coalition Website. 2006. *About us.* www.cdfi.org/aboutus.asp (April 21, 2006).

CEI Community Ventures, Inc. 2006. www.ceicommunityventures.com/ (April 21, 2006).

CFED. 2005. *Assets Newsletter* (Number 1). www.cfed.org/publications/assets/Assets%202005%20Number%201.pdf (July 22, 2006).

Center for Rural Affairs Website. 2006. *Rural Enterprise Assistance Project Loan Programs.* www2.cfra.org/reap/loan_programs.htm (July 22, 2006).

Drabenstott, Mark. 2005. Top ten rural trends for community banks. Presentation to the Independent Community Bankers of America National Convention, San Antonio, TX.

Edgcomb, Elaine L., and Joyce A. Klein. 2005. *Opening opportunities, building ownership: Fulfilling the promise of microenterprise in the United States.* Washington, DC: Aspen Institute.

Grinstein-Weiss, Michal, and Jami Curley. 2003. Individual development accounts in rural communities: Implications for research (Working Paper No. 03-21). St. Louis: Center for Social Development, Washington University at St. Louis.

Hanc, George. 2006. The future of banking in America. *FDIC Banking Review.* www .fdic.gov/bank/analytical/banking/2004nov/article1/index.html (April 21, 2006).

Jossi, Frank. 2005. Angels we have heard on high. *fedgazette.* from http://minneapolisfed.org/pubs/fedgaz/05-07/jossi.cfm (April 21, 2006).

Kentucky Science and Technology Corporation. 2006. *Kentucky Enterprise Fund Website.* www.kstc.com/Dynamic/Investment_Portfoliox/CIF_Public_Awards.cfm (February 20, 2007).

Markley, Deborah, and David Barkley. 2003. Development of an entrepreneurial support organization: The case of the Kentucky Highlands Investment Corporation (Research Case Study Series Number 1). Columbia, MO: RUPRI Center for Rural Entrepreneurship.

The Microenterprise Fund for Innovation, Effectiveness, Learning, and Dissemination (FIELD). 2003. *2002 directory of U.S. microenterprise programs.* Washington, DC: Aspen Institute.

North Carolina Rural Economic Development Center. 2006. *Business Loan Programs: Capital Access Program.* www.rcruralcenter.org/loans/capital.htm (February 20, 2007).

PriceWaterhouseCooper. 2006. *Moneytree report 2005.* www.pwcmoneytree.com/exhibits/05Q4MoneyTreeReport_FINAL.pdf (April 17, 2006).

RUPRI Rural Equity Capital Initiative. 2001. *Nontraditional venture capital institutions: Filling a financial market gap* (P2001-11B). Columbia, MO: Rural Policy Research Institute.

RUPRI Rural Finance Task Force. 1997. The adequacy of rural financial markets: Economic development impacts of seven key policy issues. White paper completed for the Rural Policy Research Institute, Columbia, Missouri.

Schmitt, Brian. 2003 *Assessing the availability of traditional venture capital in the U.S.: A preliminary analysis* (Working Paper). New York: Community Development Venture Capital Alliance.

Ssewamala, Fred M., Margaret Lombe, and Jami C. Curley. 2006. *Using individual development accounts for microenterprise development.* (CSD Working Paper 06-08). St. Louis, MO: Center for Social Development, Washington University at St. Louis. http://gwbweb.wustl.edu/csd/Publications/2006/WP06-08.pdf (July 22, 2006).

U.S. Small Business Administration, Office of Advocacy. 2006. http://www.sba.gov/advo/stats/us_tot.pdf (April 7, 2006).

# 8

# The Difference Makers: Entrepreneurial Young People

*Craig Schroeder*

A rapidly growing number of textbooks, software, games, and other resources are available to teach entrepreneurship to young people, yet few resources are available on integrating youth entrepreneurship into community economic development strategies. This may be because youth entrepreneurship is seen as outside the traditional definition of economic development, or perhaps it is because educators and economic developers typically have not worked together. But, for communities suffering from chronic and persistent youth out-migration and economic distress, youth entrepreneurship can be an important element in attracting more young people to stay or return and revitalize the community through entrepreneurial endeavors. Therefore, this topic needs further exploration as a community-based strategy that combines the resources of education and communities in the development and support of entrepreneurial young people.

The Rural Policy Research Institute (RUPRI) Center for Rural Entrepreneurship has since 2003 focused on the topic of youth entrepreneurship and career education tied to youth leadership and adult mentoring in a systems approach to youth engagement and community economic development. This chapter explores the learning thus far on this community-based approach and describes ways community leaders can work with educators and other partners to engage young entrepreneurs and attract more young people to stay or return to rural areas. Specifically, the discussion will present observations on engaging entrepreneurial youth; discuss roles of schools, community, and adult mentors in the development of entrepreneurial young people; illustrate several emerging best practices as communities embark on youth entrepreneurship as part of their economic development game plan; and showcase young people with entrepreneurial ventures. The chapter concludes with several key points to consider on this topic.

## EMERGING TRENDS

A 1994, national Gallup survey commissioned by the Ewing Marion Kaufmann Foundation, reported that 69 percent of high school students have an interest in starting their own business (Walstad 1994). Work around the country indicates that a growing number of young people view entrepreneurship as a desirable career path, seeking entrepreneurship classes in their school and starting microbusinesses as early as elementary school age (RUPRI Center for Rural Entrepreneurship 2006). In particular, rural youth are keenly aware that markets can now be successfully reached even from the most remote community. As public access to the Internet approaches only its second decade, young people accept instantaneous global networking via the Internet and cell phones as the norm, and entrepreneurial youth who embrace technology are becoming resources for communities seeking to participate in the networked economy.

Another encouraging trend documented by the RUPRI youth survey work in rural communities is that a large percentage of junior high, high school, and college students would like to return to their hometowns if good career opportunities were available. It is common for more than 60 percent of teenage respondents to report such a desire, yet a much smaller percentage perceive that such opportunities actually exist for them (RUPRI Center for Rural Entrepreneurship 2006).

Field experience indicates that a systems approach is vital to moving from a set of interesting activities to a strategy that can impact youth out-migration trends and lead to social and economic revitalization. System design and illustrations from community-based work will be provided later.

## RETHINKING YOUR GAME PLAN

Community leaders concerned about the impact of youth out-migration trends must rethink their strategy options, beginning with an understanding of young peoples' preferences for entrepreneurial careers and desire to be part of their community now and in the future. The emerging trends just discussed, when combined with youth engagement strategies, can create significant opportunities to revitalize a community both socially and economically. Before exploring these opportunities and how to effectively engage young entrepreneurs as difference makers in the future of a community, young peoples' characteristics should be examined.

## CHARACTERISTICS OF YOUNG ENTREPRENEURS

As a starting point, it is important to understand that there is not a single definition of young entrepreneurs. Each young person has strengths, weaknesses, talents, relationships, environment, and experiences that shape who they are and will become. Certain traits or characteristics can help identify an entrepreneurial young person, however. These traits are important because entrepreneurial youth often do not automatically come to mind when thinking about young people in a community. Often, the student body president, the star football or volleyball player, or the honor roll students immediately come to mind. Some of these young people may also be entrepreneurial, so they should not be excluded, but another, not so visible, group of youth should also be identified. Characteristics of these young people and potential ways to engage them should be recognized.

Entrepreneurial young people may not be obvious because they may not be high academic achievers or may spend their free time in dad's shop inventing or in mom's craft room creating, so they are invisible. They may work in a local business after school because they enjoy it, or they may be busy operating their own small business.

One story that illustrates this comes from a participant in a recent youth entrepreneurship workshop. One gentleman had a neighbor whose son operated a Web design consulting business from his bedroom while in high school. What makes this story interesting is that he was making a higher annual income than his parents by working part-time after school and on weekends. Such budding entrepreneurs may exist in many communities and go undetected.

Sometimes entrepreneurial youth appear to be introverted. This may be because they know they are wired differently than their peers, and at this age, "fitting in" is important to them. In the adult population, only one in ten Americans is truly entrepreneurial (Minniti and Bygrave 2004). The percentage may be somewhat higher among young people due to a growing interest in entrepreneurship, but they are still likely a minority among their classmates.

While other students may focus on sports or other extracurricular activities, entrepreneurial youth think about inventing and marketing their ideas. Young entrepreneurs enjoy the creative process so much that it may explain why they are sometimes not high academic achievers. A commonly heard phrase is that "A and B students work for C and D students." Perhaps a more positive statement would be, "Smart people work for creative visionaries."

Sometimes youth entrepreneurs do poorly in subjects such as math, English, or history but excels in art, vocational, music, or computer science courses where they can apply their creative skills more directly. Again, not all entrepreneurial youth have the same traits, but this information can be an indication to teachers and school administrators. A variety of studies on youth entrepreneurial traits and economic and social impacts are available on the Internet. One excellent resource for learning more about young entrepreneurs is the Ewing Marion Kauffman Foundation.[1]

Another indicator is that entrepreneurial students may not pay attention in class because they are bored in school or daydreaming about the project on which they are working. Because they may not understand how classroom learning relates to their entrepreneurial interests, it is easy for these students to lose interest in class.

It is important to stress that these traits are not excuses for students doing poorly in school. Instead, the main point is that low academic achievement may be an indicator of a young entrepreneur and that these students can be engaged in ways that make core subjects more relevant to them.

For example, an entrepreneurship class can incorporate math, accounting, language arts, library research, and other topics into the curriculum. When entrepreneurial youth can combine these core subjects with an idea they are passionate about or a problem they want to solve, academic achievement can improve because these students can have a deeper understanding of academic subject matter through practical application (Stern 1994).

Another characteristic of young entrepreneurs is that they may already be in business. They may have one or more microbusinesses and even employ several classmates or siblings. Ask around town if people know of youth with a small business, and look for flyers in the local coffee shop. Teachers and fellow students are also good sources of information about young people who operate their own businesses.

Some rural communities have clustered these entrepreneurial youth into school- or community-based entrepreneurial ventures. An excellent example is Rothsay High School's Storefront in Rothsay, Minnesota (U.S. Department of Education, Office of Educational Research and Improvement 1995). This program began with the purchase of a hardware store and lumber yard that became a student-run corporation and reopened the community's grocery store. Students, with teacher support, combined learning from the classroom with real-world business experience.

A support structure for entrepreneurial youth is also important because students may not be well connected to adults in economic development roles, so they may not know where to turn for help in creating a business plan around their idea or accessing capital. They may also need help in one or more of the primary functions of a business—production, management, and marketing. On a scientific level, research by the National Institutes of Health Clinical Center in Bethesda, Maryland, as reported in *TIME Magazine* in May 2004, indicates that teenagers do not have fully developed brains for decisionmaking, responsibility, and risk assessment (Wallis and Dell 2004)—attributes important to successful entrepreneurial enterprise.

One way to help entrepreneurial youth develop these attributes is by creating a supportive community environment for learning and application in real-world settings. Consider several key elements to engage and support entrepreneurial young people within the context of a community-based youth engagement system.

## YOUTH ENGAGEMENT SYSTEM

A youth engagement system is a comprehensive strategy that interconnects education, real-world experience and community support. This system seeks out and *engages* entrepreneurial youth, *equips* them to succeed, and *supports* their enterprising ventures as they mature into adulthood. For a moment, consider the roles that schools, the community, and adult mentors can play in creating a system for supporting youth entrepreneurship.

### Schools

As was stressed earlier, making education relevant to young entrepreneurs is important to their academic success and preparation for adulthood. An essential element in this work is entrepreneurship education.

Ideally, entrepreneurial concepts should be integrated into the curriculum from elementary school to postsecondary education (Rasheed and Rasheed 2003). Starting early is important because young entrepreneurs begin expressing their traits at a very young age. Waiting until the junior or senior year of high school may be too late for these students. Either they will try to figure things out on their own, and in the process take their focus off school, or they will give up and go into the mainstream path of taking college prep classes, hoping to find a job that allows them to use their creative entrepreneurial talents. College may indeed be the proper path for a young entrepreneur, but it should enhance their entrepreneurial development, not be a substitute because alternatives are not available.

On a practical level, making products to sell in kindergarten, learning about local entrepreneurs in elementary school, and offering entrepreneurship programs in junior high and high school are ways to enhance the K–12 curriculum for entrepreneurial youth.

The Consortium for Entrepreneurship Education[2] is an excellent resource for identifying and evaluating curricula available. In addition, the Rural School and Community Trust[3] has extensive research on communities and schools working together to enhance place-based education. They provide tools and best practices to help schools and communities work together to engage students and enhance education.

## Community

Community support of young entrepreneurs can take several forms. One possibility is as a learning laboratory, working in concert with the local school (Hinz 1993). For example, an apprenticeship in a business related to a student's entrepreneurship class project provides real-world, hands-on experience that can greatly enhance learning. Another approach is a Youth Entrepreneur Fair where young entrepreneurs make and sell products and are recognized by the community for their innovation and achievement.

Young entrepreneurs may also be interested in nonprofit and public sector projects that address an environmental or social cause they care about. They may even blend traditional for-profit and nonprofit roles and create what are sometimes referred to as *For Social-Profit Enterprise* or *Enviropreneurship* (Stafford and Hartman 1998).

Young civic-oriented entrepreneurs can help local decisionmakers think outside the box in solving problems and improving the community. One way to do this is to provide space for youth to participate in local organizations or on government boards.

These activities are not just a learning experience for youth, however. Young people have very interesting insights about their community and what is needed to make it a better place for young people to live. Engaging young people in community leadership and service roles helps them develop healthy self-esteem and a sense of community ownership through service to others.

Positive experiences in linking community leaders to entrepreneurship education may lead more youth to consider returning to the community after college and/or some career experience. Young entrepreneurs have stated in focus group discussions that they feel they have a better chance of succeeding in their hometown where everyone knows them versus a large city where they are only one of many people competing for customers.

The likelihood of young adults returning to a community may be further enhanced by connecting young entrepreneurs with specific business opportunities, either via business start-ups or the purchase of an existing business. Community leaders working in concert with teachers can open a dialog with young entrepreneurs to determine career goals and then work to match local business opportunities with those goals. For example, a young person interested in owning a contracting business can be made aware that the community needs such a business and would support it. There may even be such a business owned by an older owner that the young person may be able to purchase with the support of the community through a community loan program or through business succession tools that help the young buyer acquire the business without excessive debt.

Another resource that can influence young people to return to their community is a college scholarship. Almost every community has one or more organizations that provide college scholarships to graduating seniors. Often, these scholarships go to students who perform exceptionally in academics, sports, or other extracurricular activities. However, if a community wants to encourage young people to return home, and perhaps start or purchase a business, a scholarship targeted at these goals is an excellent way to convey this message to interested students. Linkages such as these that connect education to career and business opportunities can be powerful tools in attracting young entrepreneurs. Scholarship applications also can provide the community with valuable information about students who have an interest in returning home.

One private company in Nebraska provides college scholarships to students in rural communities where they provide services. For years, the application has asked applicants to indicate their interest in returning home in the future. The responses were typically vague and noncommittal. In the past three years, however, since youth have become more involved in the community, the applicants are much more positive and specific about plans for coming back. For example, one young woman stated that she plans to earn a college degree in journalism and then hopes to return home to own and operate the local newspaper business.

The information from the application was shared by the corporate sponsor with local leaders, and a dialog began with this young person about how her community could help make her goal a reality. These examples demonstrate how a scholarship connected with community engagement can have a real impact on young entrepreneurs and the future of the community. When this engagement is linked with adult role models and mentors, it can have a profound impact on young people (Stone, Bremer, and Kowske 2000).

## Adult Mentors

In reflecting back on one's experiences in youth, you may recall one or more adults with fond memories. Why did they have such a significant impact? How did they interact with you? What was it that made them so important in your development? When groups of adults are asked these questions, the responses are often moving and heartfelt. Stories about a teacher, a grandparent, or a businessperson in town are common. Comments such as, "They helped me figure out who I am" or "They helped me believe in myself" are heard often.

Young people today need the same kind of support and encouragement as previous generations; however, because the pace has become so hectic in a 24/7 networked world, youth may not spend enough quality time with adults who can help them figure out who they are, how the world works, and what their role can be in society. What is the impact on a teenager who is never asked to be involved in their community or does not receive support and encouragement from an adult, especially in difficult times? Adults can be very important in the lives of youth by making time to be positive role models—to listen, encourage, guide, and support young people.

There likely are adults locally who want to be role models and mentors to young people, and for present purposes, young entrepreneurs. They may be successful business owners or civic leaders who had a mentor in younger years and want to give back by helping a young person experience what they did at an early age. Perhaps it is a retired teacher who wants to stay involved with students and has great skills as a mentor. Maybe it is a pastor, a grandmother, the mayor, or perhaps it is you!

## TYING THE PIECES TOGETHER

Thus far, the roles of schools, the community, and adults in supporting young entrepreneurs have been discussed. But to be most effective, each component must be interconnected in ways that help young entrepreneurs develop their skills, knowledge, and confidence to the point where they can create a successful business enterprise or contribute their creativity and passion through a nonprofit organization or in public service.

If a young person is involved in an entrepreneurship class at school and has the dream to start a business but perceives that the community does not support young people or even encourages them to leave, the logical response may well be, "I want to start my own business, but I will need to leave this community to do it."

Conversely, what if a community involves youth in civic leadership and service roles but does not expose them to potential career opportunities? The logical response may be, "I really like this community, but there are no jobs here, so I guess I'll need to find another community in which to live."

But, what if we interconnect entrepreneurship education, civic leadership, and service roles with adult mentoring? The response of more young people might be, "This is a great community with lots of potential and people who support me. I want to go to college and maybe see the world, but when I am ready to settle down, this is where I want to be!"

The following diagram illustrates the relationship among the elements being discussed. It ties together the interrelationships of *engaging, equipping,* and *supporting* young entrepreneurs through education and career development, youth involvement, and community support of youth (figure 8.1).

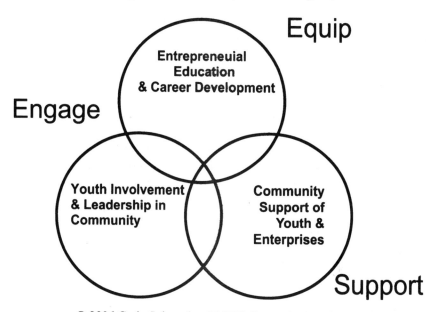

© 2006 Craig Schroeder, RUPRI Center for Rural Entrepreneurship
**Figure 8.1.   Integrated Youth Engagement System**

To help tie these concepts to one's own community work, stop at this point and draw this diagram on a large piece of paper. Think about specific programs and activities that a community and school offer within each circle that support entrepreneurial development among youth. Write down these items around the outside of the diagram in the appropriate location. If a program or activity addresses more than one topic area, record it once in an area that touches the appropriate circles.

After completing the exercise, stand back and look at the output. Where is the most activity? Is there a lack of activity in one or more areas? Are some activities and programs interconnected or is the diagram filled with disconnected elements?

Bring others into the discussion and begin to develop youth engagement goals and supporting activities with youth program leaders, young people, school administrators, civic leaders, and the business community. Consider what outcomes are to be achieved during the next two to five years, and determine how key elements on the diagram can be linked and support one another in a systematic approach to reaching the stated goals. Identify and secure additional resources and programs needed to fill gaps in the youth engagement strategy.

This integrated approach may be as straightforward as providing an entrepreneurship curriculum in the local school tied to apprenticeships with business leaders and leadership opportunities for youth in community organizations. Or, a local group may identify new ideas for engaging the school, community, and adult mentors utilizing local assets such as a building that can be converted into a youth business incubator.

Additional help is available from people with experience in this field and a community's demonstrated success. Seeing a successful program first-hand will inspire thinking and action. The RUPRI Center for Rural Entrepreneurship maintains a web-based library of entrepreneurial community success stories that can help. Another good starting point is the state department of economic development or other agencies that interact with communities on a regular basis.

RUPRI is looking across the country and internationally for community-based youth programs that incorporate the above elements successfully. It is still early to measure the real impact of a comprehensive engagement approach due to the long-term nature of working with youth in an economic development context; however, much is being learned about the elements of successful practice from young people and community leaders. Several examples that show early success follow.

## STRATEGY SUCCESS STORIES

### Ord, Nebraska

The first example is Ord, Nebraska, where, in 2005, the business development coordinator began working with thirty-four middle school age students at a parochial school. At the beginning of the school year, the students learned how entrepreneurs take their ideas and create businesses around them. The business coordinator came to class with what she calls a "Sack Full of Ideas." It was a pillowcase filled with common items gathered around her house such as Post-It Notes and a can opener with an ergonomic handle. She discussed with the students in simple terms how entrepreneurs take an existing product or service and make it better, or create something totally new.

Based on this simple description, students were then given an assignment to come up with ideas for products they would like to make and sell as a class project. During the school year, they drafted business plans, applied for loans from local bankers, met with entrepreneurs, and produced their products with help from the business program coordinator and their teachers. At the end of the school year, they held a community Youth Entrepreneurship Fair to sell their products to the public. They created radio ads with the support of the local radio station, and the students were interviewed during the fair on a live radio broadcast.

Some of the products the students created were concrete stepping stones, designer plant fertilizer, wooden toy tops, fishing lures, dog treats, and rabbit fur koozies. The students also engaged in community service projects such as planting flowers at the Senior Center, emphasizing the importance of giving back to the community. Their teachers stressed service to others as an important element of a well-rounded education.

This is a hands-on approach to teaching entrepreneurship and community service, and the students enjoyed themselves while also learning a great deal about business and their community. The business development coordinator is currently working with middle school students throughout the rural county and is facilitating a summer 4-H landscaping program to prepare young people interested in this profession while also beautifying their community.

## Big Stone Gap, Virginia

Big Stone Gap, Virginia, in the Appalachia region near the Kentucky border, has a strong CFED REAL entrepreneurship program,[4] involving seven high schools in four communities and the area technical college. During the eight years following the program's inception, twenty-four teachers gained certification in the REAL curriculum and twenty-three social programs contributed funding to support the program. The initiative has evolved to incorporate entrepreneurship concepts throughout the school curriculum.

The local Workforce Investment Board funds students to participate in the program as part of a strategy to help families move out of poverty through education and economic empowerment. Examples of student projects include the renovation of an old corn mill that is open for tours led by students. The students also mill products available for sale to tourists. The region is rich in Bluegrass music artists, so students produced a music CD of local artists that they sell along with old tinplate photographs that they found.

In their research, students learned that bats help control West Nile virus–carrying insects, so they started building bat houses to sell to area residents. The REAL program now incorporates a beauty parlor and a catering business, and, it most recently purchased a plasma cutter for manufacturing signs and other metal products. The program is a great example of the potential for a community-based youth entrepreneurship initiative and points the way for others to follow.

## Northern New Mexico

Four counties in northern New Mexico have forged an entrepreneurial support organization called the EBS Initiative for Empowering Northern

New Mexico's Business Spirit. The EBS mission statement is, "the public and private sectors uniting to create an environment that encourages an entrepreneurial mindset, models and rewards entrepreneurial risk-taking, and holistically supports the establishment and growth of small businesses" (Martinez 2005).

During the past year, the EBS Youth Entrepreneur Director has built an innovative youth entrepreneurship support structure that is already demonstrating impact. One innovative approach involves networking with established entrepreneurial firms in the region to help youth create affiliated branch businesses. The group has planned and led several community forums to help adults better connect with youth and the issues they care about. The effort also connects youth to their respective Spanish and Hispanic heritages to build bridges and respect for the different cultures in the communities that EBS serves.

A three-day EBS *You're the Boss* Conference was held in February 2006 in Española, New Mexico, at Northern New Mexico College (YoungBiz Holding USA Ltd. n.d.). Twenty educators were trained and certified in the YoungBiz youth entrepreneur curriculum during the event. The educators will teach the curriculum to students in seven school districts and in after-school organizations, such as 4-H, beginning in 2006 and 2007 (YoungBiz Holding USA Ltd. n.d.).[5]

Young entrepreneurs who show the most initiative will attend a Youth Entrepreneur Summer Camp and enter a business plan competition. The winners will receive EBS support in developing businesses. This program is well on its way to helping youth forge stronger communities and new economic opportunities in northern New Mexico.

### Putting Green, New Ulm, Minnesota

Putting Green[6] is the brainchild of a New Ulm area physician and her family. In 1997 on a family outing, they discovered that mini-golf was a fun activity that they all enjoyed together. On the way home the eight-year-old son was imagining and drawing mini golf holes in the backseat. The mother thought—"Aha! Wouldn't designing and developing a mini golf course be a great hands-on way to learn many disciplines—physics, math, art, and business?" With her passion for education and a newfound interest in sustainability—that what's good for the environment and good for business can be one in the same—sustainability education became a natural theme for the park.

The physician explains, "The blend of lighthearted family fun with the serious need to care for our environment seemed a perfect combination for success." Given what has been accomplished, it is apparent that many others agree. Putting Green, Inc. formed in 2001 as a nonprofit organization, and thanks to its many supporters and volunteers, Putting Green is an innovative center for environmental education serving south central Minnesota.

Putting Green was designed as a youth driven business. In 2001, students helped develop Putting Green's business plan. Beginning in January of 2006, Putting Green began a unique collaboration with South Central Technical College to hold a twelve-week course entitled *The Business of Putting Green: A Course for Entrepreneurs.* The course brings together high school students and local business owners to learn what it takes to be a small business owner, using Putting Green as a case study. Many of the students will form an "owner team" that will manage and operate the park.

### Highlands of Scotland

A final example is in the Highlands of Scotland where a Marketing Development Manager works with Rural Insights[7] to sponsor the ICT Youth Challenge. This is an interesting Information Communication Technology (ICT) initiative to help young people develop ideas for ICT innovations and successfully bring them to market. It is a bootstrap program that has grown to capture the interest of partners such as Microsoft.

The Highlands of Scotland is very remote and economically distressed. The concept of a youth ICT inventors and entrepreneurs program was developed as a way to revitalize the economic base of the region and create entrepreneurial career opportunities in twenty-first-century fields. The leader believes that to successfully make this transition, young people must develop ITC entrepreneurial thinking skills.

Young entrepreneurs from the Highlands give merit to the approach Rural Insights is undertaking. One group of teenagers originated an idea for using Global Positioning Satellite (GPS) tracking devices in cell phones to help emergency personnel locate accident victims in a matter of minutes even in remote and dangerous terrain. They are patenting the device and negotiating with major communication firms to license the technology.

## EXAMPLES OF YOUNG ENTREPRENEURS

Examples of what young entrepreneurs can achieve are useful in starting a youth entrepreneurship program, especially in convincing others to support a local effort. The following young people are each following a distinctive path as a young entrepreneur. Several have focused on developing their businesses while others are involved in community activities that use their creative talents and entrepreneurial passion. Many other stories in your community or region can be shared with colleagues.

## Backporch Friends

The founder of Backporch Friends[8] was sixteen years old when starting what has grown into a highly successful business. He grew up in Valentine, located in the Nebraska Sandhills, and began artistic pursuits at a very young age. Both grandmothers were avid quilters and taught him the skills needed to later design and create unique and whimsical folk art dolls. As the business grew, he employed other quilters in the region to help produce dolls under close supervision and his creative involvement in final production.

Early successes eventually led to regional, and soon national popularity. While a student in high school, he was invited to New York City to create holiday window displays in upscale retail stores. The designs are now distributed nationally and featured in the American Folk Art Museum as well as in *Country Home Magazine* and *Country Living Magazine*. Today, the Backporch products are highly collected.

## ATM

Three young students in Atkinson Public School in north central Nebraska have operated a successful lawn care business called ATM, their first initials, for the past several years. When asked if they have major competition, the response was, "Not really; other kids aren't willing to work as hard as we are." The entrepreneur who we spoke with is an engaging young man from a family of entrepreneurs and civic leaders. His family owns several local businesses and is involved in all aspects of the community.

Another family member was a high school senior last year at nearby Stuart High School. She served as a National Vice President of Family, Career and Community Leaders of America (FCCLA) and was elected governor by her peers at Girls State in 2004. She ran for both prestigious positions with a message she is passionate about: *"Youth are not only the leaders of tomorrow; we can be leaders today!"*

She tells a story about when she was little and played "Town" with cousins. Most kids play house, school, or store, but she and her cousins were big thinkers as toddlers and they ran the entire community! They named the town Greenville because their playroom had old green shag carpet. They each took turns operating the various businesses, school, library, and public utilities in their small town, and in the process, learned what it takes to make a real community work.

There is no doubt that Greenville, and the parents who encouraged their role-playing, will have a lasting impact on these young entrepreneurs. Both of these young people are growing up in a nurturing family that actively encourages entrepreneurial development and instills the importance of community service in their children.

## Girl Talk

During the 2006 Georgia Governors Entrepreneurship Summit held in Douglas, a panel of three young entrepreneurs captured the audience with their passion, humor, and energy. One particular young woman, well-known to teenage girls who read *Cosmo Girl*, shared her remarkable story. She is a student at Kennesaw State University in Georgia and an engaging young person with a heart for helping young girls discover their potential during their formative years. In 2002, she began a mentoring program in her high school to help middle school girls better address personal adolescence issues. The idea caught on and now Girl Talk[9] operates in 19 states with the goal of having programs in all 50 states by 2010.

## ELEMENTS OF SUCCESSFUL PRACTICE

We have discussed a variety of aspects of youth engagement and how they are being applied, but work with communities that are engaged in youth entrepreneurship indicates several common traits of successful programs. These "leading practices" can help inform other communities about how to develop an effective youth entrepreneur engagement strategy. Key traits include the following:

- Quality Entrepreneurship Curriculum
- Supportive Community Environment
- Peer Networking
- Pathways from Education to Opportunity

Each of these leading practices will be examined more closely with suggestions based on field experience.

## QUALITY ENTREPRENEURSHIP CURRICULUM

Teachers may use a variety of teaching styles and course materials to teach entrepreneurship. Compliance with the No Child Left Behind Act impacts elementary and middle schools nationwide and may become a requirement throughout K–12 education in the future. Curriculum that is already certified to meet these standards, is content rich, is well-organized, and does not require extensive background work by teachers to use the materials, is noted as a priority among teachers.

Teachers also appreciate the inclusion of class exercises adaptable to lesson plans. Some teachers prefer a hardcover textbook and workbooks that contain all the materials for the class. Other educators want to use a variety of resources and create hands-on class and community-based activities.

Many rural schools have insufficient resources to dedicate an entire course and teacher to entrepreneurship, so this topic is presented as a section of Business Law, Family Consumer Science, or Current Events. It can also be challenging to fit entrepreneurship into the class schedule among other required electives for college-bound students. Again, incorporating entrepreneurship into existing courses has been a solution to this constraint.

As noted previously, the Consortium for Entrepreneurship Education is a helpful clearinghouse of information on entrepreneurship curricula and supporting resource materials. Before engaging in a conversation with school administrators or faculty about offering a class, it would be useful to review the curriculum descriptions presented on their Website. It may also help to refer educators to this Website so they also have a better idea of materials available for teaching entrepreneurship.

### Supportive Community Environment

Communities can partner with schools as a learning laboratory where students practice the knowledge gained in the classroom. This may involve apprenticeships, selling products at school events, interviewing local entrepreneurs, or undertaking a community service project.

Another element involves utilizing local experts to work with young entrepreneurs. For example in Ord, Nebraska, two local bankers worked with students in preparing loan applications for their class projects. A marketing professional based in the community helped students design marketing plans. The radio station owner worked with the student to produce advertisements that played on the air.

In addition to these roles, community leaders taking an interest in young entrepreneurs can change attitudes among young people about the community and their future. Building relationships with students who want to be involved in the community, supporting their efforts, and celebrating their community and entrepreneurial projects can help them develop into productive citizens and also make a community more attractive to young people as a place to stay or return.

### Peer Networking

Just as with entrepreneurial adults, youth entrepreneurs need a "place" to associate with peers who think the way they do. Providing a space for them to interact with other young entrepreneurs allows them to feed off each other's energy and create even better ideas and inventions. This space may simply be a parent's garage or basement family room during an evening with pizza and soda.

### Pathways from Education to Opportunity

Communities can help young entrepreneurs transition from the learning process to tangible business opportunities by helping them clarify goals and develop a plan, connect with opportunities that are a good fit, and support them as their enterprises develop.

This work may involve compiling an inventory of soon-to-retire business owners looking to sell their businesses during the next several years, or it may include using an existing revolving loan fund to help a capable young person without adequate cash or equity get into business. Each young entrepreneur is unique. Determining the help they need to move ahead and filling those gaps is key.

## CONCLUSION

Much ground has been covered in this chapter exploring the subject of young entrepreneurs in the context of community economic development. In closing, it may help to emphasize several key points.

First, youth entrepreneurship needs to be a priority within a community economic development strategy for it to succeed. This is a long-term engagement process. Some of the youth will not graduate for another 4 to 13 years. Further, if they plan to attend college and gain career experience, they may not return for an additional 4 to 10 years or more. Entrepreneurship development requires a sustained effort in a fast-paced world that expects immediate results.

Equally important is the short-term impact youth can make in a community when there is room for them at the table. One high school student we worked with put it this way, "We don't mind painting the picnic shelter; we just want to help pick the color!" What she was expressing simply is youth want a role in determining the future of their community. Young people can have great ideas, and they know what a community needs to attract more young people to return. If youth attraction is a goal, then listening to youth and supporting their ideas with action are key.

In moving forward, keep in mind the process discussed for *engaging* young entrepreneurs, *equipping* them to succeed, and *supporting* them in their entrepreneurial ventures. There are a variety of ways to approach each of these key elements, but they all are needed to be the most successful.

In summary, this work is really about building relationships with young people. Take time to listen to them, encourage them, and support them. The impact will last a lifetime!

## NOTES

1. Ewing Marion Kauffman Foundation, 4801 Rockhill Road, Kansas City, MO 64110, www.kauffman.org.
2. Consortium for Entrepreneurship Education, 1601 W. Fifth Ave. #199, Columbus, OH 43212, www.entre-ed.org.
3. The Rural School and Community Trust, 1530 Wilson Blvd., Suite 240, Arlington, VA 22209, www.ruraledu.org.
4. Kim Pate, Director of Field Development, CFED, 777 N. Capitol St. NE, Suite 800, Washington DC 20002, www.cfed.org.
5. Ron Martinez, Youth Entrepreneur Director, EBS Initiative, www.bizport.org.
6. Dr. Laurel Gamm, Executive Director, Putting Green, P.O. Box 91, New Ulm, MN 56073, www.puttinggreen.org.
7. Bryan Fraser, Marketing Development Manager, Rural Insights, 16 Academy Street, Fortrose Ross-shire Scotland IV10 8TW, www.ruralinsights.com.
8. Backporch Friends, 27 N. Main St., Valentine, NE 69201.
9. Girl Talk, 3400 Peachtree Road NE, Suite 1750, Atlanta, GA 30326, www.desiretoinspire.org

## REFERENCES

Giroux, Henry A. 1994. Slacking off: Border youth and postmodern education, *Journal of Advanced Composition* 14(2): 347–66.
Hinz, Lisa. 1993. *The Community and School as an Economic Development Team*, Positive Directions for Schools and Communities, University of Minnesota, Extension Service.
Martinez, Ron. 2005. *EBS Initiative*. www.bizport.org (November 29, 2006).
Minniti, Maria, and William D. Bygrave. (July 2004). *Global Entrepreneurship Monitor, 2003 Executive Report*, 6.
Rasheed, Howard S., and Barbara Y. Rasheed. 2003. *Developing entrepreneurial characteristics in minority youth: The effects of education and enterprise experience*. Wilmington: University of North Carolina.
RUPRI Center for Rural Entrepreneurship. 2006. *Youth engagement toolkit*.
Stafford, Edwin R., and Cathy L. Hartman. 1998. *Toward an understanding of the antecedents of environmentalist-business cooperative relations*. Published in *American Marketing Association Summer Educators' Conference Proceedings*. eds. Ronald C. Goodstein and Scott B. MacKenzie, Chicago, IL: American Marketing Association, 56–63.
Stern, David. 1994. *School based enterprise: Productive learning in American high schools*. San Francisco, CA: Jossey-Bass.

Stone III, James R., Christine D. Bremer, and Brenda J. Kowske. 2000. *Youth run enterprises: Successes, barriers, and policy implications.* University of Minnesota, Extension Service, 2000.

U.S. Department of Education, Office of Educational Research and Improvement. 1995. *Critical elements of school-to-work reform: Study of school-to-work initiatives, Cross-site analysis.* Washington, DC: U.S. Department of Education, Office of Educational Research and Improvement.

YoungBiz Holding USA Ltd. n.d. *You're the boss.*www.youngbiz.com (November 29, 2006).

Wallis, Claudia, and Kristina Dell. 2004. *What makes teens tick. Time,* May 10.

Walstad, William B. 1994. Kansas City, MO: Ewing Marion Kauffmann Foundation, Center for Entrepreneurship Leadership; Princeton, NJ: Gallup Organization, Inc.; and Lincoln: Nebraska University, National Center for Research in Economic Education.

# 9

# Effective Entrepreneurship Education Programs

*Joseph Kayne*

In the previous chapter, Schroeder makes the case that encouragement and support of youth is critical to the success of any local entrepreneurship strategy, providing examples of young residents who exemplify this approach. The significant short- and long-term contributions these young people make to their communities beg the question, "How do we make this kind of behavior the rule rather than the exception?" A good place to start is the local education system. We know that one of the distinguishing characteristics of successful entrepreneurs is a culture of lifelong learning, but where does this thirst for information knowledge begin?

This chapter addresses the role of education in starting students on an entrepreneurial path, the keys to an effective student experience, and the challenges to implementing an entrepreneurship education program. In particular, the chapter focuses on entrepreneurship education at the elementary and secondary school levels.

## THE CASE FOR ELEMENTARY AND SECONDARY ENTREPRENEURSHIP EDUCATION

There is a significant difference between the percentage of students who express an interest in starting or running their own businesses and the percentage who feel they have the skills and knowledge to do so (Walstad and Kourilsky 1999). As early as 1995, Marilyn Kourilsky, then–vice president of the Kauffman Center for Entrepreneurial Leadership, suggested this gap resulted from an education system focused on a "take-a-job" mentality, preparing students to work for someone else (Kourilsky 1995). Lack of self-confidence in their capacity to become successful entrepreneurs also proves to be one of the factors that may explain the difference in entrepreneurial activity across gender and ethnicity factors (Wilson, Marlino, and Kickul 2004). Entrepreneurship curriculum is viewed as one avenue to address both the knowledge gap and the self-confidence factors affecting youth attitudes toward entrepreneurship as a career choice.

These findings are not limited to the United States. In a study of the experience with YAA, an extension of the Junior Achievement program in Australia, students with exposure to entrepreneurship curriculum in secondary schools showed an increased propensity toward and confidence in starting their own business (Peterman and Kennedy 2003). Recognizing the importance of introducing students to the entrepreneurship concepts earlier in their education, the European Union (EU) sponsored a conference in 2006 titled, *Entrepreneurship Education in Europe: Fostering Educational Mindsets through Education and Learning*. In line with Kourilsky's call for a broader entrepreneurship curriculum, the participants at the Oslo conference agreed "the scope of entrepreneurship education is much wider than training on how to start a business, as it includes the development of personal attributes and horizontal skills like creativity, initiative, self-confidence, among many others" (EU, Enterprise and Industry Directorate 2006).

## ENTREPRENEURSHIP EDUCATION: FOCUS ON HUMAN DEVELOPMENT

To fully understand the importance of an education agenda as part of an entrepreneurship community strategy one must first understand the differentiating characteristics between entrepreneurship and more traditional economic development strategies based on industrial attraction, expansion, and retention. Unlike more traditional approaches to economic development, entrepreneurship focuses on human, not physical, development. It is the domain of individuals or groups of individuals who understand and can apply the mind-set and behaviors associated with creating, growing, and sustaining successful enterprises. Any community development strategy in which entrepreneurship is a pillar must therefore explore the methods and institutions through which youth and adults obtain the skills and ways of thinking that improve their odds of success.

The critical difference between entrepreneurship and other forms of economic development presented itself most clearly during a working session of the State of Minnesota team participating in the 1999 Governors' Academy on Entrepreneurship cosponsored by the National Governors Association and the Ewing Marion Kauffman Foundation. The team's charge focused on the disparity between entrepreneurship activity in urban areas—especially the Twin Cities—and rural and smaller communities across the state.

An inventory of the small business services available in the outlying communities suggested that someone in the process of starting a business could expect a reasonable level of support from public and nongovernmental organizations. What then could explain the difference in the percentage of rural residents for whom entrepreneurship was a career choice, especially in light of the fact that the responses to a series of Gallup surveys conducted by the Kauffman Foundation (Walstad and Kourilsky 1999) suggested that geography did not affect an individual's interest in starting or running a business?

The team's deliberations resulted in a new model for understanding how communities could reach their entrepreneurial potential. This new construct relied on responses to three sequential questions:

1. Do residents have the propensity to become entrepreneurs?
2. Do those residents who have the propensity also have the skills and knowledge associated with entrepreneurship?
3. Do those residents with the skills and knowledge receive the support they need to increase their probability of success?

This epiphany occurred when the team members realized that they had devoted a disproportionate share of their time and resources to the last query and little attention to the first two. Supporting businesses through technical assistance and financing programs was the traditional domain of economic development—activities most economic development organizations had conducted for a considerable period of time and for which they considered themselves competent.

The individual development of future business owners, this human aspect of the economic development process, fell outside the boundaries of the historical economic development paradigm. Any entrepreneurship strategy that focuses only on identifying and supporting adults who want to start their own businesses ignores the largest potential audience—youth who have yet to make a career decision.

For youth to consider entrepreneurship as a career choice, especially in communities where high school graduates have historically migrated to salaried jobs, community leaders and educators must recognize that the education system and the curriculum associated with it have a significant influence over career decisions. The best example of how education can inhibit students' entrepreneurial tendencies comes from an examination of factors that influence the rate of entrepreneurial activity in EU countries.

In 2005, 56 students from the Richard T. Farmer School of Business participated in a summer entrepreneurship course at the Miami University Dolibois Education Center in Luxembourg. The students were divided into teams and then asked to compare entrepreneurship activity in each of 12 non-English speaking members of the EU with that in the United States. Using data from the 2004 *Global Entrepreneurship Monitor*, each team quickly learned that all of the nations under study exhibited a rate of entrepreneurial activity lagging behind that of the United States (Acs et al. 2004). Based on these findings, each team was then asked to identify factors that inhibited entrepreneurial activities and develop recommendations for ameliorating the identified barriers.

In two countries—Denmark and Germany—the student teams identified the education system as major inhibitors of entrepreneurial initiative. In Denmark, the issue revolved around the reinforcement throughout the education system of the national philosophy of collective good—*janteloven*.[1] Students are discouraged from deviating from a standard that suppresses personal initiative, a central characteristic of entrepreneurial societies. To the contrary, the curriculum in many, especially nonurban, Danish schools appears to reinforce the status quo, a highly unionized workforce, and reliance on the central government for most goods and services.

In Germany, the defining issue was the early career tracking of German students. Based on standardized testing, German students are placed in career paths at an early age, often by the time they are 12 years old. The remainder of their school experience is then tailored to ensure a high level of technical competency within the assigned employment category. Rather than encouraging students to explore the broadest range of career options or professional opportunities, including starting their own businesses, the career counseling function within the German education system often restricts lateral thinking and focuses on competence rather than innovation.

The Danish and German experiences demonstrate how easily education systems can encourage youth to drop out of an "entrepreneurial pipeline" through which the student progresses from awareness to competence to action. In the United States, elementary and secondary education represents the weakest section of this pipeline. If students maintain interest in entrepreneurship until their college years, they have access to an increasing number of colleges and universities with an entrepreneurship curriculum.

In 2004, Jerome Katz reported 1,600 schools of higher education in the United States offering over 2,200 entrepreneurship courses, representing a ten-fold increase from a decade earlier. Yet, experience shows that only a small fraction of the approximately 50 million students currently enrolled in elementary and secondary schools remain in the pipeline long enough to take advantage of this resource. Therefore, introducing students to the rewards, requirements, and challenges associated with entrepreneurship prior to high school graduation provides a major opportunity to increase the number of young Americans who pursue an entrepreneurial career and lifestyle.

## The Dual Role of Entrepreneurship Education

In the fact-based movie *Searching for Bobby Fischer* (Paramount Pictures 1993), chess prodigy Josh Waitzkin develops his talent through relationships with mentors who introduce Josh to the two competing aspects of becoming a grandmaster. Josh's initial interest in chess results from a chance encounter in New York's Washington Square Park with Vinnie, a drug addict, who has mastered the game of speed chess.[2] Bruce Pandolfini, a chess enthusiast hired by PBS in 1972 as an analyst for the Boris Spassky-Bobby Fischer world championship match in Iceland, develops Waitzkin's understanding and application of the technical aspects of the game. While Vinnie teaches Josh the importance of passion and risk-taking, Pandolfini counters with the need for knowledge and discipline.

In many ways, *Searching for Bobby Fischer* is the perfect metaphor for entrepreneurship education. It sheds light on the two roles—motivation and technical competence—entrepreneurship education plays in developing students who aspire to entrepreneurial lives.

Waitzkin's introduction to and education in the game of chess provide some valuable clues. How do we ensure that the emergence of the next generation of entrepreneurs is not based on chance encounters? Where do we find the "Vinnies" who will ignite the passion for entrepreneurship that lies dormant in so many youth? And finally, where and how do these future entrepreneurs gain the knowledge and discipline which improve their odds of success? As Pandolfini tells Josh's father, Fred Waitzkin, "To put your son in a position to care about winning and not to prepare him is wrong!" The intersection between motivation and competence becomes the central theme as one thinks about the educational path that best leads students to first understand their own entrepreneurial potential and later to develop the competencies that give them a greater chance of success.

## Keys to Effective Entrepreneurship Education

With the major contribution of entrepreneurship to regional and national economies and the increasing visibility of successful entrepreneurs, one might expect a proliferation of entrepreneurship education at the elementary and secondary levels similar to that at U.S. colleges and universities. This has not been the case for a number of reasons. Unlike the natural sciences, there are no formulas or algorithms which, if followed closely, guarantee a predictable outcome. In addition, many tenets of entrepreneurship are counterintuitive to traditional thinking, requiring both students and teachers to question their perspectives on education, their career, and life in general. Finally, the emphasis on creativity and lateral thinking can create chaos and confusion in an environment where order and discipline are valued.

A conceptual discussion of the keys to an effective entrepreneurship program follows. It does not cover specific curriculum or pedagogy. Readers are encouraged to visit the online resources presented at the end of this chapter for additional ideas and specific examples of entrepreneurship programs and activities through which these concepts can be implemented.

### Look Everywhere for Potential Entrepreneurship Students

The first key to an effective entrepreneurship education program requires teachers and counselors to look beyond the usual suspects as the students with the most entrepreneurial potential. Conventional wisdom suggests that students with early interests in earning their own money (e.g., a paper route or lemonade stand) or a high aptitude in mathematics translates into future entrepreneurial activity. While these students should not be dismissed, a larger pool of future entrepreneurs exists among students who have shown little or no previous interest in business.

An examination of the Inc. 500 and Ernst and Young Entrepreneur of the Year candidates conducted by the Kauffman Foundation in 2001 found only 25 percent of these successful business owners had an undergraduate degree in business (Kauffman Foundation, Strategic Planning White Paper 2001). Not surprising is that many majored in engineering and the natural sciences. It is also interesting to note that a large number of America's most accomplished entrepreneurs' academic interests included the arts or social sciences.

If entrepreneurship is truly about pursuing a passion, educators should recognize that any student who exhibits commitment and initiative may fit the profile. Consider the musician or athlete who spends hours every day honing skills to deliver the best possible performance. It is this same understanding of and dedication to excellence one finds in most successful entrepreneurs.

Second only to passion is the ability to sell one's vision to others. Therefore, students who excel in language arts or participate on the debate team also deserve consideration. The lack of a formula for identifying future successful entrepreneurs, therefore, presents both a challenge and an opportunity. Unlike the European systems of placing students on career tracks at an early age, there is no aptitude test or personality profile that clearly assesses one's future entrepreneurial proclivity. That same lack of preciseness suggests the entrepreneurial pool is significantly greater than one might assume.

John W. Altman further illuminates the need to look beyond those students who show an initial interest in business. In a presentation to the Singapore Legislature titled *Mapping the Territory*, Altman (2003) identifies what he calls the requirements for entrepreneurial success—six prerequisites that improve an entrepreneur's odds of success. The first three—knowledge, networking, and experience—can be taught and practiced in an academic setting. The last three—passion, commitment, and energy—are the students' responsibility to bring to the table. This dichotomy provides an important clue about identifying students who might be candidates for an entrepreneurship course of study. The potential entrepreneurship students are not necessarily those who started a business at an early age. Rather, they are students who display passion, commitment, and energy in any undertaking.

Ewing Marion Kauffman tested and proved this concept when he was approved as owner of a new baseball franchise, which became the Kansas City Royals. Conventional wisdom suggested that he should field a team comprised largely of experienced players available through the expansion draft.

Instead, Kauffman scoured inner cities and rural areas across America in search of superb athletes who had showed no previous interest in baseball. He then established the Royals Baseball Academy at which these dedicated athletes were trained in baseball fundamentals. Graduates included all-stars such as Frank White and Willie Aiken, who were part of the World Series championship team in 1985 (Morgan 1995, 251–56).

## Focus on Attitudes and Behaviors, Not Facts

The emphasis on human development in entrepreneurship education suggests that school administrators and instructors should consider the following three overarching principles as the cornerstones for any entrepreneurship curriculum. First, entrepreneurship is not about formulas or processes. In contrast to other business disciplines, the study of entrepreneurship rests on an understanding of the individual. As Guy Kawasaki (2004) suggests in the introduction to *The Art of the Start*, "The reality is that 'entrepreneur' is no longer a job title. It is the state of mind of people who want to alter the future" (xii). In Kawasaki's world, "mind-set" is multidimensional, ranging from self-confidence to becoming a lifelong learner. Thus, the existence of an entrepreneurial economy or community does not rely on traditional economic factors such as land, labor, capital, and technology. Instead, it depends on the identification, education, and encouragement of individuals who deploy these factors of production in new and innovative ways.

In *New Venture Creation: Entrepreneurship for the 21st Century,* Jeffry Timmons and Stephen Spinelli (2006) identify the following nine core attributes of successful entrepreneurs:

1. Commitment and Determination
2. Leadership
3. Opportunity Obsession
4. Tolerance of Risk, Ambiguity, and Uncertainty
5. Creativity
6. Self-Reliance
7. Adaptability
8. Motivation to Excel
9. Courage (8)

At the collegiate level, entrepreneurship educators have created such opportunities through experiential classroom learning and a broad range of practicum activities, including internships and business consulting projects. Much of this activity is incorporated into the entrepreneurship curriculum and individual or group independent study opportunities.

At the elementary and secondary school levels, one should not expect students to achieve competence in all or even most of these entrepreneurial skills, although there are often exceptions to this rule. Therefore, the goal of entrepreneurship education at these levels should be to begin the process of making these behaviors second nature to aspiring young entrepreneurs. Unfortunately, the most appropriate place to start runs counter to much of the current curriculum and pedagogy employed in many public and private schools. People often stereotype entrepreneurs as contrarians or rebels, and to some extent that is true. Successful entrepreneurs view the world through different filters and question everything. The "chaos" created by this approach to the world does not conform to the desire for order and discipline in the classroom. Interestingly, this is the same conflict that occurs within other organizations (e.g., major corporations) when entrepreneurially minded employees push up against management.

Singer and songwriter Harry Chapin (1978) best articulates the consequences of this disconnect between creativity and discipline in his song, "Flowers are Red." On his first day of school, a young boy is asked to draw a picture in which he chooses to use all of his crayons, stating, "There are so many colors in the rainbow and I see every one." His teacher, however, responds, "Flowers are red; green grass is green. There is no need to see them any other way than the way they always have been seen." The youth is robbed of all his creative motivation to the point that when he transfers to a school that encourages lateral thinking, he becomes the one who echoes the mantra of conformity.[3] If we expect students to think and behave like entrepreneurs, are we willing to accept the chaos when we give students the chance to test their entrepreneurial wings?

There are many heuristics and techniques for rediscovering and developing one's creative and entrepreneurial capacity. Most of these, however, are based on two themes: (1) curiosity and (2) overcoming one's "voice of judgment."[4] Of the two, curiosity is perhaps the easiest to develop. It requires only that students and teachers reframe the questions they ask as part of the learning process. In particular, one can jumpstart this transformation by simply emphasizing questions as "why" versus those that ask "how." This minor adjustment in one's approach to problem solving is the difference between an elementary school student's asking, "How can I complete this assignment if I left my pencil box at home?" and one who asks, "Why isn't there some place I can borrow (rent) supplies if I left mine at home?' The first question reinforces a dependency model. Who can help me? The second represents an opportunity.

Similar examples among middle and high school students are common. A participant in the Entrepreneur Invention Society program created a business when she asked, "Why don't athletic socks have a pocket for your house key and spending money?" Another example is the two EntrePrep students who asked, "Why isn't there an agency that matches high school students with summer internships?" Each of these business opportunities began by questioning the status quo.

Silencing one's "voice of judgment" is not so easy. It should not be a surprise that after only a few years of socialization by parents, teachers, friends, and society in general, students are averse to challenging conventional wisdom or shared standards of behavior.

Once students recognize how insatiable curiosity and destroying judgment leads to previously unimaginable possibilities, the momentum is self-sustained. Furthermore, mastery of these skills provides a gateway for developing the other behaviors in Timmons and Spinelli's (2006) taxonomy. Adaptability derives from a willingness to ask, "Why should changes in external conditions derail this idea or business?" Courage and tolerance of risk flourishes when one overcomes personal and collective judgments that set the limits on one's perception of what is possible. Once introduced to these concepts, the next challenge is creating multiple and varied opportunities in which students can practice and build confidence in their own entrepreneurial capacity.

## Need for Experiential Learning Opportunities

Returning to teaching chess as a metaphor for teaching entrepreneurship, one must heed grandmaster Paldofini's observation in *Searching for Bobby Fisher* that to win the game students cannot be passive spectators. Rather, students must be "in the game." It is this imperative that has driven the most visible and dramatic changes in entrepreneurship education pedagogy at all educational levels requiring experiential-based pedagogy and extra-curricular practicum activities. It is not teacher-directed instruction that has led to the most significant teaching moments. Instead, instructor responses to students' questions that result from experiential activity provide more insight and have a longer lasting impact.

In the mid-1960s, the National Training Laboratories in Bethel, Maine, researched the average learning retention rates for different teaching techniques (Wood 2004). Student retention rates ranged from a low of 5 percent for material presented in lecture to highs of 75 percent when students applied their new knowledge and 90 percent when students were asked to share what they had learned with others. These findings affirm the value of programs such as Students in Free Enterprise (SIFE) as effective methods of teaching entrepreneurship. The SIFE experience includes student teams that support community entrepreneurship efforts through assistance to aspiring adult entrepreneurs and mentoring at-risk youth.

Only a small percentage of entrepreneurship students will start businesses immediately after graduation from high school or college. Based on our observations at Miami University, a student may spend three to five years working in a salaried position before taking the entrepreneurial "leap." The career path may be explained by two phenomena. First, only after observing a company or an industry from the inside do students begin to identify opportunities for creating additional value in the marketplace. Second, students' confidence in their ability to start a successful enterprise increases with their understanding of and experiences in the day-to-day operations of a business, especially in an industry in which they plan to compete.

This time lag between formal education and practical application of knowledge places an additional burden on entrepreneurship educators. As noted previously, recognition that entrepreneurship education is not about facts creates an advantage since research suggests students do not retain facts for even a minimal period of time.[5] Therefore, the value of any entrepreneurship education must consist of more than the transfer of information.

We believe the long-term residual value of entrepreneurship education fits into two categories. Primary is students' increased capacity as innovators and problem solvers derived from their developing the entrepreneurial skill set discussed above. To ensure that these skills do not deteriorate over time, teachers should remind students that such skills can and should be utilized on a regular basis in varied situations. For example, a summer internship or even a vacation from an entrepreneurial perspective provides an opportunity to use and further develop one's entrepreneurial skills, thereby maximizing the value of any school project.

The second way to increase lasting value is for teachers to focus on the importance of social networks as an ingredient in entrepreneurial success. Through these relationships, entrepreneurs make the connections that help them recruit management teams, identify sources for financing, and build strategic partnerships with suppliers and distributors. It is never too early to begin building a personal network. Entrepreneurship teachers should encourage students to have business cards to hand out to guest speakers or on field trips. Students should learn to follow up any meeting or introduction with a phone call or e-mail. And where possible, faculty should help students create a mentoring relationship with an area entrepreneur.

## RECOGNIZE AND OVERCOME THE CHALLENGES

Just as in any entrepreneurial venture, proponents of entrepreneurship education must face certain risks in order to achieve the potential rewards. These challenges to introducing entrepreneurship education may come from any or all of the following groups:

- Those who believe that entrepreneurs are born not taught
- Those who view the introduction of entrepreneurship as just one more intrusion into an already full education agenda
- Those who suggest entrepreneurship programs, especially in elementary and middle schools, overemphasize the role of business versus other pursuits such as public service or the arts in society
- Those who question whether the education system can afford the costs associated with another new program

Overcoming these concerns suggests that proponents of entrepreneurship education must exhibit some of the same behaviors covered throughout the entrepreneurship curriculum. They must be able to clearly articulate the value proposition; they must identify opportunities for melding the objectives of the entrepreneurship program with other education standards; and, finally, they must be able to identify, assemble, and shepherd additional resources in support of entrepreneurship.

### Nature versus Nurture

Despite the continuing demand for and supply of entrepreneurship education options in elementary, secondary, and postsecondary institutions, scholars and entrepreneurs continue to ask the fundamental question, "Can entrepreneurship be taught?" (see Lyons, chapter 6). Proponents of the "nature" side of this dialectic argue that innate characteristics such as opportunity recognition, passion, and drive are the key to successfully creating and growing commercial enterprises. The importance of genetic make-up was recently bolstered by a study of rate of entrepreneurial activity among identical and fraternal twins. The research suggests that "genes may predispose a person to develop specific traits to become extroverted and sociable that then lead to self-employment" (Yuhasz 2006).

Advocates from the "nurture" school of thought counter with the position that many aspects of entrepreneurship—making a difference, success—are inherent in most people. Therefore, individuals' decisions to start their own business versus taking a salaried job are a matter of acculturation and confidence that they have the skills and knowledge to successfully pursue the entrepreneurship option.

There is no dearth of aspiring entrepreneurs among America's youth. Between 1994 and 1997, the Kauffman Center for Entrepreneurial Leadership commissioned the Gallup Organization to conduct a series of four surveys to determine the extent to which youth were interested in starting their own businesses. Similar surveys were presented to two adult groups—(1) teachers and (2) the general population.

The survey results became the basis for a book by William Walstad and Marilyn Kourilsky (1999) titled, *Seeds of Success: Entrepreneurship and Youth*. To their surprise, Walstad and Kourilsky found "that youth have a view of entrepreneurship that was much more positive than we ever expected" (15). Among the 1,008 survey respondents, 65 percent responded yes to the question, "Do you think you would want to start a business of your own?" Positive youth response exceeded that of both the general population (50 percent) and teachers (54 percent).

Equally important, a plurality of youth (41 percent) said that their primary reason for wanting to start a business was a desire "to be my own boss." This response mirrored the rationale provided by successful entrepreneurs who regularly chose "control of their careers and lives" as the leading motivation for their career choice.

The high level of interest in entrepreneurship among America's youth, however, has not translated into a corresponding rate of business start-ups. U.S. Bureau of the Census estimates for 2003 show that the total number of students—elementary through college graduate—totaled more than 63.5 million individuals. For the same year, the Census Bureau reports just over 600,000 business formations.[6] As Walstad and Kourilsky hypothesize, "If just a third of the youth who expressed an interest in starting a business actually acted on their aspirations at some point over their lifetimes, such initiative could significantly increase new business formation in the United States!" (15).

While the Gallup survey findings do not directly clarify the "nature versus nurture" debate, they do suggest that it may be irrelevant. As part of a 2001 strategic planning exercise, the Kauffman Center characterized the entrepreneurial pipeline as a funnel in which one poured the total number of elementary, secondary, and college-age students (Strategic Planning 2001: Reference Materials 2001). At each succeeding level of the funnel, the initial population decreased significantly until one was left with only the founders of entrepreneurial growth companies (EGCs), sometimes referred to as "gazelles," who created a majority of the net new jobs in the United States.

According to the National Commission on Entrepreneurship, EGCs represent less than 5 percent of all U.S. businesses with 20 or more employees (*National Commission on Entrepreneurship* 1999). This analogy suggests that those who question whether entrepreneurship can be taught are asking the wrong question. Instead, the key appears to be whether a system of entrepreneurship education helps individuals with the propensity and desire to become entrepreneurs recognize, develop, and exploit their potential.

## Capacity Constraints

In an era when both states and the federal government promote performance-based education standards, even those who support entrepreneurship education conceptually may argue that school systems are overburdened with mandates and testing. A strong argument can be made that entrepreneurship education, rather than competing with other academic priorities, can complement and even enhance student achievement in related subjects, especially English and mathematics. For example, an evaluation of the Mini-Society participants showed a corresponding improvement in performance in mathematics knowledge (Kourilsky and Ortiz 1985). Likewise, many schools with entrepreneurship education programs use assignments, such as press releases and marketing materials, to support language and communication skills in the general curriculum.

The importance of linking entrepreneurship education to overall academic standards was tested in 2002 when then-governor Angus King invited the Kauffman Foundation to help Maine improve the environment for entrepreneurial activity, especially in the more rural areas such as Washington County. Entrepreneurship education was identified as a lynchpin for increasing interest among Washington County youth in the potential of starting and running their own businesses.

To help build the case for introducing entrepreneurship into the school district's curriculum, Kauffman Foundation staff created a matrix that linked the objectives and outcomes of various entrepreneurship education programs to the Maine education standards (Thomas 2002). This structured evidence of the complementary nature of entrepreneurship education and state standards was used by state education officials to overcome concerns about the added time and effort associated with the entrepreneurship initiative.

## Wealth versus Value Creation

The propriety of using entrepreneurship to teach math and language skills will be challenged, especially in elementary schools. At a December 1997 symposium cosponsored by the Kauffman Foundation and the U.S. Department of Education, an administrator from a Northeastern school district challenged Mini-Society creator Marilyn Kourilsky, asking whether it made sense to train young people to be "greedy capitalists." This question raised two important issues. First, is the public's perception of entrepreneurship too narrow? And second, and perhaps more important, how does one present the goals and objectives of entrepreneurship education?

The answer to the first question is obvious. The very fact that someone associates personal financial gain as an entrepreneur's driving motivation suggests that the continuous publicity about the net worth of people like Bill Gates or Mark Cuban has had an impact on public perception of entrepreneurs and why they do what they do.

In contrast to the media persona, successful entrepreneurs reiterate that the two primary motivators are control over their careers and the desire to pursue a passion. In more formal surveys of successful entrepreneurs (conducted by the Kauffman Foundation or as part of the Inc. 500 selection process), successful entrepreneurs rank monetary gain seventh or eighth among all factors (Strategic Planning 101: Reference Materials 2001).

Equally important has been the acceptance that entrepreneurship is no longer restricted to the private, for-profit sector. The recognition that entrepreneurial behavior adds value in both the nonprofit sector (social entrepreneurship) and in government (public entrepreneurship) has resulted in a proliferation of social entrepreneurship courses and centers at U.S. colleges and universities.

While the nomenclature may differ, value creation and productivity in the nonprofit and public sectors has increased because of adding entrepreneurial principles to the equation for success. Students, parents, and educators should be continuously reminded that the entrepreneurship program in their schools is not necessarily designed to channel every student into the private sector. It is about pursuing passions regardless of whether such passions involve building the next Microsoft or addressing societal needs.

## Financial and Human Resource Requirements

Finally, naysayers may argue that implementation of entrepreneurship education is unaffordable at a time when schools are already strapped for resources and are being forced to cut back on many programs, especially extracurricular activities. The extent to which proponents of entrepreneurship education are able to identify and marshal resources in support of entrepreneurship learning may be the ultimate test to whether they understand and practice entrepreneurship themselves. If, as Harvard Business School's Howard Stevenson suggests, entrepreneurship is "the pursuit of opportunity beyond the resources you currently have available" (Mahoney 2006), embarking on the design and implementation of entrepreneurship education is such an opportunity that must not wait until the resources are at hand.

There are two dimensions to the resource question: (1) financial and (2) human. To overcome the resource challenge, school administrators and instructors should not merely reallocate existing resources. Instead, identifying and marshaling the needed resources from previously untapped sources has several advantages. First, it does not create animosity from colleagues who might otherwise view the entrepreneurship program as in competition with their courses for scarce resources. Second, seeking additional resources provides an opportunity to engage community and business leaders in the program, which may eventually lead to both direct and in-kind support for the program. Finally, the resource strategy provides classroom learning moments, giving instructors a chance to demonstrate the importance of understanding customer needs, articulating a value proposition, and differentiating between a good idea and a business opportunity.

All of these objectives are satisfied when proponents of entrepreneurship education view creating the program as an entrepreneurial venture. For example, those individuals who initiate the program must be able to answer the following questions:

- Are we creating sufficient value so that individuals will take money out of their pockets and put it in our pocket for this purpose?
- Who is the customer—that is, for whom does this value proposition resonate?
- Who is the competition?
- Can we design, produce, and deliver the program at a cost that makes it worthwhile for us and the students?

When approached from this perspective, one realizes that building a self-sustaining entrepreneurship education program in local schools is, in and of itself, a visible and relevant example of social entrepreneurship. For example, this effort is an opportunity to teach the difference between customers, those who provide the resources—whether donors or investors—and end-users (i.e., the students who are the direct beneficiaries of the program) and then to articulate the value proposition to potential customers.

Target audiences include those most likely to benefit from the creation of businesses in the community—banks, realtors, accountants, and lawyers—and individuals from whom these aspiring young entrepreneurs will eventually need to buy goods and services. School administrators may be surprised at the business community's positive response to their requests. If practitioner involvement at the collegiate level is any indication of entrepreneurs' interest in giving back to the community, elementary and middle school officials will not have much of a selling job. A recent study by Jerome Katz (2004) at St. Louis University showed that entrepreneurship programs are among the most heavily endowed activities at many universities.

The second dimension of the resource issue centers on the identification and development of human resources. This challenge is amplified because entrepreneurship education does not fit a traditional "teach and test" model. At the outset, teachers will still introduce concepts; however, their primary role quickly shifts to that of facilitator, monitor, mentor, and evaluator.

Rather than providing information, teachers stimulate by asking questions for which the students find their own answers. As students test the concepts, the instructor provides guidance and discusses options with them. At the end of the process, the teacher identifies teaching moments in which the major lessons from the students' experiences can be reinforced.

Schools have used the following methods to address the human capacity issues associated with their entrepreneurship education programs:

- Identify and recruit area business owners and entrepreneurs as guest speakers and student mentors. Once engaged in the program, business people develop a sense of ownership, which often results in financial support as a consequential benefit of their initial in-kind contribution of time, knowledge, and experience. One caveat to this approach is that success in the business arena does not necessarily translate into success in the classroom. Practitioners may require some up-front instruction and coaching as they prepare for the classroom experience.[7]
- Take advantage of teacher training provided by organizations such as the Kauffman Foundation and REAL.
- Create a circuit-riding position within or among school districts to spread the cost of an entrepreneurship instructor.
- Involve SIFE students from area colleges and universities.
- Make entrepreneurship classes in high schools an option under a College Now program with a community college or local university.
- Supplement classroom instruction by encouraging students to participate in related extracurricular activities such as DECA or pursuing the Boy Scout merit badges in entrepreneurship.
- Explore the increasing number of options for online content that can be used by teachers in the classroom.

Interaction between full-time teachers and external partners has the ancillary benefit of increasing the teachers' knowledge about entrepreneurship and their capacity to become better coaches and mentors.

## Conclusion

Establishment of an entrepreneurship education program does not guarantee either generation of successful entrepreneurs or a community's economic sustainability and growth. Lack of such programs, however, greatly increases the odds against realizing either of these outcomes. In other words, entrepreneurship programs at all levels of the educational continuum are about giving young people the following chances:

- To recognize the personal and professional rewards associated with an entrepreneurial lifestyle.
- To know the satisfaction of creating value or of addressing an economic or social need.
- To understand the difference between ideation and execution, and to appreciate why some individuals can turn an idea into a new product or service while others only talk about having ideas.
- To explore their own entrepreneurial potential. A career in which individuals must set their own deadline and create their own motivation is not for everyone. Learning these lessons at an early age can save years of frustration and disappointment later in life.
- To begin building a social network that will help them immediately and throughout their professional and personal lives.
- To comprehend that entrepreneurial leadership is as much about knowing one's weaknesses as it is about knowing one's strengths.
- To pursue a passion. Above all, entrepreneurship empowers every individual to define and pursue those things that are truly important to them.

Finally, we continuously talk about education expenditures as investments in our children's future. For many struggling towns and cities, especially those in rural areas, this personal and financial investment often represents "anti-investment" to our communities since many youth believe they must leave their hometowns to take advantage of their educations. For these youth, out-migration from their hometowns is not a matter of choice but an economic necessity.

Entrepreneurship education can potentially reverse this trend by instilling the confidence in young people that they do have a future in their native communities—not as a result of employment by an absentee employer or dependence on resource-based industries such as mining. An effective entrepreneurship education program, while not guaranteeing economic success, does provide a chance to keep those with the inclination and determination to build their own economic future in the entrepreneurial pipeline.

## ENTREPRENEURSHIP EDUCATION RESOURCES

The following annotated list of resources is provided to support the design and implementation of entrepreneurship education programs. Many of these sites provide links to additional resources and entrepreneurship education partners.

### Boy Scouts of America

In 1989, the Boy Scouts of America (BSA), with support from the Ewing Marion Kauffman Foundation, created a merit badge in entrepreneurship. The official BSA merit badge site (www.meritbadge.com/mb/134.htm) provides the specific requirements. Business students at Kennesaw State University created an online resource base to help scouts fulfill the badge requirements (coles.kennesaw.edu/pages/sife/entrepreneurshipMB/).

### Consortium for Entrepreneurship Education

The Consortium for Entrepreneurship Education (CEE) is a collaboration among entrepreneurship educators to develop innovative and effective approaches to entrepreneurship instruction. CEE's mission is "To champion entrepreneurship education and provide advocacy, leadership, networking, technical assistance, and resources nationally across all levels and disciplines of education, while promoting quality practices and programs." CEE's online resources (www.entre-ed.org) include content standards for teaching entrepreneurship skills and "Entrepreneurship Everywhere: Sample Curricula across the United States."

### DECA

DECA (www.deca.org) is an organization of high school and college students interested in various aspects of business, including entrepreneurship. DECA's "entrepreneur U. Database" includes teacher and student resources for both formal education and self-directed study (www.entrepreneuru.org).

### Ewing Marion Kauffman Foundation

The Kansas City–based Ewing Marion Kauffman Foundation (www.kauffman.org/entrepreneurship.cfm) is among the world's largest supporters of entrepreneurship research and education with their goal "to further understand the phenomenon of entrepreneurship, to advance entrepreneurship education and training efforts, to promote entrepreneurship-friendly policies, and to better facilitate the commercialization of new technologies by entrepreneurs." The Kauffman Foundation is recognized as a major catalyst for the design and implementation of entrepreneurship education programs such as Mini-Society, EntrePrep, and the Kauffman Entrepreneurship Intern Program.

## Mini-Society

Mini-Society (www.minisociety.com/) is an elementary school level program designed to introduce young children to the most basic concepts associated with business and entrepreneurship. Through teacher-guided sessions, students identify opportunities for products and services that may be delivered to their classmates or to the school. Development and distribution of the product or service involves recognizing the role of opportunity costs and the allocation of resources.

## National Foundation for Teaching Entrepreneurship

Started in 1987, the National Foundation for Teaching Entrepreneurship (NFTE) (www.nfte.com) focuses on inner-city youth who are at risk of dropping out of school. Through entrepreneurship education, NFTE channels students' innate abilities toward productive enterprises, which demonstrates the relevance of classroom learning to the real world.

## Rural Education through Action Learning

Rural Education through Action Learning (REAL) (www.cfed.org/go/real) was started in the early 1980s to bring entrepreneurship education to communities, especially those in rural areas, which had little or no access to such a curriculum. REAL, which affiliated with the Corporation for Enterprise Development (CFED) in 2004, provides curriculum, training, and resources through which students learn about the requirements and rewards associated with an entrepreneurial career choice.

## Students in Free Enterprise

Students in Free Enterprise (SIFE) (www.sife.org) is an international organization through which college students in cooperation with their colleges, universities, and local business communities develop outreach programs that encourage and support free enterprise and entrepreneurship. Activities include design and development of student-owned businesses as well as mentoring of at-risk high school students.

# NOTES

1. Each of the ten rules contained in *janteloven* discourage individuals from thinking they are smarter, better, or more special than others.

2. The character Vinnie is based on Joseph Lincoln, who died of a drug overdose in 1996. Lincoln's experience further demonstrates the importance of discipline as a counterweight for the passion which, unchecked, may lead to burnout or other self-destructive behavior.

3. The first course in the entrepreneurship sequence at Miami University is "Imagination and Entrepreneurship." Its purpose is to help students rediscover the child within them who questioned everything. The instructor and students often refer to this class jokingly as "Deprogramming 101."

4. Michael Ray and Rochelle Myers coined the term "voice of judgment" in their book *Creativity in Business*. It refers to personal and societal standards and expectations that inhibit one's creativity and willingness to take risks.

5. A 1988 study at the University of Alabama administered a multichoice test to 74 undergraduate psychology students who had completed an introductory course 4 months earlier. Their results were compared to a control group of similar students who had not taken the course. The psychology students scored only 8 percent higher than the control group (70 to 62 percent).

6. Business formations include only those firms that applied for an Employee Identification Number, therefore, it does not include self-employed individuals who use only their social security number as their business identifier and only report their business activity on Schedule C of their personal income tax return.

7. Miami University has created a half-day seminar called "From the Boardroom to the Classroom" in which alumni and local entrepreneurs are trained in techniques to translate their entrepreneurship stories into effective classroom experiences. The training includes turning the personal experience into a mini-teaching case, which gives the students a chance to discuss alternative approaches to a situation.

# REFERENCES

Altman, John W. 2003. "Mapping the Territory," presentation at the Senior Management Program, Singapore Civil Service College, May.

Acs, Zoltan J., Pia Arenius, Michael Hay, and Maria Minniti. 2004. *Global Entrepreneurship Monitor 2004*. Boston/London: Babson College/London Business School, 17.

Chapin, Harry. Flowers are Red. *Living Room Suite*. New York: Elecktra, 1978.

European Union, Enterprise and Industry Directorate. 2006. Conference Proceedings on Entrepreneurship Education in Europe: Fostering Entrepreneurial Mindsets through Education and Learning, Oslo, Norway, October 26–27.

Katz, Jerome. Chronology and trajectory of American entrepreneurship education. *Journal of Business Venturing* 18 (March 2003): 284.

Katz, Jerome A. 2004. Survey of Endowed Positions and Related Fields in the United States. Kansas City, MO: Ewing Marion Kauffman Foundation.

Kawasaki, Guy. 2004. *The art of the start: The time-tested, battle-hardened fuide for anyone starting anything.* New York: Penguin Group.

Kourilsky, Marilyn L. 1995. Entrepreneurship education: Opportunity in search of curriculum. Kansas City, MO: Ewing Marion Kauffman Foundation.

Kourilsky, Marilyn L., and E. G. Ortiz. 1985. The mini-society and mathematical reasoning: An exploratory study. *Social Studies Review.* Sacramento: California Council for the Social Studies 13: 37–48.

Mahoney, William. 2000. *Entrepreneurship's wild ride: Q&A with Howard Stevenson and Michael J. Roberts, Working knowledge for business leaders.* Harvard Business School. hbswk.hbs.edu/item/1541.html (April 22, 2006).

Morgan, Anne. 1995. Prescription for success: The life and values of Ewing Marion Kauffman. Kansas City, MO: Andrews and McNeel.

National Commission on Entrepreneurship. 1999. High growth companies: Mapping America's entrepreneurial landscape. Washington, DC: National Commission on Entrepreneurship, 1.

Peterman, Nicole, and Jessica Kennedy. 2003. Enterprise education, influencing students' perceptions of entrepreneurship. *Entrepreneurship: Theory and Practice.* Oxford: Blackwell Publishing (Winter): 129–44.

Ray, Michael, and Rochelle Myers. 2000. *Creativity in business.* New York: Broadway Books.

Searching for Bobby Fischer. 1993. (Film) Los Angeles: Paramount Pictures.

Strategic Planning 2001: Reference Materials. 2001. Kansas City, MO: Kauffman Center for Entrepreneurial Leadership. CD-ROM.

Timmons, Jeffry A., and Stephen Spinelli. 2006. New venture creation: Entrepreneurship for the 21st Century. Boston, MA: McGraw-Hill Irwin.

Thomas, Nancie. 2002. Working Paper: Entrepreneurship Education and Maine Standards. Working Paper presented to the Maine Entrepreneurship Task Force, Augusta, Maine (June).

Yuhasz, Misia. 2006. Entrepreneurs driven by genes? *The Observer On-Line,* observer.case.edu/Archives/Volume_38/Issue_25/Story_865/ (April 14, 2006).

Walstad, William B., and Marilyn L. Kourilsky. 1999. *Seeds of success: Entrepreneurship and youth.* Kansas City, MO: Kauffman Center for Entrepreneurial Leadership.

Wilson, Fiona, Deborah Marlino, and Jill Kickul. 2004. Our entrepreneurial future: Examing the diverse attitudes and motivations of teens across gender and ethnic identity. *Journal of Developmental Entrepreneurship* 9(3): 177–97.

Wood, E. J. 2004. Problem-based learning: Exploiting knowledge of how people learn to promote effective learning. Higher Education Academy. www.bioscience.heacademy.ac.uk/journal/vol3/beej-3-5.htm (June 22, 2006).

# 10

# Economic Development Via Understanding and Growing a Community's Microbusiness Segment

*Michael D. Woods and Glenn Muske*

A common thread among conversations in coffee shops across the United States is "How can our community remain competitive?" Many communities are concerned with growth while the rest focus on sustainability. To attain either goal, these communities see the need to effectively generate economic growth. Today many, if not nearly all, communities have some type of economic/community development plan or initiative. The previous chapters in this book examine many of the concepts and ideas that local communities include in their discussions and development plans. The ideas discussed include entrepreneurship development, the communities' role in development, the importance of education, both youth and adult, in entrepreneurial development, and financing. Low, Henderson, and Weiler in chapter 5 examine the struggle between quantity and quality of entrepreneurs.

If one examines many local plans, a key goal often noted involves attracting the next big manufacturing facility or a large service business such as a call center or a prison. Even though the odds are low, the possibility of bringing in industry catches the interest of local leaders. Local resources are often given little attention and effort, however. In the CARE model, this involves the creation, retention, and expansion of economic resources already in place (Woods, Frye, and Ralstin 2004).

In this chapter, the authors consider those three elements in terms of microbusiness development, a key, but often forgotten, community development resource. Truly effective community development must be broadbased in approach and microbusinesses are the broad and underlying base of the economic engine in most communities. Therefore, this chapter will: (1) define microbusinesses in terms of who they are and their impact on a local economy; (2) address the issues faced by microbusinesses; and

(3) offer suggestions on how to encourage and build the community's microbusiness segment with examples of successful assistance and innovative delivery methods.

The goal of this chapter is to help community members, leaders, and decisionmakers recognize the importance of microbusinesses in a local economy. Many of the most successful economic development efforts come from developing a diversified economic structure which includes the small, and seemingly insignificant, microbusiness owner.

## MICROBUSINESSES AND ECONOMIC DEVELOPMENT

The Kettering Foundation (2000) suggests that the development of a healthy community is linked to its diversity in two forms. Authors such as those in academia (Beaulieu 2002; Emery, Fey, and Flora 2006) and popular press writers, such as Jack Schultz (2004), author of *Boom Town USA*, discuss diversity in the types of capital available in a community. These capitals include human, financial, infrastructure, social networks as well as economic diversity. A second view of diversity in the literature focuses on one segment, in this case economic diversity. The idea is that a thriving, growing economy has a mix of businesses including product and service, large and small, and new and old (see chapter 5).

Key to this idea of diversity is that economies, whether in a large urban area or a small isolated rural setting, must build on local resources (Darling 2004). Often communities look for one large manufacturing business or service firm as a core upon which other businesses are built. In other communities, the core focus involves finding the next gazelle or fast growing business as the key element for community growth. Often forgotten or ignored is the local resource of entrepreneurs. Most typically those entrepreneurs are eager and excited to start what is usually called a microbusiness.

According to the U.S. Department of Labor, new microbusiness start-ups, from 1992 to 2005, generated more than 67 percent of gross job gains (U.S. Department of Labor 2005). One estimate is that 18 million people in the United States take steps each year to start a microbusiness. Those microbusinesses, part of an economic segment called "small business," form the core of the U.S. economy. They were the building blocks of the economic boom of the 1990s and continue to represent that core today. In fact, microbusinesses have been important in economic development throughout history.

### Microbusinesses Defined

There are several ways to define a microbusiness. The most typical approach follows the U.S. Small Business Administration (SBA) (2006) lead of basing it on the number of employees. Microbusinesses would be included in the SBA's most general definition, namely small businesses have 500 or fewer employees. In the United States, this captures more than 99 percent of all businesses, or all but 17,000 of the 24 million plus firms. Those businesses employ 51 percent of the workforce, generate more than 80 percent of all new jobs, and produce 52 percent of the gross domestic product (Henderson 1997).

Microbusinesses therefore represent one part of a larger small business segment. Devins (1999) and Kangasharju (2001) offer the most commonly used microbusiness definition, namely a business that employs fewer than ten people. Using this definition, microbusinesses still include 98 percent of all U.S. businesses in 2003 (U.S. Small Business Administration 2006) and include both the nearly 5.8 million businesses that employed someone with a payroll at sometime during the year as well as 18.6 million nonemployer firms. These numbers do not even capture farm and ranch operations.

There are other means by which microbusinesses, or similar entities, have been defined. The Association for Enterprise Opportunity (AEO) (2004) defines microenterprises as those that have five employees or fewer, require $35,000 or less in start-up capital, and which do not have access to the traditional commercial banking sector. By this definition, AEO claims that there are 20.7 million U.S. microenterprises representing 16.6 percent of all U.S. employment (Walzer and Hamm, chapter 4).

Three informal methods have also been used to define the microbusiness economic segment of the economy—(1) mom and pop stores, (2) home-based businesses, and (3) at times, family businesses. Often, these types of businesses are termed *main street business* as in rural or small towns. While defining any one of these three types of business as microbusinesses may often be correct, it must be noted that this automatic assumption is not always correct.

According to the U.S. Census Bureau (2006), mom and pop stores are assumed to have no paid employees and are most often barber and beauty shops, daycare providers, real estate agents, carpenters, plumbers, tax preparers, and writers. Four groups within the mom and pop economic sector—real estate (including leasing and rentals); construction; professional, scientific, and technical services; and retail trade—generated 60 percent of all nonemployer receipts.

Home-based businesses are estimated to represent nearly 50 percent of all small businesses and vary greatly in number of employees hired and gross revenue, with only 2 percent bringing in more than $250,000 while 74 percent bring in less than $25,000 (U.S. Census Bureau 2006). Family businesses are sometimes incorrectly assumed to be similar to "mom and pop" businesses, but, according to Heck and Stafford (2001), family

businesses may represent nearly 10 million of the U.S. businesses as well
as 50 percent of U.S. business revenue. They may employ 50 percent or
more of the labor force. They are also common, with one in ten households owning at least one business.

## Microbusiness Contributions

The preceding paragraphs have begun establishing, from a quantitative
perspective, some of the underlying economic reasons why a strong microbusiness segment is important to a local economy. The 24.4 million
businesses mentioned above employ approximately 32 million people and
generate approximately $400 billion in payroll (U.S. Small Business Ad-
ministration 2007). Alone, self-employed individuals generate annual receipts of nearly $900 billion (U.S. Census Bureau 2006). A study by Bruce,
Deskins, Hill, and Rork (2007) found increases in small businesses to be
the single-largest determinant of gross state product, employment, and state
personal income.

Other microbusiness contributions to the local economy include approximately 13 percent of the income and profits in a local economy (Family Economics and Nutrition Review 2001) plus job creation. Many entrepreneurs start a microbusiness and, considering that 74 percent of
graduating college seniors want to be self-employed the businesses they
start are likely to be micro in nature. Thus, it is in the best interests of economic development planners to include this segment in any planning activity (Levenburg and Lane 2003).

Jobs are another contribution of the microbusiness. In the 1990s, businesses employing four or fewer employees added the largest percentage of
jobs with a growth rate of more than 200 percent (Halstead and Deller
1997; Sexton 1999). They also provided human capital in terms of local
leadership (Miller 1998; Sharp and Flora 1999), volunteered for local community and civic groups, served on boards and as elected officials, and provided in-kind or cash contributions to civic and charitable organizations
(Dennis 2004). In many rural areas, they represent the primary, if not only,
business segment available. Job creation is important and the most job creation occurs within the first two years of a firm's start-up (U.S. Small Business Administration 2007).

The Kauffman Foundation (2005) noted that during a three-year period,
5 percent of nonemployer businesses, about 750,000 in total, became employer businesses. In short, they "grew up" and this change is happening at
an increasing pace. In addition, the nonemployer businesses are often important in the supply chain to larger firms. With today's active push for outsourcing, nonemployer businesses are often key partners in the mainte-
nance and growth of larger businesses.

In addition to quantifiable data, microbusinesses also offer benefits of a more qualitative nature. Economic developers prefer diversity within the local economy for several reasons. First, it protects the economy from being overly dependent on one entity and, if that business falters, fails or moves, the rest of the local economy suffers. Also, a healthy economy grows by trade within the community—one business trading with another as well as with local households.

Finally, communities need an assortment of businesses, both goods and services, to meet the needs of residents and local business owners. This mix encourages local shopping, reducing the need to go to another community. Such reasons are in part why Low, Henderson, and Weiler (2005) discussed the need to examine both the breadth and the depth of entrepreneurial activity within a region.

Another reason for developing a continuous stream of microbusinesses is the practically impossible task to predict which business will be the next gazelle—that is, which business will take off in a rapid growth pattern. Economic developers across the nation are looking for the next rising star. However how does one identify that star? What allowed Amazon.com to survive and prosper while other online retail businesses failed? Why did Starbucks become a household name? A multitude of other coffee companies tried to find the right combination to grow; yet Starbucks became the gazelle. The message seems to be the more the start-ups, the better the community's chances of finding the gazelle.

So, do microbusinesses count in terms of economic development? Mark Drabenstott (2003) stated that a solid economy depends on all forms of businesses whether entrepreneurial or small in nature. He stresses that the impact of small businesses is more than just image; they indeed represent impact. He also notes that some of these businesses will make an impact on not only the local economy but on a national and international scale as well.

Microbusinesses add dollars and cents to the local economy and to the family who owns them. They also bring quality of life to a community by expanding community offerings, improving the local image and attracting outsiders to visit. In its *Rural Entrepreneurship Initiative Guidebook* (Rightmyre, Johnson, and Chatman 2004), the Missouri Rural Entrepreneurship Initiative team noted that all economic activity has value and that a community must support all businesses including the microbusiness entity. Instead of concern about the development of entrepreneurs as opposed to small businesses as Carland, Hoy, Boulton, and Carland (1984) discuss, it may be more important to support all "proprietors," thus removing the concerns about the owners' intentions (Goetz 2005).

Probably the strongest argument for including small business owners in the mix comes from *The World Is Flat* by Friedman (2005). The overarching theme in the book concerns innovation; no business will survive in today's world in the long-term. Even small rural businesses must change just to maintain themselves. If entrepreneurship matters, then microbusinesses offer a window to successful entrepreneurship.

Putting all of this together gives a clear message about who and what microbusinesses are. It also provides a strong argument for including microbusinesses in a community's economic development strategy. The next logical questions might be "What key issues do they face?" and then "How can we nurture microbusinesses?"

## ISSUES FACED

If a community accepts the fact that microbusinesses benefit a local economy, communities must then determine how best to encourage their growth and development. The first such step is to understand that microbusinesses may or may not be similar in terms of needed assistance compared with other small businesses. Seldom do microbusinesses discuss issues such as Workers Compensation costs. Nor are they as concerned with health insurance or other fringe benefits (although one could argue that these owners should be involved with these issues).

Muske and Woods (2004) show that business needs change over time and start-up businesses may differ from ongoing businesses. In a study of 193 Oklahoma businesses with ten employees or fewer, start-up business owners reported needing financial help and general business training while ongoing business owners strongly voiced a need for marketing help. The Muske and Woods study examined a sample of existing businesses assisted by four Oklahoma agencies. Trained interviewers made phone calls using random-digit dialing. A screening question limited responses to owners employing ten people or fewer. Seventy percent of the 274 owners contacted, or 193 owners, responded to the survey.

The largest single issue for both groups was the need for help to find and develop good employees, with marketing reported as the second greatest need (table 10.1). More than 30 percent of all business respondents reported these two items as a major concern. A "second tier" of items or major issues included regulations, Workers Compensation, having a business plan, and family/business conflicts. This last item, "family/business conflicts," suggests that many microbusinesses depend on participation by family members for survival but that not all family members consider the business legitimate or question its return to the family.

The National Federation of Independent Business Owners (NFIB) offers another look at reported business issues or problems (Phillips 2004). Own-

**Table 10.1.   Major Issues or Business Problems Identified by Microbusinesses**

| | All Businesses Percent (n = 193) |
|---|---|
| Employees | 39 |
| Marketing | 31 |
| Workers Compensation | 19 |
| Regulations | 18 |
| Family/Business Conflict | 17 |
| Business Plan | 15 |
| Motivation | 12 |
| Financial Reports | 12 |
| Recordkeeping | 11 |
| Privacy | 10 |
| Benefits | 9 |
| Customer Needs | 6 |
| Quality Evaluation | 3 |

*Source*: Muske and Woods 2004

ers of microbusinesses noted that finding affordable health insurance and/or liability insurance was their most difficult problem, which is similar to what has been reported by owners of other small businesses (table 10.2). Cash flow and earnings were slightly larger issues for businesses with fewer than five employees, but all microbusiness owners reported that energy costs, space costs, and taxes (both state, federal, and property) contributed to the cash flow issue.

The same study by Phillips (2004) reported the issues considered least important, and they included exporting product or services, competition from government or nonprofit organizations, competition from Internet businesses, increased national security procedures, and cost/frequency of lawsuits.

Baines and Wheelock (1998) reported that government regulations were less of a problem to microbusinesses, and firm size was related to how much of a problem it was to find, train, and retain good employees. This issue was not nearly as troublesome for firms with fewer than five employees as for larger businesses, perhaps reflecting that smaller firms rely more on family members as workers thus eliminating some recruitment and retention difficulties.

**Table 10.2.    Top Ten Problems of Microbusiness Owners**

| |
|---|
| 1. Cost of Health Insurance |
| 2. Cost and Availability of Liability Insurance |
| 3. Cost of Energy |
| 4. Federal Taxes |
| 5. Property Taxes |
| 6. Cash Flow |
| 7. State Taxes |
| 8. Unreasonable Government Regulations |
| 9. Poor Earnings |
| 10. Cost of Supplies/Inventory |

*Source*: Phillips 2004

The smaller the business, the more likely they are to report problems staying current with the market, meeting the competition from larger businesses, and dealing with pricing issues. Microbusinesses also struggled more with seasonal sales. It is interesting that microbusinesses had less concern with low employee productivity. Although not of great concern, the study also found that obtaining information is difficult for microbusiness owners. The owners were affected by anticompetitive practices, interest rates, and earning a living wage (Phillips 2004).

A recent issue of *Entrepreneur* magazine reported three of the top five concerns of small business owners as developing new products or services, expanding to other markets inside of the United States, and cutting costs. Three wild card factors they saw for the immediate future included increased competition, rising health-care costs, and new government regulations (Henricks 2007). Supporting this article is a study done by Walstad and Kourilsky (1996) of existing small business owners reporting that government regulations, financing, controlling costs, competition, and developing sales were the greatest challenges faced by small business owners.

From a slightly different perspective, a review of small business management texts discloses what professional authors consider major areas of concern for microbusiness owners. Two texts, *Homemade Money* by Brabec (1994) and *Business Savvy for Today's New Entrepreneur* by Burns and McCullough (2001), although written for general small business owners, are closest to assisting the microbusiness market. The emphasis of these books are similar to other small business management guides such as the Kaufman Foundation's (2001) *Planning and Growing a Business Venture*. All of these authors focus on market assessment and development, business planning, business structure, budgeting, and financial statements and control.

Two final issues faced by microbusiness owners—globalization and e-commerce—have not yet been discussed, and both relate to each other and often to marketing. Muske and Woods (2004) note that most owners look only to expanding sales within 50 miles of their current business location. Less than 5 percent of survey respondents reported considering international sales. Similarly, Chamberlain (2004) with NFIB found that microbusiness owners made 90 percent of their sales within the United States, and only 5 percent regularly marketed outside the United States.

Globalization has a second side, namely purchasing goods and services from international sources. Chamberlain (2004) noted that only 17 percent of microbusiness owners had tapped the global market as suppliers, and the percentage of their total purchases represented by international trade was negligible.

Microbusinesses may not be as active in the global marketplace for several reasons, starting with use of technology. Only 74 percent reported Internet access, and less than one-half of the microbusinesses had Websites. Nearly 90 percent of other small businesses had access to the Internet and 70 percent had a Website. The inactivity with respect to globalization also comes from lack of expertise in exporting (more than half reported this situation) and with finding advisors to help (Dennis 2005). It may also be the result of a lack of local technical expertise in the area.

## TYPES AND SOURCES OF ASSISTANCE

### Types of Assistance

So what type of assistance should be provided, and how, if a community desires the development, growth, and prosperity of its microbusiness economic segment? A note of caution must be offered regarding the self-reporting of assistance needed. Barkley (2003) noted that businesses respond strategically to surveys. What business owners report as needs do not, at times, come through as issues in an econometric study (Walzer 2007). Yet self-reporting still provides the best insight into the needs of the microbusiness owners. When blended with additional data provided by individuals working and supporting this group some common issues arise.

This section offers insights into commonly requested types of assistance. Business owners report that they need help in areas of cash flow management, a variety of marketing needs, and personal. Government red tape and taxes also seem high on the list of requested needs.

As noted already, another typical request by start-ups, which is supported by research (Audretsch and Keibach 2004), is a need for capital and/or financial assistance. Although research suggests that many firms successfully start with only minimal capital, this identified request has several possible underlying reasons. First, although able to start with funds the owner has available, additional capital may enhance the speed of the start-up process as well as allow it to take advantage of opportunities that come along soon in its development cycle.

Second, the financial need may not be for money per se but for assistance in developing a financial management system and then in the analysis of reports generated by such a system. Efforts to connect financial management assistance and experts from local, state, and federal tax agencies can facilitate better business decisions.

Finally, a third reason for financial start-up assistance may come not as much from the business itself but from the individual and his or her family. If the owner has quit a job to start the business, it is the family that may have the financial needs. Certainly one way to minimize this is to have family members keep working, even if only to retain medical insurance. Research has found that family businesses often intermingle money between the business and the family. Thus the need may be more personal than family (Haynes et al. 1999).

Another often identified need is in the broad area of marketing assistance. Again, this request can take many forms. It may represent help with a market analysis. Programs exist that provide guidelines for building a business plan, including a market analysis segment (FastTrac 2006). Recent efforts have focused on aid to help business owners locate market data for analysis. With the increasing availability and user-friendliness of the Internet, such information can today be readily found and manipulated using Web-based sources. At a 2006 conference, the Oklahoma Cooperative Extension Service identified sources of useful Web-based information and then showed how each source can manipulate the data to more closely fit a business owners' needs. The Internet represents a wealth of information, and the educational program provided suggestions for "best" or vetted Websites and then offered help in adding value to the data found at each site (Barta, Muske, and Woods 2006).

Businesses and communities are always seeking opportunities in local markets. Businesses want to know what new products could be offered to an existing market or what market segments are untapped. Communities are interested in identifying the types of potential businesses that might be added to the area. When businesses and communities assess opportunities, they usually ask basic questions such as "What businesses are missing?" "Where are local consumers shopping and why?" and "Are there potential market opportunities that might be considered by entrepreneurs?"

These questions can often be addressed with specific types of market analysis.

Retail trade analysis uses Census data and community-specific sales tax data to analyze markets. This type of analysis is often called *gap analysis* and is offered by consulting firms and groups such as the Cooperative Extension Service (Barta and Woods 2001). Local businesses use this type of market analysis to identify potential opportunities. Communities use the same information to build local support for entrepreneurial and small business efforts.

Additional market analyses may also be useful. The gap described above in Barta and Woods (2001) often relies on secondary data such as population from the U.S. Bureau of Census or sales tax data provided by a state agency. Often, primary data is useful for a local market analysis. Surveys of local residents can be organized and conducted.

Another method to gather information may involve convening focus groups, representing audiences like homeowners, young people, or ethnic groups, to collect data. The key to reliable and useful results in both these and other primary data collection methods is careful survey design, methodology, and data analysis. These primary survey efforts have proven to be useful market analysis tools for businesses and communities (Fisher and Woods 1987).

Marketing techniques including product packaging and visual merchandising are included in the request for assistance. Visual merchandising can be for the product itself as well as for the overall effect of the store. One innovative effort involves a visual merchandising class offered at Oklahoma State University. Student teams work with the owners of main street businesses in rural communities. These firms have requested assistance in improving some aspect of visual merchandising, from window displays to in-store displays to store arrangement. The students receive a real-world experience, and the firms receive valuable assistance and expertise in visual merchandising techniques (Muske, Jin, and Yu 2004). Related to this is a visual merchandising educational program that merchants might desire.

The visual merchandising program was in response to a rural community request for help for its main street merchants to attract more of the nearly two million visitors that visited a national recreation area on the edge of town. The effort, an example of the Kellogg Foundation's (2004) report encouraging the "engaged institution," has since become a regular class offered each semester. Except for a small amount of seed money, the program has become self-sufficient. Information on how the program might be duplicated has been provided to other states.

Yet visual merchandising can represent more than just the appearance of one store. It also covers how the community presents itself to visitors as well as to local residents. Such efforts can be enhanced through programs such as *Main Street* which work to improve the overall atmosphere and look of a community.

Community marketing though is more than just how things look. Effective marketing also includes customer service. Quality customer service can often overcome other limitations such as selection or convenience. Front-line employees can "make or break" a business, and no amount of financial planning can overcome rude or ineffective employees. The Oklahoma PRIDE program has been a successful training effort for front-line employees of rural businesses (Woods, Selk, and Rash 1997). The program (Producing Resourceful Informed Devoted Employees) includes a "train the trainer" format, so local community groups can launch a PRIDE effort. Firms benefit by having employees who not only understand that they need to be friendly, but also that they should know the firm's policies and goals.

A related tool often used by communities is a *secret visitor* program designed to capture the experiences and perceptions of visitors. An individual(s) drives through town, shops in local stores, and asks for directions or information. The experience is recorded, sometimes with pictures, and shared during a debriefing with local merchants and organizations. This is a community-wide variation of a secret shopper program. In this approach, businesses are visited and evaluated on criteria such as product, service, and accessibility. Also, communities should recognize a need for community-wide and regional efforts designed to attract visitors. For examples of these types of programs, visit the University of Illinois Website materials on *Community Swap* (University of Illinois, Community Development Toolbox 2006).

Finally, community marketing can include the events and attractions in a community and how it advertises them to others. The key in these marketing pieces is that all parts must work together. Usually no one single marketing element will make a successful microbusiness. To paraphrase Jay Levinson's book, *Guerilla Marketing* (1998), marketing is everything you do.

There remains however an important limiting factor on what all of these marketing efforts can achieve. As noted by Muske and Woods (2004), microbusinesses tend to focus only on the local market. This was especially true for businesses that already depended upon local sales. Expansion for 30 percent of owners depending on local sales meant now reaching out to the town next door. If they have not done that in the past, such a move represents a step in the right direction and should be encouraged. However, when marketing is identified as a need, another possible response would be to work with an owner to take his or her product or service statewide, nationwide or even worldwide.

The competitive environment for many of today's businesses is evolving. They may not recognize it but most are part of the global economy. Microbusinesses must consider market access via the World Wide Web as a possibility. Certainly, their competitors are doing so. Businesses in rural areas not only need an adequate technological infrastructure, but they need the training and capacity to effectively use the technology.

One recent effort to enhance educational efforts for rural businesses regarding e-commerce is a national demonstration project led by the Southern Rural Development Center (SRDC) (2006). The project is funded by the Cooperative State Research, Education, and Extension Service (CREES) and focuses on cataloging current and emerging e-commerce educational products and investing in the development of needed curricula through cooperating Land Grant University faculty.

Currently, faculty teams are developing curricula to aid in education related to e-commerce. Topics include experiential strategies for Web-based marketing, use of the Internet by farm business owners, marketing for grocers and food retailers, promoting an e-commerce niche for rural artisans, and assistance targeted to help rural communities become digitally connected. In most cases, the modules will include *PowerPoint* slides, instructor guides, and resource tools for instruction. The intent is to enhance the development and delivery of e-commerce educational activities for rural America. The Website (http://srdc.msstate.edu/ecommerce/index.html) provides more detail on this project.

Another support effort may simply involve helping local business owners and communities with basic Web and e-commerce skills. The SRDC and Cooperative Extension Service together provided a national workshop to teach local assistance providers basic e-commerce skills. The workshop, *Entrepreneurship and E-Commerce*, focused on the building blocks of entrepreneurship and discussed barriers and market opportunities for small and rural communities. The workshop was led by a group of extension educators from around the United States. The first segment of the weeklong workshop focused on tools and programs to assist potential and emerging entrepreneurs. Later sessions focused on e-commerce topics, including marketing strategies, Website design, and use of search engines. In a computer setting, participants participated in hands-on applications, training modules, and Internet techniques. (For additional information, see the SRDC Website.)

In addition, many organizations such as the Cooperative Extension Service provide hands-on courses in Website development. The University of Nebraska initiative (Technologies across Nebraska) is one example, and the Access E-Commerce training Website developed by the University of Minnesota is another.

Finally, a complete support program for business owners must include helping them develop their own networks. Many times, questions or needs of business owners can be most quickly and easily answered through an owner's contacts. Local Chambers of Commerce and/or economic development groups should encourage members to join. In addition, efforts should be made to establish informal networks where owners can meet and discuss issues.

## Sources of Assistance

Listing types of assistance represents only part of the solution. The second part involves how to offer such assistance. Perhaps some of the most helpful suggestions come from work with microbusiness development in the United Kingdom. In that research, Devins (1999) identified that businesses benefited from a one-stop shop for business assistance. Also when requesting help, Devins further identified that the assistance given must not be off-the-shelf, but a customer-led approach designed to meet business' needs. This idea does not necessarily meet business requests. A typical question from microbusiness owners is where do they turn for help. The answer they received is not one source but many providers doing multiple tasks and covering different geographical areas. This in no way says that the help provided is not or cannot be effective; rather the issue is to find it, then identify the best source of response for each potential problem facing an owner, and then putting the pieces together (Kayne 1999).

Following are several examples of potential sources for assistance found in most states. Local communities may have other agencies or resources to add to this list:

Local Cooperative Extension Offices
Chambers of Commerce
Colleges and Universities
Small Business Development Centers
Service Corp of Retired Executive sites
Vocational and Technical Centers
State Department of Commerce
Local incubators
Rural Development groups and agencies
Local elected officials
Investment capital sources
Inventors Assistance groups
State Planning Districts
Certified Development Agencies
Local community development groups
Secretary of State Offices
State Tax and Permitting Agencies
Health Departments

## THE COMMUNITY ROLE
## IN ENTREPRENEURIAL DEVELOPMENT

Local businesses and entrepreneurs do not operate apart from the rest of the environment. If they are fortunate, they operate in communities that strive to offer a nurturing environment for potential and existing entrepreneurs (see Hustedde, chapter 3). Such communities act entrepreneurially both in their efforts to help and support business owners and in their efforts to see the macrocommunity from an entrepreneurial perspective. Communities have unique resources and assets that can be categorized into specific areas, including natural, institutional, financial, and human (Woods and Sanders 1989). Successful communities, like successful entrepreneurs or businesses, combine these resources to achieve profitable and positive goals.

One of the first tasks for a community is to identify what each support entity can add to the economic development plan. Many support organizations tend to operate with a "silo" philosophy and basically offer a specific set of resources on a continual basis. There may be little, or no, recognition often by the agency of alternative resources, approaches or delivery methods. In fact, there is often no interest in coordination, cooperation, or communication and even an unawareness of other resources.

Second, there typically is no follow-up to determine if the person seeking help went to the recommended agency or whether any assistance provided was of any help (see Lyons, chapter 6). Another operational mode found among support agencies is a one-size-fits-all approach. With this method, the agency offers somewhat broader support than that offered by a "silo" but the services the business owner receives are the same whether they are a product or service business, already in business or thinking about starting, big or small, or other criteria.

A third approach to providing business support is the group education model. Here a series of courses are given to groups. Individualized support is minimal, that which occurs may be during the coffee break. Each of these approaches do not usually meet the needs of microbusinesses.

The best community strategy is to remove barriers, whether a sole set of resources, a one-size-fits-all approach, or a group education process. The community can either work with the support groups to expand their offerings or tailor a program to best support specific business owners. Most likely, the final result will be a blend of all of these methods and will probably include all of the support agencies. What differs is how each agency is brought into the mix. Often a community can find the agencies, determine what each offers, build a database of available support, and then track business owners to make sure they receive what they need and that it has answered their question(s).

The next challenge facing specific communities becomes what to capitalize on—what resources are most valuable, rare, and nonsubstitutable (Dollinger 1995). Then, a community must decide how to best use these finite resources. Finally, a community may want to identify the best steps to increasing current resources or developing new resources. Emery, Fey, and Flora (2006) provide an excellent example of this approach using community capital endowments. They offer a methodology complete with worksheets for community action as a part of the Community Development Society CD Practice Series.

Natural resources in a community include assets such as land, water, mountains, and other nature-based amenities. These are resources over which few communities have control—either they exist or they do not. Of course, recognizing the natural resources, preserving and enhancing them, and using them effectively are a key to success and often require out-of-the-box thinking.

Institutional resources, on the other hand, are created and include organizations such as local government, schools, and civic groups which form the structure for commerce, development, and civic/cultural interaction. They provide the "playing field" for programs to work in a community. Other institutional resources in a community include various fairs and events that attract others. Finally, institutional resources can include local cultural and historical elements that can offer entrepreneurial opportunities.

Financial resources are another key ingredient for local community growth. Capital is required for both firm and community development. Businesses look to both family and private/public sources of funds. Communities look to residents and higher levels of government. Increasingly, communities willing to invest in themselves, rather than rely on outside help, are seen as successful examples of community building.

Finally, human resources are also a key building block for local community efforts. Just as with individual firms, communities are often constrained by the amount and quality of labor available locally. Businesses require different labor skill sets, and all communities are not equally endowed. Not only might a business need help with human resources in terms of labor but many times could also benefit from a local coach or mentor. Such a person can gather information/resources and where to find it. Lichtenstein and Lyons (2001), note that such assistance must be ongoing and in-depth with people who can help owners identify the issue and obtain the right help.

These resource sets may help when considering policy options for growth and development. For instance, if a community lacks specific institutions or identifies a need for a specific type of capital, then local policies may address the need. Research on local policy development has found that it contributes to successful business and community development and, to be most effective, should be customer-focused (Devins 1999). If local labor needs require educational investment or redirection, then a community can take action. The community has at least two options for action: (1) address the resource need locally or (2) look externally for assistance.

Successful entrepreneurs are often seen to be reasonable risk-takers (Brabec 1994). Entrepreneurs see an idea and assemble the appropriate resources to take advantage of an opportunity. Successful communities may behave in a similar manner. These entrepreneurial communities will identify a potential opportunity and pull the appropriate resources together to seize that opportunity.

The set of four resources discussed above (natural, institutional, financial, and human) represent the ingredients available (Emery, Fey, and Flora 2006). Successful communities, like successful entrepreneurs, are innovative and reasonable risk-takers in utilizing these resources to full advantage.

There are many recent examples of rural communities that have both nurtured potential entrepreneurs and behaved entrepreneurially as a community (Barta et al. 2006). Greer County, Oklahoma, in the southwest quadrant of the state, organized a countywide planning effort to identify local assets and used the Mainstreet Program to revitalize the county seat.

Wagoner County in northeastern Oklahoma formed a medical board and has successfully obtained grant funds to provide a medical center. Early successes with the medical board convinced local leaders in Wagoner County that they could succeed in economic development as well, and a countywide economic development trust has been successfully implemented. The trust has partnered with the private sector to expand port facilities on the Kerr-McCellan Navigation System and create jobs.

Another county in northwestern Oklahoma, Alfalfa, decided to build on the rich natural resource base and is marketing agritourism experiences. It has a rich agricultural tradition and abundant natural resources. Local leaders are utilizing video and other marketing techniques to describe the bird watching, hiking, and other outdoor opportunities. Lessons learned from all these local examples include the following: (1) form partnerships whenever possible and think regionally; (2) do not give up because success sometimes takes time; (3) be aware of all the resources and build on assets; and (4) have a plan so the entire community will know what is happening.

These successful communities have a willingness to take reasonable risks and a strong desire to assess the market to see what will work in the current environment. They also aggressively seek assistance from all possible sources and build partnerships to achieve their goals. These traits and actions seem very similar to those used by successful firm-level entrepreneurs.

So how does a community make all of this happen? Many of the programs and needs identified earlier can initially be addressed with an educational program. The groups listed and the concerns identified can all be addressed initially by bringing microbusiness owners to the table to discuss their issues.

When looking more broadly at a community's economic development strategy, however, a key element involves developing a constant flow of new entrepreneurs. Again, entrepreneurship education is what can make that happen. Individuals are interested in "being their own boss." The goal is to encourage them to take the first step and to do it successfully. This means helping individuals determine whether entrepreneurship is right for them. It is not a question of whether they have the right traits to be entrepreneurs; rather, whether it is the right time for them to start a business. Entrepreneurship education also helps them find and evaluate business opportunities (Gerena 2005).

General entrepreneurship education development programs should begin with youth programs such as *Be the e: Entrepreneurship,* a 4-H program, or *Mini Society,* a program from the Kauffman Foundation's Center for Entrepreneurial Leadership. Students should continue to hear the entrepreneurial message through high school and college (Muske and Stanforth 2000). Later, entrepreneurial programs such as *Putting It All Together: Micro and Homebased Businesses* from the Oklahoma Cooperative Extension Service or *FastTrac* from the Kauffman Foundation continue the encouragement of developing one's dream. There also is a need for specific programs on issues such as marketing or opportunities such as *Basic Training* offered by the Food and Agricultural Products Center at Oklahoma State University for people interested in food-based businesses.

Several taxonomies exist that categorize entrepreneurs into a variety of types. One such taxonomy, developed by the Kellogg Foundation (2004), classifies individuals into groups of aspiring, survival, lifestyle, growth, serial, and social entrepreneurs (Dabson, chapter 2). For the overall benefit of the community, and the type of business developed is not the issue, a broad-based economic development strategy promoting all types of entrepreneurs is key. Each entrepreneur is a piece to a growing and thriving economic engine. Aspiring entrepreneurs are just that—individuals who perhaps have an idea and would like to take the leap. Survival entrepreneurs are those in business to survive or subsist. Lifestyle entrepreneurs choose a business option to support a quality of life or other choice that suits them. Growth entrepreneurs focus on income or sales and are the more aggressive type of entrepreneur. Serial entrepreneurs like to bring a concept to the market, build the business, and then move on to the next entrepreneurial activity. Perhaps they thrive on the risk and the "rush" of launching a new venture. Even social entrepreneurs add to a community's resource base as they work in the social or volunteer sectors using entrepreneurial skills to promote and pursue social goals in nonprofit and volunteer sectors that are part of all strong communities.

The goal is locating and developing the *entrepreneurial talent* that can then become successful microbusiness owners (Markley and Macke 2003). It is what this entire group offers to the economic growth possibilities in a community that is important. In *The New Architecture of Rural Prosperity* (Clinton et al. 2005), the Southern Growth Policies Board identifies the need for communities to create new businesses, retain and expand existing as well as recruit new businesses.

## CONCLUSION

The concepts and examples presented in this chapter provide strong support to encourage a community to see microbusiness development as a required element in any local economic or community development plan. Microbusinesses often are the "mom and pop" or main street stores that form the fabric binding a community together. Not only are they crucial in the sense of providing needed goods and services, but the people who own and work in these businesses represent the human capital needed for future growth. They are often the "movers and shakers" of community growth.

This chapter offers ideas regarding the needs of microbusiness owners as well as some programs that one agency in one state has used in supporting development work. The list is by no means exhaustive of what might be offered in a community to microbusiness owners or to the community itself as it seeks to establish a nurturing environment for local businesses as an opportunistic community. Being such a community builds on itself because each new idea, new program, or new business encourages others to think broadly. Examples of such opportunistic thinking and the tools that then transform such opportunities into action can be found in the rest of this book, from other service providers in the state, and from service providers across the nation.

## REFERENCES

Association for Enterprise Opportunity (AEO). 2004. *Making the case for microenterprise: AEO 2004 legislative priorities.* Arlington, VA: AEO.

Audretsch, David B., and Max Keilbach. 2004. Does entrepreneurship capital matter? *Entrepreneurship Theory and Practice* 28(5): 419–29.

Baines, S., and J. Wheelock. 1998. Working for each other: Gender, the household and micro business survival and growth. *International Small Business Journal* 17(1): 16–36.

Barkley, David. 2003. Policy Options for Equity Financing for Rural Entrepreneurs. *Main Streets of Tomorrow: Growing and Financing Rural Entrepreneurs*, 107–125. Proceedings sponsored by the Center for the Study of Rural America, Federal Reserve Bank of Kansas City.

Barta, Suzette D., Glenn Muske, and Michael D. Woods. 2006. Data resources on the web. Presented at Women's Business Conference sponsored by Rural Enterprises of Oklahoma.

Barta, Suzette D., and Michael D. Woods. 2001. Gap analysis: A tool for community economic development. *Journal of Extension* 39(2).

Barta, S., R. Daugherty, J. Frye, J. Martin, S. Ralstin, J. Williams, S. Williams, and M. Woods. 2006. *Initiative for the future of rural Oklahoma: Focus group session results*. AE 06022, Stillwater: Oklahoma Cooperative Extension Service, Oklahoma State University.

Beaulieu, Lionel J. 2002. *Creating vibrant communities and economies in rural America*. Mississippi State, MS: Southern Rural Development Center.

Brabec, Barbara. 1994. *Homemade money*. Cincinnati, OH: Betterway Books.

Bruce, Donald, John A. Deskins, Brian C. Hill, and Jonathan C. Rork. 2007. *Small business and state growth: An econometric investigation (Report #292)*. Washington, DC: Small Business Administration.

Burns, Marilyn M., and Cathy B. McCullough. 2001. *Business savvy for today's new entrepreneur*. Stillwater, OK: New Forums Press.

Carland, James W., Frank Hoy, William R. Boulton, and Jo Ann Carland. 1984. Differentiating entrepreneurs from small business owners: A conceptualization. *Academy of Management Review* 9(2), 354–59.

Chamberlain, Lara. 2004. *National small business poll: International trade* 4(1). Washington, DC: National Federation of Independent Business Owners (NFIB).

Clinton, Jim, Carol Conway, Scott Doron, Linda Hoke, and Sandra Johnson. 2005. *The new architecture of rural prosperity*. Research Triangle Park, NC: Southern Growth Policies Board.

Darling, David L. 2004. *The economic development pyramid approach to building healthy communities—MF-2665*. Manhattan, KS: Kansas State University Agricultural Experiment Station and Cooperative Extension Service.

Dennis, William J. 2004. *National small business poll: Contributions to communities* 4(6). Washington, DC: National Federation of Independent Business Owners (NFIB).

Dennis, William J. 2005. *National small business poll: The state of technology* 5(5). Washington, DC: National Federation of Independent Business Owners (NFIB).

Devins, David. 1999. Supporting established microbusinesses: Policy issues emerging from an evaluation. *International Small Business Journal* 18(1): 86–97.

Dollinger, Marc J. 1995. The resource-based theory of entrepreneurship. In *Entrepreneurship: Strategies and Resources*, 23–37. Burr Ridge, IL: Richard D. Irwin, Inc.

Drabenstott, Mark. 2003. A new era for rural policy. *Economic Review—Fourth Quarter*. Kansas City, MO: Federal Reserve Bank: 81–97.

Emery, Mary, Susan Fey, and Cornelia Flora. 2006. Using community capitals to develop assets for positive community change. *CD Practice* (13) www.comm-dev.org/ (January 29, 2006).

Emery, Mary, Milan Wall, and Don Macke. 2004. From theory to action: Energizing entrepreneurship (E2), strategies to aid distressed communities grow their own. *Journal of the Community Development Society* 35.

Ewing Marion Kauffman Foundation. 2005. *Understanding entrepreneurship: A research and policy report.* Kansas City, MO: Ewing Marion Kauffman Foundation.

Ewing Marion Kauffman Foundation. 2001. *Planning and growing a business venture.* Kansas City, MO: Ewing Marion Kauffman Foundation.

Ewing Marion Kauffman Foundation. 2001. *Planning and growing a business venture.* Kansas City, MO: Kauffman Center for Entrepreneurial Leadership.

Family Economics and Nutrition Review. 2001. Small business: Evidence from the 1998 survey of small business finances. *Family Economics and Nutrition Review* 14(1): 84–85.

FastTrac. 2006. FastTrac Programs. www.fasttrac.org (July 18, 2006).

Fisher, Dennis U., and Mike D. Woods. 1987. Consumer opinion surveys and sales leakage data: Effective community development tools. *Journal of the Community Development Society* 18(2): 69–80.

Friedman, Thomas L. 2005. The world is flat: A brief history of the twenty-first century. New York: Farrar, Straus and Giroux.

Gerena, Charles. 2005. *Nature vs. nurture.* Richmond Federal Reserve Bank. www.richmondfed.org/publications/economic_research/region_focus/fall_2005/pdf/feature.pdf (December 21, 2005).

Goetz, Stephan J. 2005. *Searching for jobs: The growing importance of rural proprietors.* Mississippi State, MS: Southern Rural Development Center.

Halstead, John M., and Steven C. Deller. 1997. Public infrastructure in economic development and growth: Evidence from rural manufacturers. *Journal of the Community Development Society* 28(2): 149–69.

Haynes, George W., Rosemary Walker, Barbara R. Rowe, and Gong-Soog Hong. 1999. The intermingling of business and family finances in family-owned businesses. *Family Business Review* 12(3): 225–39.

Heck, Ramona K. Z., and Kathryn Stafford. 2001. The vital institution of family business: Economic benefits hidden in plain site. In *Family business gathering 2001 the holistic model: Destroying myths and creating value in family business,* eds. G. McCann and N. B. Upton, 9–17. DeLand, FL: Stetson University Family Business Center.

Henderson, Jason. 1997. How important are small businesses in the 10th district? *Regional Economic Digest* 8(3): 9–14.

Henricks, Mark. 2007. A look ahead. *Entrepreneur.* January, 70–76.

Kangasharju, Aki. 2001. Growth of the smallest: Determinants of small firm growth during strong macroeconomic fluctuations. *Journal Small Business Journal* 19(1): 28–43.

Kayne, Joseph. 1999. *State entrepreneurship policies and programs.* Kansas City, MO: Kauffman Center for Entrepreneurial Leadership.

Kellogg Foundation. 2004. *Mapping rural entrepreneurship.* Battle Creek, MI: W. K. Kellogg Foundation.

Kettering Foundation. 2000. *Creating a healthy (sustainable) economy for our community.* Dayton, OH: Kettering Foundation.

Levenburg, N. M., and P. M. Lane. 2003. Beyond the business school: An interdisciplinary examination of interest in entrepreneurship. *Proceedings of the Academy of Entrepreneurship* 9(2): 15–18. Las Vegas, NV.

Levinson, Jay. 1998. *Guerrilla marketing: Secrets for making big profits from your small business.* Boston, MA: Houghton Mifflin.

Lichtenstein, Gregg A., and Thomas S. Lyons. 2001. The entrepreneurial development system: Transforming business talent and community economies. *Economic Development Quarterly* 15(1): 3–20.

Lichtenstein, Gregg A., Thomas S. Lyons, and Nailya Kutzhanova. 2004. Building entrepreneurial communities: The appropriate role of enterprise development activities. *Journal of the Community Development Society* 35(1): 5–24.

Low, Sarah, Jason Henderson, and Stephen Weiler. 2005. Gauging a region's entrepreneurial potential. *Economic Review—Third Quarter*, 61–89. Kansas City, MO: Federal Reserve Bank.

Markley, Deborah, and Don Macke. 2003. *Entrepreneurs and Entrepreneurship, Monograph 1*. Center for Rural Entrepreneurship www.ruraleship.org (July 20, 2006).

Miller, N. 1998. Local consumer spending: A reflection of rural community social and economic exchange. *Journal of the Community Development Society* 29(2): 166–85.

Muske, G., B. Jin, and H. Yu. 2004. Engaging rural retailers in visual merchandising. *Journal of Family and Consumer Sciences* 96(3): 53–56.

Muske Glenn, and Nancy Stanforth. 2000. The educational needs of small business owners: A look into the future. *Journal of Extension* 38(6). www.joe.org/joe/2000december/a4.html (July 22, 2006).

Muske, Glenn, and Michael Woods. 2004. Microbusinesses as an economic development tool: What they bring and what they need. *Journal of the Community Development Society* 35(1): 97–116.

National Commission on Entrepreneurship. 2001. *Five myths about entrepreneurs: Understanding how businesses start and grow*. www.energizingentrepreneurs.org/content/chapter_1/supporting_materials/1_000137.pdf (July 18, 2006).

Phillips, Bruce D. 2004. *Small business problems and priorities*. Washington, DC: National Federation of Independent Business Owners (NFIB).

Rightmyre, Vicki M., Thomas G. Johnson, and Daryll Chatman. 2004. *Growing entrepreneurs from the ground up: A community based approach to growing your own business*. Columbia: University of Missouri Community Policy Analysis Center.

Schultz, Jack. 2004. *BoomTown USA: The 7 1/2 keys to big success in small towns*. Herndon, VA: National Association of Industrial and Office Properties.

Sexton, L. A. (1999) Small business is good business. *Arkansas Business and Economic Review* 32(3), 18–19.

Sharp, Jeff S., and Jan L. Flora. 1999. Entrepreneurial social infrastructure and growth machine characteristics associated with industrial-recruitment and self-development in nonmetropolitan communities. *Journal of the Community Development Society* 30(2): 131–53.

Southern Rural Development Center. 2006. *The rural e-commerce extension initiative: A national demonstration project*. http://srdc.msstate.edu/ecommerce/index.html (June 2006).

University of Illinois, Community Development Toolbox. 2006. *Community Swap*. http://communitydevelopment.uiuc.eduin (April 19, 2006).

U.S. Census Bureau. 2001. *Statistics about business size*. www.census.gov/ (April 19, 2006).

U.S. Census Bureau. 2006. *Mom and pop shops increase*. http://factfinder.census.gov/jsp/saff/SAFFInfo.jsp?_pageId=tp17_business_industry (April 19, 2006).

U.S. Census Bureau. 2006. *Nonemployer statistics*. http://www.census.gov/prod/2006pubs/ns0400a01.pdf (February 6, 2007).

U.S. Department of Labor. 2005. *New quarterly data from BLS on business employment dynamics by size of firm*—#05-2277. Washington, DC: Bureau of Labor Statistics.

U.S. Small Business Administration. 2000. *Employer firms, establishments, employment and annual payroll by firm size and state.* Washington, DC: Small Business Administration. www.sba.gov/advo/stats/st.pdf (April 19, 2006).

U.S. Small Business Administration. 2001. *Statistics of U.S. businesses: Firm size data.* http://www.sba.gov/advo/research/us_tot.pdf (April 19, 2006).

U.S. Small Business Administration. 2006. 2004 statistics of U.S. businesses: Firm size data. http://www.sba.gov/advo/research/st_04.pdf (February 5, 2007).

U.S. Small Business Administration. 2006. *Statistics of U.S. businesses: Firm size data.* http://www.sba.gov/advo/research/us_tot.pdf (April 17, 2006).

U.S. Small Business Administration. 2007. Small businesses as job generators. *The Advocate* 26(2). www.sba.gov/advo/feb07.pdf (February 1, 2007).

Walstad, William B., and Marilyn Kourilsky. 1996. The findings from a national survey of entrepreneurship and small business. *Journal of Private Enterprise* 11(2): 21–32.

Woods, Michael. 2000. Diversifying the rural economy: Tourism development. In *The rural south: Preparing for the challenges of the 21st Century, #10.* Mississippi State, MS: Southern Rural Development Center.

Woods, M. D., V. J. Frye, and S. R. Ralstin. 2004. *Blueprints for your community's future: Creating a strategic plan for local economic development, F-916.* Stillwater: Oklahoma Cooperative Extension Service.

Woods, M., and L. Sanders. 1989. Rural development: A critical Oklahoma issue. *Current Farm Economics* 67(3): 3–16.

Woods, M., M. P. Selk, and D. Rash. 1997. PRIDE-A workshop to Promote Quality Customer Service. *Galaxy Summit Conference Proceedings,* 52–53. Cincinnati, OH.

# 11

## Energizing Entrepreneurs: Lessons from the Field

*Don Macke*

Rural America represents a diverse collection of landscapes, societies, and communities. This diversity is reflected in economic and social realities that vary widely as do the opportunities for development through entrepreneurial-based strategies (Macke and Markley 2005). In 1999, with support from the Ewing Marion Kauffman Foundation,[1] the Rural Policy Research Institute[2] (RUPRI), and others,[3] a team was assembled to explore possible roles of entrepreneurship in rural America. During a three-year period from 2000 into 2003, the researchers[4] traveled more than one million miles throughout North America exploring numerous landscapes ranging from the Olympic Peninsula in Washington to Downeast Maine, into rural Georgia, throughout the Great Plains, and many other rural regions.

The research approach was simple and direct—to find those rural places that were prospering and had a reputation for innovative rural development. Literally hundreds of communities were visited, and several thousand rural residents, including civic leaders, entrepreneurs, and resource providers, were interviewed. The investigations gathered major insights into why these places were doing so well and the kinds of development approaches that were making a difference.

This chapter summarizes the field work and offers insights to help communities or regions achieve greater development success through entrepreneurship. The findings are organized into three sections. In the first section, "Keys to Success and Failure," core learning from the field studies and exploration of entrepreneurial support systems in rural America is shared. The second section, "Models of Practice," reviews information on both long-standing and emerging entrepreneurial development systems. The final section, "Community Resources," provides an outline of additional information and helpful resources to assist practitioners interested in starting entrepreneurship programs.

## KEYS TO SUCCESS AND FAILURE

Defining success relative to failure is usually subjective at best. For communities in Nebraska's rural Sandhills Region, success is defined as sufficient population growth to sustain local schools, churches, and a main street. Most residents in this cattle ranching region would oppose too much development as counter to their desire for a certain type of rural life.

In southeast Georgia, the definition changes, with communities seeking to sustain growth through expanded investment and job creation. Because success and failure are defined locally in varied ways, community vitality as defined by the Aspen Institute (1996) is often used as an indicator of whether a rural place or region is doing well or not. The Aspen Institute's definition of community vitality embraces multiple indicators that a community or region can adopt to create a comprehensive and operational definition of progress. For example, a community may adopt wealth creation across class lines as a bottom line economic development outcome and treat job creation as an intermediate metric. The value of the Aspen Institute approach is that it provides a framework for communities to develop their own system of outcome goal setting and measurement.

The current research did not focus on macro indicators of economic performance; rather, it seriously examined development strategies where local residents and entrepreneurs felt they were succeeding because of the strategies employed. The project continually interviewed local residents, especially local entrepreneurs. This process, by visiting and studying multiple, different landscapes, reached an important insight, namely that the practice, not the form, of the strategy matters.

Many forms of entrepreneurial support were studied, including the following:

- Incubators
- Entrepreneurial Training Programs
- Capital Access Strategies
- Small Business Development Centers
- Coaching and Facilitation
- Project Based Development
- Business Retention and Expansion Programs
- Microenterprise Strategies

Success and failure, and everything in between, were found in each of these forms of entrepreneurial support. No clear pattern of when one strategy or approach achieved greater impact over another was uncovered. What was found within all of these forms of entrepreneurial support, however, is a set of practices that resulted in energizing entrepreneurial talent and in stimulating development. Many attributes of these practices have been documented previously (Macke and Markley 2004). The overarching and five most important attributes of successful practices will be discussed next:

1. A focus on entrepreneurs, not businesses
2. The right geography, capitalization and strategy
3. Use of the right approaches
4. Use of business services
5. A systems approach—performance driven and accountable

## Entrepreneurs

A majority of successful efforts are more about people development than business development. Businesses are the means to an end while entrepreneurs are the key creative force. The implications of this orientation are important. Addressing the technical issues of business creation, development, and growth is not enough to ensure success. More importantly, helping individuals and their teams acquire the knowledge, skills, and attitudes essential for business creation and development becomes a primary focus. This view is similar to America's embrace of a liberal arts education. Educating people broadly and helping them learn to think will place them in a stronger position to thrive through life's many challenges and opportunities.

The same is true with investing in the entrepreneur as a person. The attitude, aptitude, and networks of entrepreneurs will allow them to find the best possible answers for business success. The challenge is not helping the entrepreneur find the right marketing strategy; rather, it is helping an entrepreneur become good at finding the right marketing strategy today, tomorrow, and in the years ahead given changes in the marketplace.

## Geography, Capitalization, and Strategy

Helping entrepreneurs requires relationship building and a one-on-one connectivity. Entrepreneurial development does not work well in a mass produced or supported approach. Effective statewide support systems were studied that reaped limited results because they lacked these relationships. Instead, they focused on technical needs like capital and business planning and failed to address the human and creative needs of entrepreneurs.

The realities of following the wrong approach play out in many ways. Using the correct geographic area that can be served at a human scale proves to be very important. The right geography is subjective but does have important boundaries. It must be an area where the support system can create a one-on-one relationship with entrepreneurs but large enough to allow robust resources and entrepreneurial networks to emerge and grow. Creating these kinds of human resource intensive systems demands adequate program capital with a strategy that can effectively manage resources at a personal level over a regional landscape.

### Right Approaches

Since most economic development is funded directly or indirectly by local, state, or federal governments, tight fiscal times demand efficiency and effectiveness. Such demands have moved many public programs away from individual help to group assistance or mass approaches using Web-based resources. Many of these programs and resources have good track records, but they perform better with that one-on-one element. Interviews with successful entrepreneurial approaches found that entrepreneurial networks, mentoring, peer groups, small groups, and customized assistance work best. In these environments, the full needs of entrepreneurs can be more readily identified and addressed.

In addition, those programs with the greatest impact understood the implications of a human development, rather than a strictly business development, approach. More personal support issues such as life balance, goal clarification, and preference management (e.g., the entrepreneur wants to produce but not manage finances) can be addressed more effectively; however, as with education or healthcare programs, these kinds of entrepreneurial development systems are expensive and difficult to build and sustain.

### Business Services

Some policymakers might argue that most economic progress occurs outside of development programs, which are housed mainly in the private sector. The availability and level of private business services differs widely in rural and urban areas, and these services can be important in local economic development. Urban areas have a rich environment of private business services, ranging from basic (e.g., help with taxes) to sophisticated (e.g., patent attorneys). Most rural areas, on the other hand, may offer some basic services, but sophisticated business services are usually only located in urban centers. Not only is access an issue, but there is a cultural barrier as well. Most rural entrepreneurs are not familiar with these services, do not know how to access them, or do not know the rules of engagement (e.g., fee for services).

The RUPRI study found that places with successful strategies worked hard to connect and graduate entrepreneurs into the world of private business services. Successful locations had built regional business service networks and created an understanding of, and pathways to, external and more sophisticated resources. They brokered and connected entrepreneurs to the right services, both public and private, at a fair price and at the right time.

## A Systems Approach

Creating and growing a venture is a challenge and it truly takes a system to grow an entrepreneur. Meeting the needs of entrepreneurs with different types and levels of entrepreneurial talent requires a support system that can easily connect entrepreneurs to the resources needed on a real time basis (see Lyons, Lichtenstein, and Kutzhanova, chapter 6). That means, providing access to resources and support when crises arise, whether at night or on the weekends. It also means connecting and coordinating service providers so that entrepreneurs can access appropriate services from any door to the system, i.e., there is no wrong door.

A systems approach also recognizes that entrepreneurs exist within a community and that a supportive policy environment is needed. The system must include programs or activities that promote a new culture of entrepreneurship in the community or region, beginning with K–12 education and extending to state and regional policymakers.

Most entrepreneurs readily admit that failures were usually their most powerful teachers. The same can be said with entrepreneurial programs. Programs viewed today as highly successful can share horror stories of missteps, challenges, and incorrect approaches from which great learning was realized. Many lessons were learned in the RUPRI-sponsored field research, but five main reasons for why entrepreneurial efforts come up short were identified:

1. Traditional economic development repackaged
2. General versus specific support
3. Too few resources
4. Limited staying power
5. Failure to target entrepreneurial talent

### Repackaged Development

Experiences in the field support the perception that many, if not most, rural communities and regions do not participate effectively in the economic development process. They do not have an adequate commitment, investment, or strategy to even have an opportunity to succeed. Most rural communities engaged in economic development continue to focus on natural resource industry preservation, tourism, and/or business attraction.

Even though many rural communities embrace the idea of entrepreneurship, very few have invested adequately in this approach. For many, entrepreneurship initiatives fail because they exist in name only with current development efforts simply repackaged and renamed as entrepreneurship. In reality, these efforts come up short because they do not address the critical elements necessary for success outlined earlier.

### General versus Specific Support

A repetitive theme in this chapter is that entrepreneurial development requires a customized approach. Many other efforts have realized limited success because of the general approach they employ. Often, these programs focus on addressing a narrow set of business inputs or skills such as capital access or business training. While these resources are part of the overall picture, they alone are rarely sufficient to create an entrepreneurial society and/or economy capable of moving a community or region forward economically. By contrast, more successful programs provide real-time and specific help to meet the critical needs of specific entrepreneurs.

### Under Resourced

As noted previously, successful entrepreneurial approaches are human and capital resource intensive. Providing customized and sophisticated real-time assistance to hundreds of entrepreneurs on an ongoing basis requires staff, volunteers, and dollars. Many programs, even those with a great design, are less successful because of inadequate capitalization. Some areas, however, have overcome this obstacle. For instance, in very rural Valley County, Nebraska (pop. 4,500), entrepreneurial programs work in part because of a staff of three, dozens of dedicated volunteers, and more than one-half million dollars in economic development investment.[5]

### Limited Staying Power

It is relatively easy to understand why efforts fail when they are short-lived, and this is true of all development, but especially of entrepreneurship programs. Since entrepreneurship is a human resource development approach, it requires consistent and long-term commitments. Even the most respected programs such as Coastal Enterprises in Maine (www.ceimaine .org) or the Delta Corporation (www.ecd.org) took years to refine their approaches before realizing systemic outcomes. A three-year program is not long enough; a generational commitment is mandatory if significant change and progress are desired.

### Failure to Target Entrepreneurial Talent

Any successful business has learned to find a competitive niche. Part of this formula for success involves understanding the customers and doing the best job in meeting their needs at a competitive price. The same is true with entrepreneurial development. A key dividing line between less and more successful programs is entrepreneurial talent segmentation. Successful programs understand that an aspiring entrepreneur with no prior business experience has very different developmental needs than an existing business seeking to grow into a national market. Less successful entrepreneurship programs tend to treat all entrepreneurs the same and try to address their needs through similar approaches. As entrepreneurial skills and success increase, entrepreneurs require more customized and specialized assistance.

Combined, these five attributes of success and five reasons for failure begin to paint a picture of the core elements in cutting-edge entrepreneurial development systems and environments. The next section describes models of successful rural entrepreneurial development systems.

## MODELS OF PRACTICE

Entrepreneurship is part of our American heritage, with Ben Franklin serving as a model entrepreneur at the time of the American Revolution. Despite this legacy and history, focused and intentional entrepreneurial local economic development is relatively new. The oldest programs are only twenty to thirty years old. This section explores five long-term programs and five new promising initiatives. Each of these initiatives has learned the lessons outlined earlier in this chapter.

### Long-Standing Programs

There are about two-dozen long-standing entrepreneurial development systems in rural America that could be highlighted. Five have been selected to illustrate important factors underlying their success. They exhibit diverse approaches as well as different areas of the United States:

1. Kentucky Highlands Investment Corporation
2. Coastal Enterprises of Maine

3. Northern Initiatives of Michigan
4. Sirolli's Enterprise Facilitation
5. Economic Gardening in Colorado

*Kentucky Highlands Investment Corporation*

Like many of the other long-established programs, Kentucky Highlands was created when the federal government was investing heavily in rural America to address issues of chronic poverty and lack of economic opportunity. Located in a multicounty region of Appalachian Kentucky, Kentucky Highlands began as a capital access strategy and grew into a comprehensive entrepreneurial development system. Over time, it was discovered that creating access to capital was not enough; intensive one-on-one work with entrepreneurs was essential.

Kentucky Highlands also assumed the role of a regional development corporation, addressing the issues of community culture and attitude toward business development. It helped to create other initiatives (e.g., microenterprise programs) that collectively created a continuum of development support for start-ups to high-growth entrepreneurs (Markley and Barkley 2003).

The Center for Rural Entrepreneurship's case study of Kentucky Highlands documents the collection of subsidiaries, programs, and strategies that have been created over time. The organizational chart with its many related elements looks complicated and reflects significant evolutionary sophistication. Kentucky Highlands is resourceful in connecting with available private and public resources and programs that can address specific needs of the entrepreneurs within their portfolio. The staff of Kentucky Highlands not only know how to "do" business deals, but they are able to (and do) take over and manage a company in which they are investing. The challenge for Kentucky Highlands in this time of declining state and federal economic development program resources will be to find new sources of funding to sustain program needs.

*Coastal Enterprises of Maine*

Coastal Enterprises Inc. (CEI) of Downeast Maine recently celebrated twenty-five years of success. It started as an antipoverty development agency and continues to support a broad mission, ranging from childcare facilities to commercial development. CEI, matching the economy and society of rural Maine, also undertook cutting-edge work in agriculture, fisheries, forestry, and other sectors central to the Maine economy.

CEI is also a leader in microenterprise development crafting, some of America's cutting-edge microcapital programs, including training resources.

These strategies addressed entrepreneurial needs at the start-up and early stage business end of the continuum. This focus and accomplishment in the microlending and training arena reflect Maine's tradition of self-employment.

CEI has moved beyond microlending to address the capital, human, and technical needs of existing and expanding entrepreneurial businesses. Their employment of state and federal capital programs link investment and technical resources to these ventures. With the exception of the far north, the Western Mountains of Maine are economically distressed and very rural. There is a sense of being disconnected from the state and the growth centers of the Bangor/Portland Corridor and the Downeast Coastal communities. CEI, partnering with existing western Maine development organizations, created a field presence in western Maine to extend credit and expertise to entrepreneurs in this rural landscape.

CEI, like Michigan's Northern Initiatives, also pioneered sectoral or industry-specific development strategies. Maine, as is true with many rural states, has deep roots in natural resource industries such as fishing and farming. CEI worked with area commercial fishing interests to establish a fish market in Portland when the closest market was in Boston. Its other work with timber and agricultural interests has fostered important progress from raw commodities to emerging value-added industries.

CEI, unlike many traditional development organizations, was not obsessed with job creation as its primary outcome metric. It understood Maine, the residents, and the communities, and the need to help self-employed and small businesses find greater economic security and higher incomes as important. Greater job creation could only come if existing enterprises were doing better and had greater sustainability.

There are many chapters in the CEI story. An important new development in CEI's history is its geographic reach moving beyond its home county in Downeast Maine to western Maine and other parts of New England. CEI understands that if it is to have systemic impact, organizational scale is very important. Today, it is extending its reach to the entire New England region (Rowley 2003).

## Northern Initiatives of Michigan

Northern Michigan, especially the fifteen counties north of the Mackinac Bridge, is a very rural region rooted in mining, fishing, forestry, manufacturing, and tourism. All of these industries are undergoing profound changes that challenge the very future of this area. Northern Initiatives (NI), which is affiliated with Shore Bank of Chicago and the University of Northern Michigan, is a highly networked organization that partners widely to achieve its mission.

Partnerships range from work with the Nature Conservancy (ecotourism and landscape preservation) to manufacturers. This association has benefited NI in pioneering work with youth entrepreneurship, small business development, and sectoral development. NI was one of the first rural development organizations to embrace cluster strategies. Today, NI is a primary player, stimulating and supporting an entrepreneurial culture in northern Michigan (Bauer 2004b).

NI provides a variety of fairly conventional development corporation services ranging from microlending, to entrepreneurial training, to peer groups for existing growth businesses, to near equity financing and deal development for larger businesses. It also engages in strategic community work. For example, through its partnership with tourism interests, it has explored how to shift tourism in the region from high impact and low value to lower impact and higher value. NI is innovative and strategic in pursuing new answers to this challenged region's need for development.

NI has also been a pioneer in youth entrepreneurship. Its long-standing and robust engagement with schools in the region has promoted entrepreneurship education within school walls and access to prime time with kids. The number of schools and kids involved highlights the impact and effectiveness of NI (Bauer 2004b).

## Sirolli's Enterprise Facilitation

Ernesto Sirolli, a well-known economic development speaker in the United States and internationally, created the Sirolli Institute and Enterprise Facilitation (EF) as a pioneering *entrepreneur-focused* economic development strategy (see www.sirolli.com). Possibly one of the best opportunities to study how EF works is in Kansas. The RUPRI Center for Rural Entrepreneurship, in partnership with EntreWorks, recently completed a multiyear evaluation of Sirolli projects in Kansas.

The State of Kansas through its Department of Commerce became interested in EF in the 1990s. The State financially seeded five multicommunity EF projects in rural Kansas. The Sirolli Institute was retained to design, train, and support these projects. These projects benefited from EF's latest learning and offered a great opportunity to see how EF could work in five relatively different rural landscapes. The State required multicounty and community collaborations to come together as part of this pilot initiative.

Overall, one project (located in southeast Kansas) achieved especially significant economic and social impacts. It enabled a very poor and economically distressed region to come together and stimulate development. At the other end of the state, the Western Kansas Project struggled due to vast distances, limited entrepreneurial talent, and a decade-long drought harming the business climate. Despite these challenges, this project stayed together and realized important development results.

The other three projects have achieved relatively good impacts. Compared with microenterprise development and business attraction, EF has proven to be somewhat higher in cost than microenterprise programs (based on cost per job created) but significantly lower in cost than business attraction incentives. The RUPRI case study provides lessons learned with summary statistics on costs and impacts.[6]

The remaining key lesson to be learned from Kansas is whether these projects survive and thrive past state funding. Over time, state funds have declined and forced these projects to press financially strapped local resources for more funding.

## Colorado's Economic Gardening

For nearly twenty years, Chris Gibbons has almost single-handedly created a major entrepreneurial movement called Economic Gardening (EG) in Littleton, Colorado, a wealthy suburb of Denver (see www .littletongov.org). The lessons learned have been adapted widely and are taking root throughout the United States and the world. Most of the adoption of EG has been in larger communities such as Chico, California, or Loveland, Colorado; however, experiences in rural areas, such as Wyoming, clearly suggest the secrets learned can be employed even in remote regions. EG is very strategic in its work with entrepreneurs, focusing on market research support and helping entrepreneurs find competitive niches (Bauer 2005).

The five approaches just discussed all employ practices that are central to impacting entrepreneurial programs and all demonstrate sustainability and capacity. They have learned over the years and have created mature strategies that work and here changed local and regional economies over time. A review of key findings from these five mini–case studies offer clues on the keys to building a successful entrepreneurial strategy:

- All of these efforts focus on individuals or teams and their personal as well as business needs.
- There is a clear understanding that the potential for economic development impact is rooted in the ability of these individuals/teams to grow, sustain, and eventually build competitive businesses.
- Most of these systems provide access to capital (Sirolli's EF does not) as a core way to connect to entrepreneurs and help them grow. They also have learned that capital access alone is not enough.
- Equally important to capital access is deal polishing or the process of taking a good idea and team and evolving it into a great idea and team. This is a hallmark of these systems. The impact numbers being realized by these systems are directly tied to their ability to engage entrepreneurs in the polishing process.

- Most of these systems see importance in youth entrepreneurship. They understand that youth can and do play an important role in transforming culture. These initiatives represent a long view and commitment to the future and realize that bottom line economic impact metrics come slowly from youth entrepreneurship. These systems believe, however, that youth strategies can improve the culture for an entrepreneurial economy over time.
- Many of these systems engage in civic entrepreneurship. They are collaborative, network well, and link to strategic partnerships. Coastal Enterprises, Inc. cannot, on its own, attract venture capital to Maine, but it has learned how the venture markets work in Boston and how to link deals with investors. In turn, these systems build civic capacity to support entrepreneurial development.
- All of these systems are entrepreneurial themselves. They are led by strong entrepreneurs seeking to change their worlds. Their visions are expansive, and they are more interested in systemic change than simply organizational survival.
- Most of the systems are very good at optimizing available public and private resources. They aggressively explore how various programs from community banking to the federal government's New Markets Tax Credits can be used to advance mission priorities.
- All of the systems understand their markets. They know the cultures and communities where they labor. This deep knowledge allows them to build appropriate strategies that work with area cultures.
- Finally, most of these established systems engage in policy development and advocacy by advising public policymakers (ranging from local to federal) on how policies and programs can be more helpful in building entrepreneurial cultures in their landscapes.

A very positive thing is happening at the dawn of the twenty-first century. Interest and exploration of entrepreneurial development is showing up throughout North America and rural regions from Scotland to Western Australia. The experience of five of these promising new entrepreneurial initiatives shows the breadth of these innovations.

## Promising New Initiatives

Just six years ago, when the current research initiative began, very little new entrepreneurial activity could be identified. Yes, there were programs, organizations, and places that were experimenting, but the field was still emerging and was poorly defined. In only a half-decade, there has been an explosion of activity as demonstrated by five promising new initiatives that highlight this new movement in rural development:

1. Northern California
2. Nebraska's HomeTown Competitiveness
3. Georgia's Entrepreneurial Communities
4. North Carolina's Entrepreneurial Development Network
5. Fairfield, Iowa's Entrepreneurs Association Approach

## Northern California

A remarkable rural landscape located in Northern California is sometimes referred to as Redwood Country or the Lost Coast. It is rugged, beautiful, and isolated, with industries such as timber in decline and with economic restructuring a significant challenge. In Humboldt County, a group of partners, including the Humboldt Area Community Foundation, has come together to build an entrepreneurial economy and society. They are realizing very interesting successes. Now, this effort is branching out to include other communities in this region, with new partners, including Humboldt State University, the College of the Redwoods, local development groups, and local governments.[7]

The core strategy focuses on specific industries, such as timber, agriculture, or business services, and the coalition has taken the time to learn from and engage leaders in these industries. This learning process has brought deeper insight and relationships. The coalition, rooted in this knowledge, is working to build resources to address the needs of these industries and the businesses within them. Issues of capital access, a trained workforce, infrastructure, marketing, and branding are all part of the package being developed in this remote landscape in Northern California.

## Nebraska's HomeTown Competitiveness

The Northern Great Plains, a land of small farming communities, has been in demographic retreat since the 1930s and the Great Depression. Nebraska, for example, has 365 communities with an average size of approximately 350 residents.

HomeTown Competitiveness (HTC) was created to support sustainable, appropriate, and entrepreneurial development in communities and regions like those in the Northern Great Plains Region. HTC focuses on helping communities build core development capacity (i.e., leadership, financial resources, youth, and entrepreneurship). Started in 2000, HTC now has a positive track record in partner communities in Nebraska, Missouri, and Kansas.[8] The number of communities embracing and investing in HTC continues to grow, and bottom line results from one of the early adopting communities, Valley County, Nebraska, sheds light on the types of outcomes being realized. Figure 11.1 is from Valley County's recent development reports.

### VALLEY COUNTY
ECONOMIC DEVELOPMENT BOARD

*Accomplishments 2000-2006*

**Business Recruitment and Development**
- Recruitment of **Val-E-Ethanol, LLC** in 2005
- 35 FTEs – payroll of $1.4 million annually
- Additional 73 secondary jobs created
- $1.2 million increase in retail sales annually
- $500,000 in personal property taxes in 1st year
- Increase in corn price for local farmers

To help service the anticipated increase in truck traffic Trotter Truck & Tire now open. Arby's and Trotters Whoa & Go scheduled to open in July—50 employees.

Recruitment of **Timberline Total Solutions** in 2002. From 2002-2005, TTS paid more than $4.7 million in total payroll. Each year since it has opened, college students return and reunite with the community. In summer of 2005, 20 high school and college students employed.

Business Retention & Expansion visits in 2005 showed 20 PT and 2 FT positions were added from January-May. Capital Investment—21,400 square feet of business expansion.

Two new full-service banks added—Pathway Bank opened 2005 and BankFirst expanded to new location 2006.

**Sales Tax Loans**
14 Loans totaling $658,157 with 46 New and 31Retained Employees

| Sales Tax Loans | Loan Amt | # of Employees |
|---|---|---|
| 2003-01 | $ 40,000 | 3 New |
| 2003-02 | 200,000 | 14 New |
| 2003-03 | 62,000 | 6 Retained |
| 2004-02 | 17,500 | 9 Retained |
| 2005-01 | 50,000 | 18 New |
| 2005-02 | 30,000 | 2 Retained |
| 2005-03 | 40,000 | 1 New, 4 Retained |
| 2005-04 | 16,720 | 5 New |
| 2005-05 (2 loans) | 100,000 | 1 New, 8 Retained |
| 2006-01 | 70,000 | 2 New, 1 Retained |
| Total | $626,220 | |
| Re-Use Loans | 6,500 | 1 New, 1 Retained |
| 2004-01 | | |
| 2004-02 | 20,000 | (See above) |
| 2004-03 | 5,437 | 1 New |
| Total | $ 31,937 | |

**Figure 11.1.   Sample HTC Communit Outcomes Report Card**

## Increase in Retail Sales, Personal Income, & Per Capita Income

From 2000 to 2004, retail sales in Valley County increased 20% compared to the state average of 16.2%. From 2000 to 2003, personal income increased by 20.9% in Valley County compared to 10.8% statewide. In addition, during that same time period, per capita income in Valley County increased by 21.9% versus the 9.2% state average.

## Grants Received—$566,890
- Award of $17,000 BECA Grant for youth attraction in 2006.
- Award of $75,000 Kellogg Grant for Valley County HomeTown Competitiveness in 2005.
- (This was part of a $2 million grant awarded to Nebraska HomeTown Competitiveness.)
- Finalization of $399,890 in housing rehab grant for Valley County in 2005.
- Award of $50,000 USDA RBEG grant for technical assistance in 2004.
- $25,000 Planning Grant for Downtown Project in 2003

## HomeTown Competitiveness Pilot Community—2002 to Present
*Entrepreneurship*
- Business Boot Camp, 2004—8 businesses participated
- EDGE Class in 2005—14 businesses participated
- First Valley County Job Fair in 2006
- Job Service for employees and employers
- Completion of 140 business visitations with NE DED
- Business Development Coordinator position added in 2004
- Immediate response to all business prospect inquiries and business assistance requests.

*Youth*
- Youth Entrepreneurship Program/Business Fair at St. Mary's 2005
- Girl Scout Project 2006

*Leadership*
- Leadership Quest Program 4 years—87 graduates

*Charitable Assets*
- Establishment of Valley County Founders Club—67 members

## Awards &Speaking Engagements

Selected as 2005 Governor's Showcase Community; selected as the first "Certified Community" in Nebraska in 2005; speaker at numerous HomeTown Competitiveness Workshops and ED Conferences yearly

## Publications

New York Times, Nov. 14, 2005, "In Ord, Neb., the Latest Success Is 20 New Residents" USA Today, Omaha World Herald, Grand Island Independent, W.K. Kellogg Foundation Annual Report and Web site.

## Population Increase in Valley County (Number of Households—based on Kay Payne's surveys)

|  | 2006 | 2001 |  | Growth |
|---|---|---|---|---|
| Arcadia Area | 243 | 226 | 108% | 8% |
| North Loup Area | 243 | 218 | 111% | 11% |
| Ord Area | 1439 | 1426 | 101% | 1% |
| Total | 1925 | 1870 | 103% | 3% |

Valley County is clearly a leader with respect to the impacts realized through the HTC Development Framework, but other communities are beginning to see similar results. Typically, an HTC community moves through the following phases as they build an entrepreneurial economy:

- Discovery and strategy building
- Organizational development, including engagement of stakeholder groups increased development funding, and expanded professional staffing
- Early economic development results, including business saves, expansions, and attractions
- Early metrics, including increased business profitability, job creation, and new investment—eventually, there will be more job creation, business expansions, macro income growth, and tax base improvements.

### Georgia's Entrepreneurial Communities

Rural Georgia is the land of industrial development and attraction, but one of its greatest entrepreneurial champions is a former Chamber of Commerce executive. Don Betts and other leaders have built a remarkable local and statewide entrepreneurial strategy. At the state level, there is now an Office of Entrepreneurship and Small Business and regionally there are now a series of sector-focused innovation centers.

Locally, Georgia has created the "Entrepreneurial Friendly Communities" program. An economic development transformation is occurring across Georgia as rural communities and regions add entrepreneurship to their portfolio of development tools.[9] Currently, the Georgia effort focuses on increasing community awareness with engaged communities, building strategies and capacity. Over time, indicators of bottom line economic impacts related to business growth, job creation, tax base expansion, firms moving to external markets, and business competitiveness will become apparent.

### Entrepreneurial Development Network in North Carolina

Parts of North Carolina are booming with the new economy while other regions continue to struggle with the loss of textile and apparel manufacturers. Like most other states, the state is in a profound economic transition.

Rural North Carolina has benefited from a strong partner over the years, namely the North Carolina Rural Economic Development Center (Rural Center) (see www.ncruralcenter.org). The Rural Center carefully researches an issue before launching a new initiative as was the case several years ago when it began to explore entrepreneurship as a rural development strategy.

The research laid the groundwork for a new initiative starting at the Rural Center, but which now embraces development partners, including the state government, higher education, and local communities.

From the ground up, North Carolina is building an entrepreneurial development system based on lessons learned from across the nation during the past twenty to thirty years. Impressive progress has been made, but this is an emergent effort with more to come over time (Bauer 2003). North Carolina has proven that there is considerable community interest in entrepreneurship. They have trained hundreds of community leaders and developers. They have seeded innovative initiatives, allowing communities to experiment with possible strategies. It is still too early to document bottom line impacts, but the early adopters are building strategies and capacity. Another year should begin to show evidence of impact in North Carolina.

*Fairfield, Iowa's Entrepreneurs Association*

Fairfield, Iowa (pop. 9,500), is a small regional trade center community located in southeastern Iowa with corn, hogs, and manufacturing representing the economic mainstays. An informal group of local entrepreneurs started the Fairfield Entrepreneurs Association (FEA) in the early 1990s (Chojnowski 2006).

The FEA has created an informal but strategic support system for area entrepreneurs based mainly on networking. Many factors have contributed to Fairfield's success in becoming the "entrepreneurial capital of Iowa," but this networked approach to identifying and matching entrepreneurs to mentors, peer groups, and resources has realized significant development (Bauer 2004a). FEA does not offer established entrepreneurship programs; rather, it has built a "networked environment" where entrepreneurs can find other entrepreneurs with insight, answers, and resources.

Fairfield is like a large family with much business expertise. Want to go into business? Do not bother to go to a state workshop; instead find someone in the family with the right expertise to help you down this path. Entrepreneur forums foster learning on key topics such as marketing, but, more importantly, they allow folks to become acquainted and build their own resource networks.

Obviously, many other innovative, promising, and emergent entrepreneurial initiatives exist throughout North America and the world. In fact, there are too many for the small RUPRI research team to even track, let alone document, in the time available. Those interested in exploring entrepreneurship further should take the time to not only research these historic and promising initiatives but also visit some of these places. Often, only through visitation is it possible to fully understand reasons why these efforts are achieving results.

## Community Resources

The past decade has seen an explosion of new resources that can help communities become more entrepreneurial. Some of these resources are highlighted in the next section.

### RUPRI Center for Rural Entrepreneurship

The RUPRI Center for Rural Entrepreneurship was created mainly to provide a one-stop shop for community entrepreneurship information. Several community-friendly resources that can help local leaders in pursuing a successful entrepreneurship initiative are as follows:

The Website (www.energizingentrepreneurs.org) compiles a great deal of information on local entrepreneurship together in one location. It is free, is updated regularly, and it contains easy-to-use information with links to the other resources discussed in this chapter.

The *Rural Entrepreneurship Newsletter* is also free and is available electronically every three weeks. It contains information organized in short sections that allows for a quick review of important topics related to entrepreneurship development. This newsletter provides cutting-edge applied research, a calendar of upcoming events, and, most importantly, electronic links that connect readers to potentially interesting resources.

*Energizing Entrepreneurs: Charting a Course for Rural Communities.* This community guidebook is a serious resource for practitioners. It can serve as a community guide in building a strategy, and it complements the Website where additional information, tools, stories, and other resources can be located quickly. This guidebook provides a comprehensive, easy to read, and logical approach for community leaders seeking to pursue entrepreneurship as a development strategy. The book is supported by a Website, www.energizing entrepreneurs.org, with real-time and more in-depth information.

## National Practitioners Network

Interested practitioners can join (also free) the National Practitioners Network. This network can help connect practitioners with others undertaking similar work. This informal network helps users find answers to specific questions, meet colleagues, find mentors, and become connected. Ultimately, this approach will enable people in very remote places interested in entrepreneurship to be on the inside of the field through critical connections with other practitioners and resources.

## Jurisdictional Groups

Many national associations address entrepreneurship, and groups such as the National Governors Association, National Association of Development Organizations, and the Appalachian Regional Commission have all done excellent work and provide valuable resources for communities. The following groups have especially useful materials:

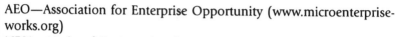

- AEO—Association for Enterprise Opportunity (www.microenterprise-works.org)
- NBIA—National Business Incubation Association (www.nbia.org)
- SBA/SBDCs—U.S. Small Business Administration (www.sba.gov/) and your state's Small Business Development Centers (www.asbdc-us.org/)

Contact information for these and other resources is available on the National Center Website listed above (www.energizingentrepreneurs.org).

## Think Tanks

Many research organizations and foundations have picked up the entrepreneurship call. Four organizations deserve special attention:

1 The Ewing Marion Kauffman Foundation of Kansas City
2 The Edward Lowe Foundation of Michigan
3 CFED (formerly the Corporation for Enterprise Development)
4 The W. K. Kellogg Foundation of Michigan

Again, contact information can be found on the National Center's Website (www.energizingentrepreneurs.org). For information on youth entrepreneurship, a special resource page on the Web can provide guidance.

## Resources Closer to Home

Chances are that many resources to help in launching entrepreneurship efforts exist closer to home. Contacts with the regional or state Small Business Development Center, Cooperative Extension, regional universities or colleges and/or state economic development agencies can be very helpful. Likewise, many utilities and trade groups, such as financial institutions, can also help. Entrepreneurship may represent the most profitable basis for development in the twenty-first century. Communities seeking to explore ways for entrepreneurship to make a difference in the local economy and society are strongly advised to do their homework. Invest time and money exploring research and gaining a deeper understanding of how entrepreneurship can help your community develop. Look around and explore communities in regions that seem further ahead of others. Learn from others who are pioneering entrepreneurship strategies. Finally, make room in your community for a shared discovery process that enables a broad cross-section of the community to become part of *your* strategy.[10]

## CONCLUSION

Thomas Friedman (2005) in *The World Is Flat* makes a powerful case for how a globalizing economy and society are impacting all of us. Rural America ranges from attractive landscapes adjacent to growing metropolitan areas to very isolated and challenged places in the Northern Great Plains. Development opportunities in a world economy and society will vary greatly depending on which rural region one calls home.

Whether you are in a struggling rural community or one experiencing growth opportunities, the RUPRI field research supports the view that entrepreneurship may offer one of the best strategies for sustainable and appropriate development. Investing in local people and supporting their entrepreneurial talents can enable a more diversified and prosperous economy and healthier society to emerge over time. This chapter provides many resources that can help community leaders in their pursuit of effective entrepreneurial programs and initiatives, keeping in mind that local action is essential to achieving results.

## NOTES

1. For more information, contact www.kauffman.org.
2. For more information, contact www.rupri.org.
3. Other support was provided by the Nebraska Community Foundation in Lincoln Nebraska; Partnership for Rural America; the National Rural Development Partnership; and the National Commission on Entrepreneurship.
4. Members of the RUPRI field team included Don Macke, Deborah Markley, Erik Pages, and Jay Kayne. Numerous other individuals and organizations greatly contributed to this work.
5. Information on Valley County and HTC can be obtained through the HTC Website at www.htcnebraska.org.
6. A copy of the Center for Rural Entrepreneurship/EntreWorks case study of the Kansas Sirolli Project can be obtained by contacting Taina Radenslaben at taina@ruraleship.org.
7. For more information on Northern California, check out www.ruraleship.org, the Library, and Eship Across America/California.
8. Additional information on HomeTown Competitiveness or HTC can be found at www.htcnebraska.org.

9. For more information on Georgia, see www.energizingentrepreneurs.org/content/chapter5.php?id=241&sel=3.

10. Additional information on community strategies can be found at www.energizingentrepreneurs.org.

## REFERENCES

Aspen Institute. 1996. Measuring Community Capacity Building—A Workbook in Progress for Rural Communities. Version 3–96. Washington, DC: Aspen Institute, Rural Economic Policy Program.

Bauer, Lisa. 2003. *Institute for Rural Entrepreneurship in North Carolina*. RUPRI Center for Rural Entrepreneurship. www.energizingentrepreneurs.org/content/chapter_5/stories/1_000092.pdf (January 29, 2007).

Bauer, Lisa. 2004a. *Northern Initiatives*. RUPRI Center for Rural Entrepreneurship. www.energizingentrepreneurs.org/content/chapter_5/stories/1_000096.pdf (January 29, 2007).

Bauer, Lisa. 2004b. *Iowa Town Booms in Eastern Ways*. RUPRI Center for Rural Entrepreneurship. www.energizingentrepreneurs.org/content/chapter_6/stories/1_000208.pdf (January 29, 2007).

Bauer, Lisa. 2005. *Economic Gardening in Littleton Colorado*. RUPRI Center for Rural Entrepreneurship. www.energizingentrepreneurs.org/content/chapter_6/stories/1_000114.pdf (January 29, 2007).

Chojnowski, Burt. 2006. Open-source rural entrepreneurial development. *Rural Research Report* 17(2). Macomb: Illinois Institute for Rural Affairs, Western Illinois University.

Friedman, Thomas L. 2005. *The world is flat: A brief history of the twenty-first century.* New York: Farrar, Straus and Giroux.

Markley, Deborah, and David Barkley. 2003. *Development of an entrepreneurial support organization: The case of the Kentucky Highlands Investment Corporation.* Lincoln, NE: RUPRI Center for Rural Entrepreneurship.

Macke, Don, and Deborah Markley. 2004. *Energizing entrepreneurs—The practice.* Lincoln, NE: RUPRI Center for Rural Entrepreneurship.

Macke, Don, and Deborah Markley. 2005. *Understanding rural America.* Lincoln, NE: RUPRI Center for Rural Entrepreneurship.

Rowley, Thomas D. 2003. *Just don't call it entrepreneurial.* Columbia, MO: Rural Policy Research Institute.

# 12

## Transforming Rural Economies through Entrepreneurial Networks: A Case Study

*June Holley*

While support for individual entrepreneurs—such as state venture funds and incentives for technology firms—may be effective in urban centers, such approaches are unlikely to be sufficient to transform many of our troubled rural economies into places of prosperity. What strategies and policy suggestions can we offer that address the depth of the economic restructuring that is needed in rural regions?

One approach that increasing number of scholars are exploring draws from complexity theory, network analysis and recent studies of innovation (Kauffman 1995; Rogers 2003; Watts 2003; Axelrod and Cohen 2000; McDaniel and Driebe 2005). These theories describe a set of dynamic processes that, with small initial investment, can generate powerful forces capable of shifting rural regions with little business activity into prosperous entrepreneurial regions. Rather than focus on the individual entrepreneur in isolation, this approach emphasizes the importance of the relationships between entrepreneurs and supportive organizations in the region and the capacity of these entities to self-organize in ways that result in economic advantage both for the entrepreneur and the region (Cooke, Bockholt, and Todtling 2000; Haragon 2003; Kelly 1998; Saxenian 2000; Rosen 2000; Holley 2005; Krebs and Holley 2004).

In an earlier chapter, Dabson noted that regions are now the critical unit of economic activity and entrepreneurship and innovation are key in the process of mobilizing local assets into regional advantage. He also discussed the various types of entrepreneurs and how their efforts must be supported. Hustedde discussed the importance of an entrepreneurial environment within a region to foster local business start-ups and expansions. Lyons and others have stressed the idea that a systematic approach is needed to meet the needs of various entrepreneurs. Markley described various ways to finance entrepreneurial ventures and the importance of involving local financial institutions.

This chapter uses a case study to explore the factors previously described as essential to successful entrepreneurship and the dynamics of regional entrepreneurial economies in greater depth. A case study format is used to the transformative processes that occurred in one region—Appalachian Ohio—and outlines the policy implications that can be drawn from that region's successful experimentation.

The chapter explores the intriguing changes that occurred in this region during the last decade, from the initial formation of a specialty food cluster to the current operation of the Appalachian Ohio Regional Entrepreneurship Network. The first section describes how a local economic development organization implemented an entrepreneurial strategy to add value to the region's agricultural assets through the organization of a cluster—a system of support for specialty food entrepreneurs. This cluster-formation consisted of three dynamic processes: (1) building networks, (2) encouraging innovation, and (3) involving many groups in collaborative efforts.

The next section describes how the success in the specialty food sector became the foundation for the development of a regional innovation economy. The major vehicle for this transformation was the emergence of a regional flavor cluster where artisans and food businesses joined with tourism bureaus and other community organizations to combine their offerings and open large regional markets. The final section explores the potential of two regional entrepreneurship networks to expand the impact of local successes through policy and learning.

## A SPECIALTY FOOD CLUSTER EMERGES
## IN APPALACHIAN OHIO

Like many other local economies during the 1990s, Appalachian Ohio lost businesses and jobs as lower cost international suppliers made Ohio businesses, especially small manufacturers, less competitive. For example, in less than a decade, Athens County (pop. 60,000), saw the demise of three grocery stores, a Japanese seat belt manufacturer, a plastics manufacturer, and a shoe factory, resulting in the loss of more than 1,000 jobs. However, a small group in the region began to explore options that would provide jobs and wealth less susceptible to these large international forces.

### A Kitchen Incubator

In 1992, a group of farmers approached the Appalachian Center for Economic Networks (ACEnet), a regional nonprofit that operated a small business incubator and was organizing business networks to increase jobs in the region. The farm group wanted to add value to their farm products but was overwhelmed by state regulations for food processing. An ACEnet staff member had recently attended a National Business Incubation Association (NBIA) conference and had learned about a *Kitchen Incubator* project in Spokane, Washington (the first of its kind in the country). Kitchen Incubators are processing facilities where entrepreneurs can rent the use of a wide range of equipment—a bottling line, ovens, or catering space—to process their products. After hearing the idea, the farmers agreed to work in collaboration with ACEnet to set up a Kitchen Incubator in their community that would help them become specialty food entrepreneurs.

Kitchen Incubators are an example of facilities that focus on providing services to groups of entrepreneurs in a specific cluster. Other cluster-focused incubators work with artisans, technology businesses, or wood products businesses. They usually provide shared equipment, offices or workspaces, storage, and access to technical assistance related to that cluster. These services mean that an entrepreneur does not have to invest scarce start-up dollars in equipment or real estate but can use those funds for working capital and more rapid expansion.[1]

Kitchen Incubator initiatives have the greatest impact on rural economies when they combine low-cost access to equipment with three other key services: (1) identifying needs of entrepreneurs and working with others in the community to create new services to meet those needs; (2) building networks among entrepreneurs, so they begin to collaborate to gain economies of scale; and (3) providing innovation services and market access so that entrepreneurs generate substantial sales and profits.

During the three years needed to access funds, find a building, and complete required renovations to develop a regional Kitchen Incubator, ACEnet staff held literally dozens of *joint design sessions* to gather input. These design groups—which included farmers, food artists, Ohio University's food service director, food specialists from Cooperative Extension, local grocery store managers, and consultants—provided input and ideas that were used to design the floor plan, select equipment, and determine rates. The diversity of the design groups enabled potential food entrepreneurs to build relationships with many individuals and experts who could help them succeed with business ventures. The relationships formed during this design process were the beginning of the *regional network development* that became so critical in the coming years: dozens of individuals from many different types of organizations and businesses got to know and trust each other and learned the basic skills of successful collaboration.

The resulting ACEnet Kitchen Incubator facility was a 12,000 square foot space with 3,000 square feet of processing space. One room contained equipment for bottling jarred products; another was filled with ovens, stoves, and preparation tables; and two smaller spaces were reserved for drying and cooling products. An even larger space was used for storage and had palletized areas that entrepreneurs could rent to store bulk items such as jars or raw materials.

The facility also contained large walk-in coolers and freezers where entrepreneurs rented sections or shelves. A large area next to the two loading docks served as a staging area where finished products were palletized to be picked up by distributors. Since there were usually at least several trucks at the loading docks, this area became a *networking hub* where entrepreneurs congregated, shared news, and discussed joint projects. Such informal networking spaces proved to be essential in fostering self-organized collaborations among the entrepreneurs.

The front of the incubator included business offices rented by several entrepreneurs, a library with trade journals and regulations, a copier and fax, and the offices of ACEnet's three-person technical assistance staff. Eventually, the facility became self-sufficient; rental fees covered the costs of operations.

### What Is a Cluster?

ACEnet decided not to limit its services to the food manufacturers who used the Kitchen Incubator. Instead, ACEnet would serve the entire specialty food and agricultural cluster in the Appalachian region, including food manufacturers with their own facilities, locally owned restaurants, and farmers interested in exploring specialty crops. The incubator also included businesses that provided services (such as graphic designers and accounting services), markets (from larger grocery stores to convenience stores), and distributors.

Finally, the cluster included many nonprofits and support agencies such as the Small Business Development Center and Cooperative Extension Service. ACEnet helped them to customize their services to more effectively serve food-related businesses. Defining the specialty food cluster to include food producers, their markets, and organizations that supported their success was an important step. From the start, the cluster included many of the services entrepreneurs would need for continued growth and development.

Most of the partners became engaged in the cluster through involvement in one of the many projects organized to develop a new *cluster infrastructure*—a set of permanent services or programs that enabled more food cluster entrepreneurs to start-up and then continue to expand over the years. Examples of cluster infrastructure, described in a later section, include festivals, regional brands, and an innovation fund. Over the years, ACEnet introduced new approaches gleaned from conferences, the Internet, or from the vast network of relationships with individuals around the country. In this way, several subclusters, such as agritourism and freshwater shrimp, were formed.

## Cluster-Focused Services

During the three years required to complete the Kitchen Incubator, ACEnet staff set up a basic array of *cluster-focused services* that dramatically increased business survival rates. The most crucial services were all intended to ensure that entrepreneurs operated at the high end of markets, where they could maximize profits.

### Product Innovation

From previous research[2] ACEnet knew that businesses developing new products and processes tended to grow more rapidly every year, create more and higher quality jobs, and be more resilient during economic downturns. Because of these findings, *product and process innovation* was a central part of the technical assistance program provided by ACEnet. The results have been impressive—more than fifty new businesses started each year, and annual sales of existing food businesses grew by an average of 45 to 65 percent during the past two years.

The most successful of the twenty or so salsa businesses participating in the ACEnet network (each offering specialty salsa with unusual flavors such as apple verde or blackberry chipolte), for example, could charge three to ten times the price of typical grocery salsas. Since the ingredients cost only minimally more than those of commodity brands, the products made the businesses very profitable, often at an early stage of business development.

Somewhat surprisingly, entrepreneurs found that higher prices often increased rather than decreased the volume of sales. Consumers desiring high-quality, innovative, authentic regional products represent one of the fastest growing market niches in the food industry, and higher prices often signal to consumers that a product fits this profile.

Much of what makes products high-end is appearance, so ACEnet staff identified several graphic artists willing to develop appealing labels and introduced them to the entrepreneurs. Initially, the entrepreneurs hesitated to pay the cost of graphic design. Finally, Crumbs Bakery, one of the businesses in the incubator, agreed to work on a new label for a tofu pasta. While working on the label in the incubator conference room, staff encouraged other entrepreneurs to come in, meet the designer, and give feedback on the design. The resulting label was stunning, and product sales increased dramatically—even though the pasta was now being sold for twice the price of the product with the old look. Even more exciting was the fact that in the next three months, 14 previously resistant businesses suddenly decided to adopt new labels and appearances for their products.

The production of food is fraught with issues of safety and shelf life. ACEnet staff used this need for caution to introduce entrepreneurs to the benefits of food science. Here, ACEnet linked entrepreneurs with food scientists from university programs and consulting businesses who not only worked with them to develop safe production processes but assisted with a wide range of difficult issues, from separation in salad dressings to flavor deterioration. Tackling these issues gave entrepreneurs the knowledge essential to ongoing product innovation and taught them the rewards of using experts to improve product quality.

ACEnet's food production staff was extremely innovative and continually encouraged entrepreneurs to conduct extensive trials on new product ideas, often using feedback from other entrepreneurs and staff in the incubator, which, in turn, increased those individuals' appreciation for the nuances of product quality and innovation. Finally, through workshops and the food-net group e-mail, ACEnet provided information on trends—not just in the specialty food industry, but also in related areas such as wellness and health, resulting in several product breakthroughs such as the development of health-oriented teas and heart healthy soy pasta.

This spread of new practices is an example of the many vital *innovation diffusion processes* that occurred in the specialty food cluster. Because the network of entrepreneurs was very effective in spreading word of successes— such as those with high quality labels—a whole set of new practices that increased sales and profitability were quickly adopted by a large percentage of the entrepreneurs, eventually creating a *culture of quality and innovation.*

*Networking Entrepreneurs*

The other critical cluster service involved building *networks* among entrepreneurs. ACEnet staff spent considerable time listening to entrepreneurs—often in informal conversations as they met in the halls of the incubator. Staff identified needs and opportunities and then, rather than try to meet that need themselves, introduced entrepreneurs to people who could help them solve the problem or explore the opportunity. When one entrepreneur needed a way to remove seeds and bitter skin from a local fruit (pawpaw), ACEnet staff brought in a food scientist from the Ohio State University who found the appropriate machine, which he lent to ACEnet to use for this purpose.

ACEnet staff also encouraged entrepreneurs to share information and resources with each other. One of the powerful dynamics of successful entrepreneurial networks is the use of *complex reciprocity,* or what anthropologists call a *gift economy,* to keep knowledge and resources circulating in a way that results in extraordinary economic value. First, staff share generously—providing important information about trends, markets, people, and so forth. Entrepreneurs quickly translate this information into economic gain; they buy a piece of used equipment for much less than they had expected, they draw on the know-how of an experienced entrepreneur to develop superior products, or they gain entrée into a large grocery chain very quickly because someone shares the name of a key contact.

Next, staff encourage entrepreneurs to share generously among themselves, knowing that this behavior primes the pump of exchange and results in much more knowledge and resource sharing by others back to them. It is amazing how quickly the transition to this type of mutual sharing behavior occurs, even though entrepreneurs continue to compete fiercely with each other in many ways.

Entrepreneurs quickly learn how to identify those areas where it makes sound financial sense to cooperate. With staff assistance initially, they begin to form *collaborations*. At first, many of these are *twosies*. For example, two entrepreneurs agree to jointly purchase jars to obtain a much lower price or two entrepreneurs agree to take turns driving their products to a nearby city for delivery. Joint activities tend to be low risk at first, involving little or no money and with little chance of adverse results if things go wrong. Entrepreneurs use these activities to test other entrepreneurs—they quickly find who they can trust for which activities. For example, one entrepreneur may be an excellent partner on product innovation but may not be able to deliver products reliably. ACEnet staff help process the results of the joint activities so that entrepreneurs realize that almost everyone can be trusted—but perhaps only to deliver on certain activities. This ability to trust others selectively means that many more people can be a resource.

As the cumulative knowledge about an individual's capacities spreads around the network, a huge informal knowledge bank is formed. Entrepreneurs need only go to a fellow entrepreneur or two to find the name of a person appropriate to join with them to make some activity or scheme more likely to succeed and more financially viable. Of course, some people are more likely than others to know what is happening in the larger network, and entrepreneurs contact them first when they need information. As entrepreneurs gain the skills needed for successful collaboration—accurate assessment, negotiation and clarification of expectations, dealing with misunderstandings, and other issues—they start to form larger collaborations that can really have a substantial positive impact on their business. For example, the unit price drops substantially when six or eight entrepreneurs join in purchasing a tractor trailer load of jars.

Crucial to the building of these networks are *networking hubs* where entrepreneurs naturally meet each other. They are sufficiently unstructured spaces so that entrepreneurs have the time to share information and negotiate deals. The design of incubators and other business assistance offices must consider the importance of connections. For example, as mentioned, the loading docks at ACEnet are an important networking spot. Restaurants run by ACEnet-assisted entrepreneurs have also become effective networking hubs, where entrepreneurs delivering supplies encounter entrepreneurs enjoying a meal.

The *tipping point* of these entrepreneurial networks occurred when ACEnet staff began to hear about dozens of collaborations that had received no assistance from them. At this point, the economy was *self-organizing*—entrepreneurs were able to identify needs and quickly draw together similarly interested entrepreneurs to meet those needs.

Contrast this environment with the more typical training approach to microenterprise development, where a local organization provides six or eight weeks of training in starting a business, then usually has little contact with entrepreneurs later. In a networked approach, staff provide technical assistance in customized small doses as questions and issues arise, ensuring that the assistance is immediately applicable. Staff have long-term relationships with the entrepreneurs—they not only help a business start-up but work with entrepreneurs to continue business growth and profitability.

Finally, because resources for technical assistance staff are limited, ACEnet works to ensure that more experienced entrepreneurs assist those with less experience. Why do experienced entrepreneurs do this? They know that these same entrepreneurs will soon be valuable partners in joint ventures, and they see their mentoring as a long-term investment. In addition, they tend to enjoy helping others and knowing that their actions will build a stronger local economy.

The result is that more businesses survive and prosper, adding jobs and wealth to the region. ACEnet currently assists almost 200 food entrepreneurs a year, and the network includes many more organizations that are actively engaged with other businesses in ways that enhance their productivity and profits.

## High-Impact Collaborations

Peer networks among entrepreneurs are a powerful force, but they are seldom able to coordinate the development of new services, programs, and institutions that can dramatically increase business success and accelerate business growth. These more complex collaborations require the involvement of a wide range of area organizations—from banks and chambers of commerce to cooperative extension and tourism bureaus—that commit to becoming *entrepreneur support organizations*. This means that they are willing to work with others in their region to create a *cluster infrastructure* and an *acceleration infrastructure*.

A cluster infrastructure focuses on a single cluster, such as specialty food or tourism, while an acceleration infrastructure helps entrepreneurs continue to expand their business and can help entrepreneurs in many clusters by dealing with large gaps in the system. For example, lack of access to capital is a huge barrier to business growth in Appalachian Ohio, where banks are lending to small businesses at a rate two to four times less than the national average.[3] Realizing this problem, the region collaborated by creating new institutions and services to ensure that entrepreneurs could access the kinds of capital they needed: ACEnet formed a high risk loan fund; Ohio University supported the start-up of a venture fund with more than a dozen investors; several organizations worked together to identify angel investors; and the Oak Hill Bank applied for and received a New Market Tax Credit, enabling it to set up a low interest loan fund for distressed communities. Although each project had a lead organization, virtually all of these new institutions resulted from collaborations among many regional organizations.

The regional capacity to collaborate was built over many years. The first collaborations focused on the Kitchen Incubator, where area organizations learned to listen to the needs of entrepreneurs and share their expertise effectively in joint design sessions. Then, a series of small joint projects emerged. For example, during the development period of the Kitchen Incubator, Hocking College—a regional technical school—allowed entrepreneurs to have access to its culinary kitchen to begin prototyping products. Local newspapers worked closely with staff and journalism students to generate frequent stories about food entrepreneurs. Then, projects became larger: entrepreneurs joined with local volunteers to develop a regional brand—*Food We Love*—and urged more than eighty regional stores to set up Buy Local displays; and several communities joined with entrepreneurs and area organizations on festivals, most notably the Pawpaw Festival and the Chili Pepper Festival. Finally, groups of organizations began to help in the formation of subclusters. The agritourism cluster, for example, brought together tourism bureaus from several counties that worked with ACEnet on workshops to help farmers set up farm-based tourism activities—such as corn mazes and hayrides—to supplement their income.

ACEnet partnered with Ohio State Cooperative Extension on workshops for farmers interested in the production of freshwater shrimp, then worked closely with the health department to approve the Kitchen Incubator shrimp and fish processing. Hocking College then joined this cluster to help with a Jambalaya Jam at the Hocking Festival to celebrate the first successful harvest. Currently, area organizations and entrepreneurs are involved in dozens of joint projects every year, ranging from festivals and marketing brochures to new sources of capital and regional Websites.

## THE FORMATION OF A REGIONAL FLAVOR CLUSTER

### What Is a Regional Innovation Economy?

Clearly, a new type of economy was emerging in Appalachian Ohio. This economy was based on a subtle shift by a substantial number of businesses—especially restaurants and specialty food businesses—from being *local* businesses to becoming *regional* businesses. What made the businesses regional? A regional business tended to have a passionate, local customer base but also drew from larger nearby urban centers (such as, in this case, Columbus and Cleveland). These customers often felt that they were part of the business, offering suggestions, lending money at less than market rates, and acting as informal marketers.

In addition, the regional businesses were distinctive and authentic—they used local ingredients; they offered exciting, innovative products and services; and their owners and employees were known for their engaging personalities. They networked with other area businesses, which were suppliers or worked with them on joint purchasing or marketing. They often used innovative technology to streamline business processes and to connect more effectively with customers. They helped create a more supportive environment for themselves and other regional businesses.

Casa Nueva, a worker-owned Mexican restaurant in Athens, is an excellent example. This business not only purchases almost 90 percent of its raw materials from area farmers and food processors, it highlights this fact in its menu. The staff develops a new menu, full of culinary surprises, for each season. In addition, Casa Nueva manufactures many of its salsas, which are sold throughout the region. Casa Nueva has a devoted customer base that stays in touch through the business' Website. When these customers move to other cities, they often demand that local stores carry Casa Nueva products.

Casa Nueva plays an important role in expanding the entrepreneurial economy, particularly the arena of the cultural creatives, which Richard Florida points out is a magnet for a high quality workforce (Florida 2002). For example, the restaurant displays the works of local artists, and the cantina provides a venue for area musicians and poets. Casa Nueva helped form an Independent Restaurant Association that organizes joint purchasing, supports local growers, and donates to local charities. The restaurant is now one of the most profitable in town, employing more than eighty workers, many of them owners as well.

In the past century, urban areas have become increasingly isolated from surrounding rural communities, with urban and rural commerce and culture seen as vastly different and mutually exclusive. The new regional innovation economy is healing this unnatural divide. This economy began with the notion of buying food locally, a behavior that has morphed into a movement, with sales of locally grown products experiencing growth rates higher than that of organic foods. Urban residents quickly realized that Buy Local meant not just purchasing food grown in their city, but purchasing food products from the rural regions around the city as well. When a region includes one or more urban areas and the surrounding rural areas, an individual's regional purchases can become a substantial percentage of his or her spending. Plus, dollars spent in a region tend to stay in the region, circulating again and again and creating local jobs and local wealth. Regional economies usually transport goods less than 200 or 300 miles, unlike typical food or clothing items which often travel several thousand miles.[4]

Regions become wealthy through two major drivers: (1) exporting outside their region to bring in income and (2) increasing the circulation cycles of regional dollars. By paying attention to the development of the internal economy of the region as well as its external economy, communities can become more vibrant and resilient. An added bonus is that the collaboration required to develop a regional innovation economy will also increase the capacity of communities to creatively confront the energy, health, and diversity issues that seem certain to be major challenges as this century unfolds.

## Culture of Innovation

Many of the emerging regional businesses are *innovation leaders*. They tend to be extremely innovative—developing new products and processes every year—which often sets them on a powerful growth trajectory. This innovation is not only important for business success, but it helps create a *culture of innovation* that sets up a virtuous cycle of economic health and prosperity.

Only 5 to 15 percent of businesses are innovators in most regions; however, when more than 50 percent of the businesses in a region become innovators (usually by connecting the innovators to less innovative entrepreneurs), the economy becomes increasingly prosperous and resilient (Audretsch 2003). In such an economy, the top performers among the regional businesses—in all sectors—will often move into the traded or export economy.

Prosperity does not come simply from high tech businesses; it occurs when there are breakthrough businesses in many sectors. For example, restaurants move into the *traded economy* by manufacturing some of their food offerings. A dry cleaning business may innovate by developing a new green process for cleaning and have the potential to develop a national franchise. A beauty parlor may have developed hair care training programs for employees that could be offered nationally. In rural communities or urban cores with few biotech or information technology firms, economic developers can still build a regional innovation economy by helping existing local businesses become master innovators.

## Developing a Regional Flavor

But how does a culture of innovation develop? How does an area build a sense that it is a distinct and dynamic region? The story of AORIC and Regional Flavor offer some clues.

Several years ago, several organizations—ACEnet, Rural Action, the Foundation for Appalachian Ohio, the Ohio Arts Council, the Ohio University Voinovich Center, and People for Adams County Tomorrow (PACT)—formed the Appalachian Ohio Regional Investment Coalition (AORIC) to explore this shift from local entrepreneurship to a dynamic regional economy. AORIC designed a strategy called *Regional Flavor*. The idea was to link food entrepreneurs with artisans and entrepreneurs in tourism-related businesses with the hope that they would—through dozens of collaborative projects—develop a distinctive and attractive sense of the region. They saw Regional Flavor emerging from the area's natural and heritage assets: the beautiful parks and recreational amenities, the many musical venues, the rich history related to the Underground Railroad and the coal fields, and the work of skilled artisans using local woods.

When local assets are combined into unique sets of experiences, activities, and stories, the region becomes very appealing: residents become more strongly committed to the region, others are drawn to move to the area, and visitors to the region develop long-term emotional bonds. This process increases economic activity as residents purchase more regionally made products and services; new arrivals bring much-needed skills and resources; and visitors return again and again, spending dollars on each visit. The region, as well as the businesses, become more innovative and entrepreneurial.

*Quilt Barns and Birding Trails*

When AORIC tried to identify examples of Regional Flavor projects already working, they discovered an amazing collaboration in Adams and Brown Counties, two relatively isolated counties in western Appalachian Ohio. For years, bird watchers (one of the most prosperous of all tourist groups) had been coming to Appalachian Ohio to watch bird migrations, but they spent very little money in the region.

The local Audubon Society decided to produce a brochure and map that would include birding spots but would also point out retail shops and bed and breakfast operations. In a serendipity typical of regional innovation economies, this project developed a unique twist. One board member had a mother who was part of a quilting group. This group had the novel idea that area artisans might paint large quilt patterns on local barns. If the brochure included the location of the barns, they reasoned, the birders might take more time to meander through the counties and spend even more dollars in the region.

A public relations firm in nearby Cincinnati embraced the quilt painting idea. They donated the design for a map/brochure, and 30,000 copies were distributed to nearby urban centers. The project was such a success that several barn owners set up gift shops in their barns, and artisans began to make quilt puzzles and potholders to sell in local stores along the quilt barn trail. The local bed and breakfast added cabins and a restaurant to meet demand. Thus, from the unlikely partnership of birds and barns emerged a lovely sense of Regional Flavor and significantly increased entrepreneurial activity.

### Yellowroot: A Regional Innovation Fund

Seeing how a small amount of money and a somewhat unusual collaboration had catalyzed this Regional Flavor project, AORIC decided to set up a new but promising piece of infrastructure whose purpose would be to jumpstart this kind of collaborative innovation. The concept was a small but powerful *innovation fund* called the Yellowroot Fund. This fund provided small seed funds—from $300 to $3,000—to projects that involved both entrepreneurs and at least two supporting organizations.

During the past few years, several dozen projects received money from the fund. These projects ranged from a mural corridor project—a joint brochure by five collaborating counties that included 17 large outdoor murals in communities around the region—to a grant to replicate the quilt barn map in another part of the region. The idea was to offer seed funds to many newly formed collaborative groups so that they could start an experiment. If they could succeed at something small, the theory went, they would be able to attract the attention of funders with larger pools of funds and take the project to scale. This in fact happened as the quilt barn concept spread rapidly throughout the region, and as several projects used their successes to leverage substantial additional dollars.

Several projects began to create what are being called *microregions*. For example, a group of nearly a dozen small former coal mining towns spanning the borders of three counties became the Little Cities of the Black Diamonds. A collaboration of several small nonprofits and area artisans, restaurants, and bed and breakfasts joined to develop a series of tours, some highlighting the region's coal legacy (the CIO of the AFL-CIO was first organized here), while others visited artisan shops or nature trails. The Yellowroot Fund supported a brochure describing these tours.

As the experiment with Regional Flavor progressed, AORIC began to realize that Regional Flavor does not mean one consistent, packaged theme
imposed on the entire region, as often happens with regional brands generated by outside consultants. Regional Flavor, instead, emerges from the
crafting of dozens of microregions, such as the Little Cities of the Black Diamonds, linked by cross-cutting themes such as the heritage mural corridor
or the Underground Railroad activities.

These small projects are powerful, but often neglected, ingredients in an
entrepreneurial regional economy. They create the foundation for transformation of the economy in several ways. First, the projects build new leadership. People involved in these projects gain new project development
skills and find that they can make important things happen. At the same
time, the project participants learn to work together and build trust and understanding. Perhaps most importantly, they learn that when they see an
opportunity or a problem, they can join with others to do something that
makes a difference for themselves and their communities. Once people succeed on a few small projects, they tend to become more ambitious and start
tackling larger and larger opportunities and problems as the next section
describes.

*Mobilizing Regional Businesses: Regional Brands and Regional Support Services*

Linking artisans, food businesses, and recreation to create a new style of
experiential tourism can prime the regional economy pump, but it is insufficient to turn around an economy in chronic decline. This level of transformation requires several major shifts, including the development of regional markets and market pathways, the creation of regional brands, the
implementation of services to enable local businesses to become regional,
and the ongoing support of projects that enhance Regional Flavor.

The first step is to develop a substantial market for regional goods and
services that convinces people, especially in urban areas, to demand regional products, and ensures that those regional products and services are
easy to access. This approach requires development of new retail outlets—
online, in local communities, and in urban centers—and partnerships with
existing stores.

Development of effective regional distribution systems is also necessary.
Currently, distribution systems for most products are national. It is usually
easier for small food manufacturers to place their products on the shelves
of a natural food store in Utah than to sell to *all* the stores—grocery, convenience, specialty, natural, and farmers market—in a town fifty miles away.
Already, enterprising entrepreneurs who deliver their products to a nearby
city also take the products of other businesses, and they make a profit from
this activity. Entrepreneur support organizations can identify these entre-

preneurs and help them work together to create reliable regional distribution systems?

Next, the products of thousands of small food and artisan businesses need to be organized into regional brands. These Regional Flavor brands are quite different than typical brands. For example, *Food We Love*, the Appalachian Ohio food brand, is an umbrella brand for a wide assortment of products. The only things these products have in common are that they are each unique, are very high quality, and are made in Appalachian Ohio. They constitute an inviting and engaging Regional Flavor stew, not a consistent and bland purée. The brand helps very small businesses get into large grocery chains, and it provides several congregate sites in the store where common branding draws people to the displays. The brand also helps organize tastings, where customers can try the products and get to know the entrepreneurs. This interaction helps consumers develop a long-term, emotional bond to the entrepreneurs, the region, and the brand, which tends to generate repeat purchases and informal marketing of the products among their friendship networks.

At the same time that regional brands are implemented, entrepreneur support organizations work to help businesses become regional rather than local. An area of huge potential for many communities is to provide the assistance that enables artisans to become small entrepreneurial manufacturers. Appalachian Ohio is home to more than a thousand artisans, but most of them sell only in limited venues such as craft fairs. The first step is to reposition artisan products not as gifts or knickknacks but as ingredients in a Regional Home where the food, dishware, furniture, and art are all created in the region and, through the sense of the region that they reflect, add to the beauty and enjoyment of one's home.

Regional economies are built from the ground up. The community of Nelsonville (pop. 5,000), a former coal mining town that several years ago had an unemployment rate of 16 percent and an almost empty, but architecturally attractive, town square, is an example. Several local benefactors offered subsidies to entrepreneurs willing to open shops on the square, and soon there were twenty-five shops, including several potters' galleries, an artisan cooperative, a yarn shop, and an art gallery. A coffee shop opened at one end of the square, and Hocking College's culinary school established a gourmet restaurant.

ACEnet then worked with shop owners on a brochure, with funds from the owners leveraging grants from the Yellowroot Fund. The marketing piece highlighted the heritage of the area (the region was home to many brick manufacturers early in the century, including the stunning Starbrick) as well as the artisans and included a walking map of the square.

Staff of the shops on the square were trained and encouraged to tell the story of the business, the artisans, and the region. Shopping became an authentic and enjoyable experience and an important part of building the Regional Flavor in the customer's mind. Store staff were also encouraged to cross-sell—identifying the interests of their customers and referring them to other shops and activities that they might enjoy. The shops now sell the products of more than 200 area artisans.

The next step was to identify those entrepreneurs interested in growth and link them to new regional markets to start the expansion process. ACEnet created a Website that featured Regional House and Home products. The galleries assisted entrepreneurs with product innovation and quality, then warehoused and shipped the artisans' products. As a result, the galleries have increased their income streams, strengthened their interest in quality, and became a source of aggregated purchasing trends for area artisans.

The galleries also encouraged entrepreneurs to emphasize regional aspects of their products, through design and hang tags or brochures that tell stories containing the products in the region's heritage and culture. For example, the Starbrick Clay gallery commissioned an artisan to make pottery coasters and trivets using the Starbrick design and then told the story of the early twentieth-century brickmaker to people who stopped by the shop.

## How a Region Can Support Innovation and Regional Flavor

The media, local and regional leaders, and area consumers all can play an important role in building a regional innovation economy. Marketing in a regional innovation economy works because it generates buzz—people become passionate about a new regional restaurant and urge their friends and coworkers to try it. Thus, it makes sense for entrepreneur support organizations to understand how buzz, or *innovation diffusion*, works. ACEnet involved a group of area women who had large networks of friends in the community in the development of the *Food We Love* logo and store materials. These women developed a sense of ownership of the brand and shared their excitement with friends. Basically, they became an informal sales force for the brand. Consequently, when the products arrived in stores, many shoppers were already familiar with them, and sales were brisk from the start. ACEnet developed a mailing list of people who expressed interest in buying local products and sent out frequent notices of new products or the entry of the brand into additional stores. The media also played an important role in supporting the emerging regional innovation economy. Almost every week, area newspapers or radio featured stories of entrepreneurs and community collaborations. During the start-up of the *Food We Love* brand, one paper ran a weekly column, written by ACEnet staff, that provided information about the value and importance of purchasing regional products.

Regional leadership is also crucial to the success of regional innovation economies. The director of the Governor's Office of Appalachia, for example, provided crucial funding for several Regional Flavor projects and created a regional Web portal that helped link and incorporate a large number of regional sites.[5]

## REGIONAL NETWORKS

Several new network structures were developed in Appalachia to support the emergence of a regional innovation economy. The first was a small learning network among a group of entrepreneurship organizations. The second was the formation of an *Appalachian Ohio Regional Entrepreneurship Network*, a loose network of entrepreneurs, entrepreneur support organizations, and government officials and policymakers.

### A Multi-State Learning and Policy Network: The Central Appalachian Network

The Central Appalachian Network (CAN) was formed more than a decade ago by a group of entrepreneur support organizations in Appalachian Ohio, West Virginia, southwest Virginia, and Kentucky. This group has primarily served as a learning, knowledge-building, and innovation diffusion network.

CAN periodically selects areas where members want to deepen their understanding, then it convenes *CANtanks* with speakers and interactive sessions. Periodically, the groups share successful innovations with each other and provide mentoring in the application and adaptation of these initiatives. In addition, CAN sets up joint capacity building activities that enhance the operations of the organizations.

More recently, the groups delved into the policy arena. Each organization selected a local policy objective and, at the same time, a joint Central Appalachian initiative was chosen by CAN members. The results of these experiments led to a policy white paper, *Strategies for Sustainable Entrepreneurship*, that included policy recommendations derived from the experiences of the CAN members. The document described five key insights identified by the groups as crucial to successful regional entrepreneurship, shared stories about entrepreneurs to illustrate the insights, backed up their findings with research, and then made policy recommendations.[6] This document was presented at a CAN Roundtable at which policy influentials from the five states heard from national innovators and area entrepreneurs, discussed the policy recommendations presented in *Strategies for Sustainable Entrepreneurship*, then met in state delegations to identify next steps. These delegations have continued to meet in many of the states, leading to the development of new entrepreneurship initiatives and/or statewide entrepreneurship networks.

## The Appalachian Ohio Regional Entrepreneurship Network

A *regional entrepreneurship network* (REN)—the loose network of entrepreneurs, entrepreneur support organizations, and public officials/policymakers—is critical to the long-term success of regional economies. A REN is a vehicle for identifying emerging needs of entrepreneurs; creating, modifying, or coordinating new services to meet those needs; and engaging policymakers to develop policy drawn from what the region has learned about supporting entrepreneurs.

Many areas believe that they can organize a regional entrepreneurship network by convening a large group of people and suggesting that they form a network. This seldom works as the relationships, skills, and understanding needed for the group to work together as a whole have not yet been developed. The relationships that are developed as organizations and entrepreneurs work with others in the region on dozens of small collaborative projects are the crucial foundation for larger regionwide efforts.

The Appalachian Ohio Regional Entrepreneurship Network has been built in this way. In addition to the many collaborative projects described in this chapter thus far, several other key actions helped weave the network. For example, Ohio University's Voinovich Center for Public Leadership, which has a long history of providing training to local public officials, piloted a daylong workshop that introduced public officials and local organizations in several counties to entrepreneurship.

Local officials and economic development staff have, for decades, based their hopes for jobs on recruitment strategies—convincing manufacturing operations from outside their region to locate in their community. With the outsourcing of manufacturing to low-wage regions of the world, this dream became unsustainable.

Entrepreneurship is a more complex strategy than recruitment, however. For success, it requires that organizations become entrepreneur-focused and work together effectively to support those entrepreneurs. It requires continual innovation and adjustment. Thus, having a trusted partner such as the Voinovich Center provide training and mentoring is essential in developing the strong local support so critical to an effective regional network.[7]

Network formation has taken a decade in Appalachian Ohio. Only recently has the network come together to contemplate its future. At a gathering of approximately 100 entrepreneurs and support organizations from around the region, AORIC members invited a panel of diverse entrepreneurs to discuss what they needed to grow and to increase profitability. This was followed by a presentation based on research on the state of entrepreneurship in the region. The gathering then subdivided into small groups, each generating ideas for enhancing the entrepreneurial environment in the region. Unfortunately, the continued development of a regional network is constrained by a lack of resources to convene and coordinate the group.

## Implications for Policy

The major implication of the approach described in this case study is that effective entrepreneurship policy needs to include investment in developing entrepreneurial networks, not just assistance to individual firms. Such networks can take several forms. Clusters—sets of entrepreneurs with a particular market focus and other businesses and organizations that support them—are a basic building block of regional entrepreneurial economies. Funding for clusters is likely to be most effective when a pool of funds is available for collaborative projects that generate cluster infrastructure. For example, a pool of funds for an artisan cluster might support the creation of an arts incubator, joint marketing brochures, and the development of a regional arts festival. In addition, funds for cluster organizers (usually agile and innovative nonprofits such as ACEnet), *network weavers* (individuals who take responsibility for introducing arts entrepreneurs to each other and to support organizations) and for cluster communication systems are critical for success.

Broader Regional Entrepreneurship Networks are also key to successful regional economies. Effective entrepreneurship policy will support one or more organizations who catalyze and coordinate such networks in a region. Such organizations can identify broad regional needs of entrepreneurs and organize collaborative projects to fill those gaps. In addition, they can introduce entrepreneurship concepts and practices to local officials, and build skills needed for network building and collaboration. They can also develop new evaluative and accountability processes, especially those that track and enhance the quality of the regional networks. Network mapping software and metrics are available that can be used for these purposes. Finally, such organizations can help build a new relationship between policymakers and practitioners so that entrepreneurship policy is flexible enough to support local experimentation and is capable of moving local successes to scale. In this way, rural regions, through their own self-organized efforts, will be able to create prosperous entrepreneurial economies.

## NOTES

1. For more information, visit the National Business Incubator Association Website: www.nbia.com.

2. Innovation and Firm Performance, Session C and Giulio Cainelli, et al. Technological innovation and firm performance in Italian traditional manufacturing sectors, Conference Innovation and Enterprise Creation: Statistics and Indicators, France, 23–24.11.2000 ftp.cordis.lu/pub/innovation-smes/docs/statconf_paper_e.pdf and 2003 European Innovation Scoreboard: Technical Paper No. 1, Indicators and Definitions, Nov. 11, 2003 trendchart.cordis.lu/scoreboards/scoreboard2003/ pdf/ eis_2003_tp1_indicators_definitions.p. "Innovative small and medium-sized enterprises and the creation of employment" in Entrepreneurial Innovation in Europe: A review of 11 studies of innovation policy and practice in today's Europe" www .cordis.lu/innovation-policy/studies/ca_study4.htm; www.hhh.umn.edu/img/assets/ 9140/year2_report1.pdf.

3. See www.ffiec.gov.
4. See the 100 mile diet at www.100milediet.org/.
5. See www.appalachianohio.com.
6. See www.cannetwork.org.
7. See www.voinovichcenter.ohiou.edu.
8. See www.networkweaving.com/blog.

# REFERENCES

Audretsch, David B. 2003. Entrepreneurship policy and the management of places. In *The emergence of entrepreneurship policy governance, start-ups, and growth in the U.S. knowledge economy*, ed. David Hart, 20–38. Cambridge: Cambridge University Press.

Axelrod, Robert, and Michael Cohen. 2000. *Harnessing complexity: Organizational implications of a scientific frontier.* New York: Basic Books.

Central Appalachian Network. 2005. *Strategies for sustainable entrepreneurship.* Central Appalachian Network.

Cooke, Philip, Patries Boekholt, and Franz Todtling. 2000. *The governance of innovation in Europe: Regional perspectives on global competitiveness.* London: Continuum International Publishing Group.

Florida, Richard. 2002. *The Rise of the Creative Class.* New York: Basic Books.

Haragon, Andrew. 2003. *How breakthroughs happen: The surprising truth about how companies innovate.* Boston, MA: Harvard Business School.

Holley, June. 2005. Transforming your regional economy through uncertainty and surprise. In *Uncertainty and surprise in complex systems: Questions on working with the unexpected,* 153–64. New York: Springer.

Kauffman, Stuart. 1995. *At home in the universe: The search for laws of self-organization and complexity.* New York: Oxford University Press.

Kelly, Kevin. 1998. *New rules for the new economy: 10 radical strategies for a connected world.* New York: Viking Press.

Krebs, Valdis, and June Holley. 2004. Building smart communities through network weaving. www.orgnet.com/BuildingNetworks.pdf (January 26, 2007).

McDaniel, Jr., R. R., and D. J. Driebe, eds. 2005. *Uncertainty and surprise in complex systems: Questions on working with the unexpected.* New York: Springer.

McVay, Mary, and Madi Hirschland. 2001. *Making the connection: Appalachian Center for Economic Networks (ACEnet)*, Access to Markets Case Study Series/No. 1 (FIELD) Washington, DC: Aspen Institute.

Rogers, Everett. 2003. *Diffusion of innovations*. New York: Free Press.

Rosen, Emanuel. 2000. *The anatomy of buzz*. New York: Doubleday

Saxenian, Annalee. 2000. *Regional advantage: Culture and competition in Silicon Valley and Route 128*. Cambridge, MA: Harvard University Press.

Watts, Duncan. 2003. *Six degrees: The science of the connected age*. New York: W. W. Norton.

# 13

## Getting Started in Community-Based Entrepreneurship

*Scott Loveridge*

Previous chapters in this book describe various trends, approaches, and obstacles involved in improving entrepreneurial performance, especially in rural areas. The chapters bring "lessons learned" and perspectives on enhancing the performance and success of entrepreneurs. This chapter ties the previous information together and provides individuals with practical first steps toward establishing a *community-based* entrepreneurship program. Why community-based? While dialog and reform at the state or national level can be useful, it should be clear from previous chapters that the most immediate impacts can be obtained by many small groups working locally.

The chapter begins with a brief description of techniques to determine whether a focus on community-based entrepreneurship is warranted. Assuming the answer is, "Yes, we do need community-based entrepreneurship!" a series of steps and questions will help readers identify assets from which to build a program and also which areas need improvement. Finally, key strategies for creating coalitions for community-based entrepreneurship are explored.

### DOES MY COMMUNITY NEED COMMUNITY-BASED ENTREPRENEURSHIP?

Before implementing an economic development strategy, it is important to assess the community's situation. Resources expended in one area can often mean less for other strategies. Entrepreneurship competes for resources with industrial recruitment, amenity-led development, technology-led development, infrastructure development, and, to a lesser extent, business retention and expansion. All of these approaches may be appropriate for a community, depending on the situation.

Probably the most important asset in a community is the available time of its leadership—a resource that is often undervalued in assessing economic development strategies. Communities tend to look at costs per job created in terms of costs of subsidies (e.g., tax abatements and other benefits) extended to a firm. Forgotten are the time costs of leaders who plan and implement the economic development strategy.

In community-based entrepreneurship, the time costs are likely to outweigh the out-of-pocket expenses required to help firms. This can be positive and, because entrepreneurial firms require fewer formal subsidies than recruited firms, the community can be more self-reliant. The outcome translates into a potentially more sustainable economic development system. Once such a system becomes part of the local culture, it can be sustained with less effort, whereas the costs of recruiting firms have risen (CFED 2007).

Nevertheless, it is important to consider time costs before committing local leadership to an entrepreneurship effort. The initial phases will take time, and results may not appear for a while. Thus, entrepreneurship strategies require substantial long-term commitment, and research has shown that people are fairly impatient for results with respect to economic development (Loveridge and Loy 1998). So, the case for supporting an entrepreneurship approach must be made.

How does one decide, then, whether there is a need to establish a stronger community-based entrepreneurial system in a specific area? It is perhaps best to start with the state. How does the state stack up against others in terms of entrepreneurship? Goetz and Freshwater (2001) conducted a statistical analysis of various indicators with a formal model ranking states, while the Small Business Foundation of Michigan (2004) used a broad array of indicators to construct a "grade" for entrepreneurialism (table 13.1). While the two studies differ in data sources, assessment techniques, and in years covered, there is surprising consistency in the results (with some notable exceptions, e.g., Georgia and Montana). California, Utah, and Virginia received "A-" grades and were also in the top ten in the Goetz and Freshwater analysis, so high scorers in both systems also seem to follow common knowledge. All three states have reputations as vibrant, entrepreneurial places.

Clearly, states differ in performance and reputation with respect to cultivating entrepreneurs even if the differences in the two studies do point to a need to develop an agreed-upon and scientifically defensible way of rating a state's performance. Still, if a state scores well on both measures, there can at least be some confidence of positive community role models in the region and a reasonably favorable state climate.

Table 13.1.  **Assessments of Entrepreneurial Climate**

| State | Rank | Grade | State | Rank | Grade | State | Rank | Grade |
|-------|------|-------|-------|------|-------|-------|------|-------|
| AL | 18 | C- | MA | 21 | B | OK | 20 | C- |
| AK | 47 | C | MI | 28 | D | OR | 27 | C- |
| AZ | 8 | C | MN | 16 | C | PA | 25 | C- |
| AR | 12 | B- | MS | 32 | C- | RI | 24 | C+ |
| CA | 4 | A- | MO | 38 | D | SC | 34 | D+ |
| CO | 3 | D+ | MT | 48 | B+ | SD | 22 | B |
| CT | 49 | C- | NE | 7 | C- | TN | 39 | C |
| DE | 33 | B- | NV | 30 | B | TX | 10 | C+ |
| FL | 5 | B- | NH | 29 | B- | UT | 6 | A- |
| GA | 2 | D+ | NJ | 13 | C | VT | 50 | D+ |
| HI | 44 | C | NM | 37 | C- | VA | 1 | A- |
| ID | 40 | C- | NY | 35 | B- | WA | 14 | C |
| IL | 19 | D | NC | 23 | C- | WV | 36 | D- |
| IN | 26 | D | ND | 45 | C | WI | 46 | C- |
| ME | 43 | C- | OH | 31 | D+ | WY | 42 | C |
| MD | 11 | C | | | | | | |

*Sources*: Ranks from Goetz and Freshwater 2001; Grades from Small Business Foundation of Michigan 2004.

If a state scores poorly on both indices in table 13.1, it may be more important to engage in state policy discussions and to look out of state for positive community models. In this case, use table 13.1 to choose a state with similar social and economic characteristics but that has a score higher than your state on entrepreneurship climate.

A statewide assessment is not enough; entrepreneurial culture, and therefore performance, may vary substantially by region within a state. It is important to determine how well a local area supports entrepreneurs. Henderson, Low, and Weiler (chapter 4) provide a solid overview of conditions that seem to give rise to a strong entrepreneurial climate; these factors, together with *local attitudes and practices*, form the basis for future growth.

Lichtenstein and Lyons (2006) suggest a simple conceptual approach to thinking about a community's entrepreneurs, and they make several very compelling points. First, entrepreneurs can be found in all sizes of business. Most entrepreneurial support programs, including those described by several chapters in this book, focus almost exclusively on "small,"[1] especially start-up firms. Second, there is interdependency among small and large firms. Small firms benefit from the existence of large firms for a customer base and as role models.

Third, to become large, businesses must first be midsized, but to become midsized, they must start operations. Firms of all sizes go through a life cycle and, ultimately, most die. Those that do not die may change form dramatically and may leave the area of their birth. For example, Nokia, the successful cell phone company, started as a pulp mill, then became a boot manufacturer before moving into electronics. Along the way, Nokia moved from its rural hometown to a suburb of the Finnish capital, Helsinki (Huuhtanen 2006).

Similarly, Gerber started with baby food in rural Fremont, Michigan, but now makes a wide array of products and is headquartered in New Jersey.[2] Rural communities are especially vulnerable to losing entrepreneurial firms to relocation as the growing firm develops and its needs change.

These "life cycle" issues mean that within a community there is a need for what the Lichtenstein and Lyons (2006) call a "pipeline" of entrepreneurs, and start-ups are critical to keeping the pipeline filled. A specific community may experience gaps in its pipeline at other levels, however; in these cases, a focus on recruitment or expansion may be most appropriate. The model proposed by Lichtenstein and Lyons is mainly conceptual; they did not present empirical evidence to help determine appropriate levels of entrepreneurs at each stage.

Loveridge and Nizalov (2005) used the Lichtenstein and Lyons conceptual model to conduct an empirical test of the optimal distribution of firm sizes within a local (county) economy in Michigan. Their findings show that the optimal distribution of firms' growth should be skewed toward the smaller end of the scale. While the Loveridge and Nizalov results involve only one state, and so must be interpreted with caution, a rough rule of thumb from the study is that if a local economy has less than 20 percent of its employment in the one to four employee size firm, it may benefit from increased support for entrepreneurs at the start-up stage.

A logical step in assessing the need for increased emphasis on community-based entrepreneurship is to examine available data for the county. In most communities, data about geographic areas smaller than counties is extremely limited. Labor markets and economic linkages in today's world extend well beyond township or city lines, so functional economic areas are based on counties or larger. Finally, county government provides many important local institutions, and it is important to include these in increasing support for entrepreneurship.

The U.S. Census Bureau publishes *County Business Patterns* annually (www.census.gov/epcd/cbp/view/cbpview.html). To determine whether a county has enough small businesses to support an entrepreneurship program, download the county's information and perform the calculation. Because the U.S. Census Bureau does not publish employment by firm size, one can only determine an estimated *range* of the percentage of employment in small firms and, since small firms are often only one person, it is safest to assume the true percentage is toward the smaller side of the range. A sample calculation for Kalamazoo, Michigan, in 2003[3] follows:

1. Number of firms with 1 to 4 employees: 2,620
2. Total countywide employment: 112,823
3. Minimum percentage of employment in small firms: 2,620/112,823 = 2.3%
4. Maximum percentage of employment in small firms: (2,620 × 4)/ 112,823 = 9.3%

With these simple data, one might conclude that Kalamazoo should try to increase the number of small firms regardless of the distribution of firm sizes within the one to four employee size firm category.

A counterexample is Keweenau County, also in Michigan. The county experienced a copper boom in the 1860s and went into a steep population decline after the last mine closed. The area is now home to artisans who enjoy the picturesque shoreline and cheap housing. In Keweenau County, the number of firms with one to four employees is 59, while total countywide employment is 245. This makes the range of employment in small firms from 24 to 96 percent.

Clearly, Keweenau County is an extreme case, and the higher end of the range is completely unrealistic. It does illustrate, however, that some counties would benefit more from attention to expansion of existing firms than by focusing on start-ups. In this case, growth could perhaps best be stimulated through better marketing, an apprenticeship program, formation of artist cooperatives, recruiting a midsize firm that might supply the many artists, or perhaps a resort-type hotel to provide new customers for the artists.

On the other hand, the community may have adjusted to its lifestyle and may prefer to maintain its current status as a place where rugged individualists can come to develop their craft. It is therefore important to understand community preferences before launching major economic development initiatives.

The *small firm employment to total employment* ratio provides a quick reality check and is a first step in determining how much a specific area might focus on encouraging additional start-ups, and in helping existing small businesses survive. As the Keweenau County example shows, practitioners can still pursue an entrepreneurial development strategy even if there are sufficient numbers of small firms; it is just that the strategies will focus more on other sizes of firms. If an area has identified a deficiency in small businesses, the next step is to conduct an asset-mapping exercise.


## ASSET-MAPPING FOR
## COMMUNITY-BASED ENTREPRENEURSHIP

Many community development initiatives have failed in the past because they started with a needs assessment and moved directly to intervention to address those needs. A problem with this approach is that it ignores local capacities that may be available to support the initiative (Kretzmann and McKnight 1993). It is important to consider local capacities because the alternative is outside assistance, which may be beneficial but likely not sustainable. The Aspen Institute has published a free workbook on the basics of measuring community capacity (2007), and the ABCD Institute also has a widely used manual (Kretzmann and McKnight 1993). Inventorying knowledge, skills, and abilities available locally is a critical part of the intervention planning process (Kretzmann and McKnight 1993). If these local capacities can be brought to bear on the issue, the initiative is more likely to succeed, with requirements for outside assistance eliminated, reduced, or more focused.

Convene a brainstorming session or visit individuals one-on-one and ask what they and the community have to offer entrepreneurs. Ask what has led to the success of existing businesses in the area. Ask if there are other individuals or organizations that exist locally or elsewhere in the region who can provide support to entrepreneurs. Ask what they do well. Ask about positive entrepreneurial aspects of the community in general. And, as Holley (chapter 12) suggests in her chapter, ask people about their networks to support entrepreneurs in order to identify and begin to weave a stronger pattern of local linkages.

Through the asset-mapping process, community support questions raised in this book and in a special issue of the *Journal of the Community Development Society* can be answered. The next section provides details on these questions that form a more complete assessment and help identify areas for further development of community-based entrepreneurial systems in the region.


## KEY QUESTIONS IN FORMULATING A STRATEGY
## FOR COMMUNITY-BASED ENTREPRENEURSHIP

The ability of a community to produce and support the growth and development of local entrepreneurs is multidimensional, and no two communities are alike in capacities. In what follows, key questions identified in this book are grouped into three broad categories. First, questions about *Community and Networks* help develop an understanding of important baseline conditions to organize a community's ability to help entrepreneurs help each other. Second, *Finance and Regulations* questions relate to providing entrepreneurs with adequate capital and reducing the red tape associated with doing business. Third, *Training and Mentoring* questions help community leaders understand how to position local resources most effectively to help entrepreneurs improve their businesses. Each of these dimensions is important in creating a total system of entrepreneurial development.

## Community and Networks

1. *Is there a network of entrepreneurs for peer-to-peer support and idea generation* (Korsching and Allen 2004; Lichtenstein, Lyons, and Kutzhanova 2004; Muske and Woods 2004)? A network of entrepreneurs is increasingly viewed as crucial to community-supported entrepreneurship for several reasons. Peers are "living" the same problems, so their solutions to problems are viewed by entrepreneurs as more credible than other types of advisors. Through sharing, entrepreneurs learn that seemingly insurmountable obstacles can be overcome. Finally, peers can support each other with contacts and business in ways that other organizations cannot.

2. *Is there a locally based and locally controlled single-mission organization focused on improving the community's entrepreneurial climate* (Korsching and Allen 2004)? A danger here is that an existing organization, such as the Chamber of Commerce or the local economic development agency will say, "That's us," but on further exploration, one finds that the agency has many missions, among them general business support. Korshing and Allen (2004) suggest a stand-alone organization to develop many of the items listed in this chapter, separate from recruitment and promotional activities. Such an organization can function without having to worry about filling up the industrial park or planning the downtown's "Sidewalk Days."

3. *Are activities to support entrepreneurs well-coordinated across service providers* (Lichtenstein, Lyons, and Kutzhanova 2004; Muske and Woods 2004; Woods and Muske, chapter 11)? The asset-mapping exercise suggested earlier in this chapter helps to identify gaps in service provision. Based on observation, the needs for service outstrip any one organization's capacity to deliver, so service providers should not, in principle, be threatened by this question; in practice, it may cause some of them anxiety. Better articulation among service providers means that businesses come to each "helping agency" ready to use the information available. Such articulation can help save time per customer and yield greater overall impacts as more are served.

*4. Is there an ombudsman or mentor who can help guide microbusinesses through all the early steps of business formation and growth* (Muske and Woods 2004)? Often, a local Small Business Development Center (SBDC) offers these kinds of services, but localities and states vary in the level of matching dollars for this federally supported system. If the area does not have a local SBDC office, sometimes an arrangement can be made for regular visits by area SBDC staff. Other organizations that might offer ombudsman services are the local Extension office, the Chamber of Commerce, financial institutions, or the local economic development authority (LEDA). It is relatively straightforward to determine whether these services exist locally. It is critically important to have access to these services within the area.

*5. Is there a mechanism for learning about and acting upon emerging needs of the community's entrepreneurs* (Muske and Woods 2004; Warner and Daugherty 2004)? Frequently, the LEDA conducts regular business retention and expansion visits with larger employers in their territory. A shortcoming to this approach is that most LEDAs take a "Lone Ranger" approach to problem solving, attempting to address a specific firm's issues on the spot. While that is fine as far as it goes, missing elements are consistent tracking of the small problems faced by many firms and broader community action to address the problems. Some local economic developers establish a database to identify themes across businesses; more practitioners should adopt this strategy.

A second weakness of the "Lone Ranger" approach is that a focus on larger employers can mean that issues faced by start-up and second stage firms can go unnoticed. Community-based business retention and expansion programs (e.g., Loveridge and Morse 1997) address this shortcoming by leveraging the resources of the local LEDA with a broader cross-section of community opinion leaders in a comprehensive action-oriented examination of business issues. If done well, a community-based business retention and expansion program can boost the political capital of the LEDA to accomplish results as well as help to uncover issues that may have hampered overall business development.

*6. Is the community welcoming to newcomers* (Levitte 2004; Henderson, Low, and Weiler, chapter 4)? Newcomers are critical to the continued health of the local economy. They bring ideas, contacts, and experiences that may not otherwise be present. Newcomers also provide replacements for people who leave an area through life cycle changes such as going to college, transfer, and other reasons. Moreover, one school of thought says that certain creative types are highly mobile and seek a tolerant and welcoming atmosphere (Florida 2002). Thus, it is an important question, but not one of the easier ones on this list to answer.

Some insights might be obtained by asking recent arrivals questions such as "What helped you adjust when you moved here?" but that provides only a partial picture because it does not provide an understanding of what those who did not come or did not stay could have used. Practitioners should review and evaluate services offered to international migrants, who are the source of population growth in many areas. Immigrants are more entrepreneurial than people raised in the United States (Henderson, Low, and Weiler, chapter 4; International Migration Policy Program 1997).

*7. Are entrepreneurs counseled on appropriate ways to use social capital and avoid social capital traps* (Kayne, chapter 8; Levitte 2004)? Social capital is a term used to describe feelings of connectedness between individuals and is beneficial when individuals use it to make business connections; however, when local ties are too strong, social capital can prevent businesses from seeking support from external sources. Furthermore, as Levitte (2004) demonstrates, sometimes jealousy or other negative feelings can interfere with productive economic relationships to the detriment of the entire community. To assess this characteristic in a community, one can ask service providers and entrepreneurs themselves whether people go outside the community when they cannot meet needs locally and whether they continue to do business with individuals they do not like if it makes business sense.

*8. Are knowledge clusters (people who know a great deal about a type of product, a specific part of the production and marketing process, or how to support entrepreneurs) identified and fostered* (Jackson 2004)? Important to emphasize here is that knowledge clusters can cut across sectors, and great potential for mutually beneficial improvements can come from such exchanges. For example, individuals who handle advertising for diverse businesses might learn more from each other than a network of used car dealer public relations departments. The latter would compete on many levels and thus be less willing to share information, and would not have the diversity of experience within the former type of group. Determining whether these clusters exist locally would take the form of questions such as "Do you ever get together with a group to help figure out better ways to do business?" "Tell me a little about the group."

*9. Are knowledge clusters engaged in intercluster learning and exchange* (Henderson, Low, and Weiler, chapter 4; Jackson 2004)? Continuing the advertising example, the people in this cluster might benefit from knowing what changes are occurring in information technologies. So for the assessment, follow-up questions might include, "Does that group ever compare notes with other groups?" "Tell me about those groups."

*10. Does the community deliberately foster growth of leaders who can play a positive role in the development process* (Muske and Woods 2004)? Most often, this approach takes the form of leadership development programs regularly offered by Chambers and county extension offices. It is important to recruit diverse individuals into these programs to foster development of deep local networks.

*11. Does the community's current leadership have a vision for entrepreneurship* (Dabson, chapter 2; Emery, Wall, and Macke 2004)? While this question may sound difficult to answer, it should be relatively easy to assess in the context of an asset-mapping exercise. Simply ask, "What would you like to see happen here to facilitate entrepreneurial development?" If community leaders give consistent answers, then there is a vision, which is an asset for forward movement. Dabson (chapter 2) emphasizes sustained *productivity* growth as key to regional development. Are local leaders focused on productivity or activity?

*12. Does the community support businesses that are risk-takers* (Emery, Wall, and Macke 2004)? Can the community identify instances in which it supported a business with an unproven product or process? Innovative, risk-taking businesses are best poised to achieve high growth. Businesses may need support through several failures before ultimately getting the formula right. These failures are important learning tools for entrepreneurs.

*13. Does the community treat all businesses equally or does it focus additional resources on businesses with high expectations of entrepreneurial activity* (Dabson, chapter 2)? Nearly every community has "lifestyle" businesspeople who prefer limited engagement in their enterprise. They may be retirees who "need something to do," or they may have family or other commitments that make them desire a short work week. Or they may simply have already achieved their financial goals and wish to avoid the headaches that come with expansion. While lifestyle entrepreneurs merit access to some business support services, it is important to recognize that they will not grow significantly. By focusing additional services on businesses with a high desire to grow, communities maximize the impact of entrepreneurial support efforts.

*14. Are the community's infrastructure investments, including telecommunications, sufficient to support entrepreneurs* (Henderson, Low, and Weiler, chapter 4; Muske and Woods 2004)? Inadequate roads, air service, and Internet access can hobble otherwise viable plans for entrepreneurial growth. Consistent efforts to upgrade these connections to markets and other resources (e.g., information, technical assistance) are key in planning for development. It is important to touch base with entrepreneurial firms to determine *their priorities* in establishing community priorities. All too often, limited public infrastructure investment dollars are targeted toward large industrial parks not needed by local entrepreneurs. The same dollars allocated toward more general purpose infrastructure can improve business productivity and raise the overall quality of life in the community.

*15. Do existing entrepreneurial development strategies complement and build on the natural and cultural assets in the region* (Dabson, chapter 2; Holley, chapter 12)? Consideration of existing natural and cultural assets can help identify areas of natural competitive advantage. An earlier chapter provides an example of building upon a little-known fruit that is indigenous to the region (Holley, chapter 12). Focusing on the PawPaw fruit has generated value-added enterprises and tourism dollars. Other regions, where the Paw-Paw fruit does not grow, will find it difficult to compete head-to-head with the area.

## Finance and Regulations

*16. Are bank loans available for start-ups* (Lichtenstein, Lyons, and Kutzhanova 2004; Muske and Woods 2004; Woods and Muske, chapter 11)? While Lyons, Lichtenstein, and Kutzhanova (chapter 5), point out that capital is not the major source of start-up funding for entrepreneurial businesses, communities that provide these kinds of financial services are likely to see an increased level of start-ups.

*17. Does the community have an Individual Development Account (IDA) program to help entrepreneurs build start-up capital? Does the community have a revolving loan fund program for business start-up and expansion? Does the community support the formation of peer-lending programs? Does the community take full advantage of Small Business Administration financing programs such as the guaranteed loan programs and intermediary lending program?* Markley (chapter 6) provides an excellent overview of these financing tools. These tried-and-true models can be replicated in other communities to solve the often intractable problem of obtaining capital to start or grow a business. While capital may not be the primary barrier to increasing the local supply of entrepreneurs, it is probably the largest problem in the minds of many business owners, so financing programs may provide real assistance and signal to owners that the local leadership takes their concerns seriously.

*18. Has the community created a Community Development Financial Institution (a private financial institution whose mission is community development) and a Community Development Venture Capital Institution to assemble and distribute venture capital* (Markley, chapter 6)? These newer models of formalizing channels for financing of entrepreneurial development are worthwhile to explore, especially if a community already uses the methods outlined in question 17.

*19. Are external assets in entrepreneurial development such as foundations, the Heartland Center, the Rural Policy Research Institute Center for Rural Entrepreneurship, the Cooperative Extension System, and the SBDC network engaged with the community* (Macke, chapter 9; Markley, chapter 6)? It is important to benefit from lessons that others have learned the "hard way" through trial and error. If a community is not aware of, or does not use the educational assets listed above, then it may make critical mistakes in its efforts to grow and sustain entrepreneurs. Similarly, foundations, such as Ewing Marion

Kauffman, Edward Lowe, and Kellogg, have models for improved entrepreneurial support systems and are eager to share them.

20. *Does the community help entrepreneurs understand finance, recordkeeping, and government regulations* (Muske and Woods 2004)? Keeping abreast of these basic challenges in running a business can be difficult in the start-up or growth phases of the enterprise. Timely interventions can avoid situations that put a business in jeopardy.

21. *Are regulations favorable for start-ups, expansions, and transitions* (Lichtenstein, Lyons, and Kutzhanova 2004; Warner and Weiss Daugherty 2004)? Many business frustrations involve permitting and zoning practices. Making sure that these requirements are as *clear* and simple as possible can greatly assist businesses. This is an area where an ombudsman can work effectively to help untangle and streamline local permitting processes. It should be pointed out that loosening regulations is often not what is needed. Making regulations easy to understand and processing requests quickly are often enough.

22. *Are local regulations applied fairly and consistently* (Warner and Weiss Daugherty 2004)? Haphazard application of local regulations can reduce morale on the part of the affected businesses, causing them to abandon plans for expansion or to contact other communities for a new location. It is especially galling to existing businesses to see nonlocal competitors offered relaxed local regulations or tax breaks as part of an attraction package.

### Training and Mentoring Systems

23. *Do activities focus on entrepreneurs or businesses* (Dabson, chapter 2; Lichtenstein, Lyons, and Kutzhanova 2004; Muske and Woods 2004)? It is important to focus on developing the capacities of entrepreneurs because businesses may come or go depending on factors beyond the control of a community. If a business opportunity fades, a high capacity entrepreneur will switch to creating jobs in another way. Focusing on building the capacity of entrepreneurs is therefore more likely to pay off in the long run.

24. *Is sufficient attention given to increasing the supply of entrepreneurs? Does the community reject the "entrepreneurs are born not made" attitude toward entrepreneurial development* (Dabson, chapter 2; Kayne, chapter 8; Lichtenstein, Lyons, and Kutzhanova 2004; Lyons, Lichtenstein, and Kutzhanova, chapter 5; Rosenfeld 2000)? A region needs a steady supply of entrepreneurs to succeed. Communities must seek the next generation of entrepreneurs through networks and mentoring. Lyons, Lichtenstein, and Kutzhanova (chapter 5) provide a powerful set of arguments against assuming that some people are born with innate entrepreneurial ability.

25. *Does the educational system support entrepreneurship* (Emery, Wall, and Macke 2004; Hanham, Loveridge, and Richardson 1991; Kayne, chapter 8;

Schroeder, chapter 7)? Positive examples for integrating entrepreneurship into formal educational programs exist. Integrating entrepreneurship into the curriculum may occur through examples, activity-based learning, formal courses, or projects, and it should permeate every level of education from kindergarten through advanced studies. Kayne and Schroeder, in this volume, provide solid discussions of educational principles and practical resources for entrepreneurship development. In addition, the national network of Centers for Economic Education and Junior Achievement provide many easy-to-adapt learning materials. School boards can institute a "no child without a business plan" approach in curriculum revision.

26. *Do club-based entrepreneurship development opportunities for youth exist* (Emery, Wall, and Macke 2004)? The Cooperative Extension system, through its 4-H program, offers entrepreneurial experiences (Woods and Muske, chapter 11) as do many other youth organizations. If existing clubs do not offer these experiences, new clubs might be formed around this theme.

27. *Do local enterprise managers help train youth for business ownership through internship-type opportunities* (Emery, Wall, and Macke 2004)? Internships with local businesses can help youth explore careers as they learn about the daily life and challenges of entrepreneurs. While they tackle challenges with fresh perspectives, interns can help business owners understand youth in terms of a potential market and managing future employees. Some interns may become valued employees as they learn about a career path and tailor their educational experiences to fit the business's needs. Interns who start their own businesses later may become suppliers or customers of the mentor firm.

28. *Do local enterprises encourage and support spin-offs* (Illeris 2000; Nylander and Brown 2004)? Existing enterprises are a surprisingly frequent source of new enterprises. Business owners can benefit in several ways from mentoring their staff to develop spin-off enterprises. For example, some internal operations can be outsourced to the new local firm at a lower cost due to economies of scale. Say firm X needs photocopier repairs, has a staff member who is good at fixing the photocopier, but the photocopier only breaks down every three months. By helping the staff member start a photocopier repair service, overall costs can be reduced even while the company pays the (former) staff member more per hour. At the same time, a new service is extended to other firms in the area, improving their efficiency.

29. *Do local enterprises rotate responsibilities so that more people can learn the complete operation* (Nylander and Brown 2004)? This kind of cross-training exercise can be important for sustaining businesses in a time when key people transition (sometimes without warning) out of the business, but also in helping various parts of the business understand each other as the business grows. As each part of the business comes to a better understanding of the

processes and difficulties of the other, mutually beneficial solutions can arise. Finally, cross-training can help relieve boredom that may set in after one has done a job for too long. This can improve overall attitudes in the workplace, reducing turnover.

30. _Do local business owners actively encourage the rest of the family to be part of their business_ (Nylander and Brown 2004)? As with job rotation within the company, involving family members in the business can help the business survive life cycle changes. Also, as family members gain entrepreneurial skills, they can apply them in other businesses. Trust levels can be higher among family members, so critical business strategy information can be shared more easily. If a family member starts a complementary business, the connections can result in contracts or bridge financing that can help stabilize a business in its early years.

31. _Do managers actively mentor youth who are not employees_ (Emery, Wall, and Macke 2004; Kayne, chapter 8)? The benefits of this activity are very similar to the case of internship programs mentioned above. Also, as Kayne points out in this volume, the opportunity to explain principles increases the learner's retention, so a mentoring program fits well with entrepreneurial short courses.

32. _Are entrepreneurial support activities driven by funding agencies or the clients_ (Lichtenstein, Lyons, and Kutzhanova 2004)? First, is the support offered on the business owner's time frame? If the support is a business plan development class offered every six months with limited follow-up, then the answer is "no." Owners need answers to their questions as they arise, twenty-four hours a day, seven days a week. Second, do the agencies coordinate or duplicate services? It can be confusing and frustrating for business owners to have to navigate three or four systems to identify which one is best positioned to provide assistance. There is plenty of work for all agencies to do. There is no need to duplicate in one area while other areas go unserved.

33. _Are assistance programs tailored to a business owner's technical, managerial, entrepreneurial, and personal skill sets_ (Lyons, Lichtenstein, and Kutzhanova, chapter 5; Muske and Woods 2004)? A one-size-fits-all approach to technical assistance is simply not workable in an environment where one person is starting a business because the output from a craft activity is starting to fill up the basement (focus on getting money back from a craft activity/new to owning a business), while another entrepreneur wants to build and sell a second or third 50-employee business (job creation focus/seasoned entrepreneur).

34. _Do programs for entrepreneurs focus on training or implementation_ (Lichtenstein, Lyons, and Kutzhanova 2004; Warner and Weiss Daugherty 2004)? Many existing entrepreneurial programs focus on providing training around a set of tried-and-true business practices. While this might be valu-

able background information, a more action-oriented approach of helping entrepreneurs implement a solution for today's pressing issue is likely to have greater community impact and be more valued by clients. This approach represents a win-win situation as clients' needs are better served, translating to better local political support for service providers.

35. *Are entrepreneurial support systems customized to a community's unique situation* (Lichtenstein, Lyons, and Kutzhanova 2004)? Communities should realistically assess their own strengths and weaknesses and tailor support systems accordingly. If a region produces marketable fruits and vegetables but has few points of interest for tourism, then a focus on assisting value-added agricultural enterprises might be better for enhancing local employment growth than a strategy providing services for tourism businesses.

36. *Are support systems geared for all phases of the business life cycle (birth, small, medium, large, spin-off, and succession)* (Emery, Wall, and Macke 2004; Korsching and Allen 2004; Lyons, Lichtenstein, and Kutzhanova, chapter 5; Schoeder, chapter 7)? Again, the notion of articulation becomes important. The provider of choice may differ depending on the life stage of a business. To draw an analogy from education, a Nobel-prize winning scientist might not be an effective Kindergarten teacher, but he or she may be very good with university students pursuing advanced degrees in the subject. If one person or one provider works with businesses at all skill levels, some will probably not receive the support they need. Some providers should focus on basic skill levels, freeing others to work intensively to fully develop high performers.

37. *Are entrepreneurs and the community-based organizations that support them making full use of advanced products and processes* (Jackson 2004)? While it may be difficult to determine the extent to which entrepreneurs in the region use advanced products and processes, the use of technology for communications and information processing by service providers is easy to assess. Standards change very quickly, and if providers do not keep pace, they will find it difficult to keep clients informed about best practices.

Local leaders are often reluctant to take on technology investments, preferring instead to invest in human resources or higher profile capital projects. Overcoming the political challenges that work against technology investments is important in making the best use of local business opportunities, thus reducing barriers to business growth. For example, a business may be frustrated when there is no immediate answer to the question of which parcels of land might be zoned appropriately for their new venture. A nearby community that has invested in integrating its land use plan into a geographic information system might provide an answer in minutes, encouraging an entrepreneur to expand there.

38. *Are informal coaching systems fostered for smaller and more remotely located businesses* (Emery, Wall, and Macke 2004; Macke, chapter 9)? In rural

areas, services tend to concentrate in county seats or in regional population centers. While this helps serve the largest number of residents at the least cost and makes use of the most sophisticated infrastructure, it can be difficult for more remote businesses to access critical coaching services. This situation, in turn, can lead to lost opportunities and uneven growth within a community.

Similarly, many services are dedicated to keeping and growing the area's largest businesses because a major plant closing can be devastating. Ignoring small businesses, however, again leads to lost opportunities. A consistent effort to maintain contacts with, and provide services to, remote and smaller businesses is an important part of a comprehensive community-based entrepreneurship strategy.

39. *Does the community provide assistance with marketing* (Muske and Woods 2004; Woods and Muske, chapter 11)? Smaller businesses often are not adept at navigating channels to identify how to sell their products to more people. Marketing goes well beyond Website development or advertising; businesses must be coached on these practices but also in identifying appropriate markets and pricing structures. Some may also benefit from consolidating the efforts of many small businesses into a larger pool for marketing purposes.

40. *Does the community provide assistance with employee management* (Muske and Woods 2004; Woods and Muske, chapter 11)? As an entrepreneur advances from one person doing it all to a larger enterprise, the required skill sets change. Innovators with great technical skills may have no clue about managing personnel. This situation places the business at risk as the wrong people are hired, as employees are poorly trained, as labor laws are not followed because the owner is unaware of them, or as potentially good employees become dissatisfied due to underdeveloped communication and reward systems. Assisting a firm as it grows and engages more people can keep the business on track for the future.

41. *Does the community help entrepreneurs expand the geographic area of their market* (Muske and Woods 2004)? A classic local economic development strategy is to expand exports from the region (Shaffer 1989). Many businesses stop growing because the local market is saturated. Helping businesses move from meeting demand in their immediate area to selling to more distant areas can be key to increased sales and employment growth.

## CONCLUSION

This chapter has synthesized major findings from across the United States and several other countries on enhancing the performance of local economies through systems to support growth and development of entrepreneurs. The challenges in this arena remain great. Existing traditions of using tax abatements and related strategies to *recruit* rather than *build* capacities are strong and will not be supplanted for some time to come. Significant resources are deployed toward industrial recruitment, and vested interests in agencies do not wish to see their programs end. The entrepreneurial road must be traveled without the same kinds of resources that benefit recruitment strategies.

It is not likely that any community can currently answer "yes" to *all* of the 41 questions raised in the previous section. Based on field experience, any number above 30 would be an exceptional score. There is much room for improvement in almost every community. As communities move forward in adopting the approaches listed above, perhaps the average score will rise and we will begin to know which of the questions associate most strongly with improved economic performance. Our science still has some ways to travel in this regard.

The list will likely acquire some new questions as new techniques for stimulating the emergence and development of entrepreneurs are invented and tried. The good news, as earlier chapters in this book have shown, is that the science and practice of encouraging entrepreneurship now have significant champions in various sectors of society: forward thinking communities setting positive examples, as well as the government, public agencies, universities, and foundations. Our knowledge will improve.

Communities must move forward based on the best current thinking on the subject, and this volume provides an excellent summary of the state-of-the-art in entrepreneurship development. Communities have important external partners available to them, but true success in enhancing local business development starts with building an effective local coalition that can then tap the outside resources documented in this book.

The changing economy requires new skill sets, flexibility, and an understanding of how global forces are changing business strategies. As several chapters in this book have demonstrated, entrepreneurship is a key part of keeping communities viable. Transitioning from an old-style economy to an entrepreneurial economy requires a cultural shift that will take time, but the time to begin to implement the change in strategies and attitudes is now.

# NOTES

1. "Small" is subject to interpretation. For example, the U.S. Small Business Administration (SBA) defines the upper limit of "small" for eligibility for its programs to be anywhere from 150 to 1,500 employees, and up to $32M in sales, depending on the industry. See SBA's Website, www.sba.gov/size/sizetable2002.pdf, for size standards by NAICS classification.

2. See Gerber's corporate history at www.gerber.com/history.
3. There is typically a lag in data availability, but, in general, the size distribution of firms within a county does not change dramatically from year to year. Exceptions may occur if large firms go out of business, so one should take those situations into account.

## REFERENCES

Aspen Institute. 2007. *Measuring community capacity building: A workbook-in-progress for rural communities.* www.aspeninstitute.org/atf/cf/{DEB6F227-659B-4EC8-8F84-8DF23CA704F5}/Measuring%20Community%20Capactiy%20Building.pdf (July 27, 2006).
Corporation for Enterprise Development (CFED). 2007. *2006 development report card for the states.* www.cfed.org/focus.m?parentid=34&siteid=1581&id=1582 (July 27, 2006).
Emery, Mary, Milan Wall, and Don Macke. 2004. From theory to action: Energizing entrepreneurship (E2) strategies to aid distressed communities grow their own. *Journal of the Community Development Society* 35(1): 82–96.
Florida, Richard. 2002. *The rise of the creative class.* New York: Basic Books.
Goetz, Stephan, and David Freshwater. 2001. State-level determinants of entrepreneurship and a preliminary measure of entrepreneurial climate. *Economic Development Quarterly* 15(1): 58–70.
Hanham, Alison Chisholm, Scott Loveridge, and Bill Richardson. 1991. A national school-based entrepreneurship program offers promise. *Journal of the Community Development Society* 30(2): 115–30.
Huuhtanen, Matti. 2006. Nokia, the town, gives city workers mobile phones. *San Diego Union Tribune,* May 8. www.signonsandiego.com/uniontrib/20060508/news_mz1b8cellpho.html (July 27, 2006).
International Migration Policy Program. 1997. Immigrant entrepreneurs. *Research Perspectives on Migration* 1(2): 3–11. Washington, DC: Carnegie-Mellon University. www.ceip.org/programs/migrat/rpm2.pdf (July 27, 2006).
Illeris, Sven. 2000. Adapting to foreign competition: The textile and clothing industry in the Herning-Ikast Area of Jutland, Denmark. In *Small town and rural development: A case studies approach,* ed. Peter Schaeffer and Scott Loveridge, 243–50. Westport, CT: Praeger.
Jackson, Edward T. 2004. Community innovation through entrepreneurship: Grantmaking in Canadian economic development. *Journal of the Community Development Society* 35(1): 65–81.
Korsching, Peter F., and John C. Allen. 2004. Local entrepreneurship: A development model based on community interaction field theory. *Journal of the Community Development Society* 35(1): 24–43.
Kretzmann, John, and John McKnight. 1993. *Building communities from the inside out: A path toward finding and mobilizing a community's assets.* Evanston, IL: Institute for Policy Research, Northwestern University.
Levitte, Yael. 2004. Bonding social capital in entrepreneurial communities—Survival networks or barriers? *Journal of the Community Development Society* 35(1): 44–64.

Lichtenstein, Gregg A., Thomas S. Lyons, and Nailya Kutzhanova. 2004. Building entrepreneurial communities: The appropriate role of enterprise development activities. *Journal of the Community Development Society* 35(1): 5–24.

Lichtenstein, Gregg, and Thomas Lyons. 2006. Managing the community's pipeline of entrepreneurs and enterprises: A new way of thinking about business assets. *Economic Development Quarterly* 20(4): 377–86.

Loveridge, Scott, and Beth Loy. 1998. West Virginia attitudes towards economic development. Paper presented at the annual meeting of the Western Regional Science Association, Ojai, Calif. February.

Loveridge, Scott, and Denys Nizalov. In review. Does firm size distribution matter? An empirical test of the entrepreneurial pipeline theory.

Loveridge, Scott, and George W. Morse. 1997. *Implementing Local Business Retention and Expansion Visitation Programs*. University Park, Pennsylvania: Northeast Regional Center for Rural Development, Pennsylvania State University.

Muske, Glenn, and Michael Woods. 2004. Micro business as an economic development tool: What they bring and what they need. *Journal of the Community Development Society* 35(1): 95–116.

Nylander, Albert B. III, and Ralph B. Brown. 2004. Familial networks and regional entrepreneurs in northeast Mississippi's upholstered furniture industry. *Journal of the Community Development Society* 35(1): 135–48.

Rosenfeld, Stuart. 2000. Educating for industrial competitiveness and rural development. In *Small town and rural economic development*. eds. Peter Schaeffer and Scott Loveridge, 123–32. Westport, CT: Praeger.

Shaffer, Ron. *Community economics.* 1989. Ames: Iowa State University Press.

Small Business Foundation of Michigan. 2004. *Michigan entrepreneurship scorecard 2004–2005. . . . Towards an entrepreneurial economy.* Lansing, Michigan. www.sbam .org/sbam0304/documents/MIEntSCCompositeDocumentforWebsite.pdf (July 27, 2006).

Warner, Mildred, and Christine Weiss Daugherty. 2004. Promoting the "civic" in entrepreneurship: The case of rural Slovakia. *Journal of the Community Development Society* 35(1): 117–34.

# Index

# About the Editor and Contributors

Adee Athiyaman, Ph.D., is professor of marketing in the Illinois Institute for Rural Affairs at Western Illinois University. His research on marketing models has been published in more than 30 scholarly journals such as the *Australian Journal of Marketing Research, European Journal of Marketing, Australasian Journal of Regional Studies, New Zealand Journal of Applied Business Research, and Marketing Intelligence and Planning.* His current research involves an examination of the various scenarios and contextual factors that affect entrepreneurial development and action.

Brian Dabson is research professor at the Harry S. Truman School of Public Affairs, University of Missouri (Columbia). He is president and CEO of the Rural Policy Research Institute (RUPRI) and codirector of the RUPRI Center for Rural Entrepreneurship. He holds an undergraduate degree in planning and a master's degree in social sciences from the University of Birmingham, England. Before coming to the University of Missouri, he was president of CFED (formerly Corporation for Enterprise Development), a Washington, D.C.–based national nonprofit organization dedicated to expanding economic opportunity through asset-building, entrepreneurship, and economic development. He has written and presented extensively on various aspects of economic development policy and practice, with a special focus in recent years on entrepreneurship and economic development in rural America. He served two terms as president of the Organization for Economic Cooperation and Development's (OECD) Forum on Social Innovations.

Gisele F. Hamm, M.S., manages the MAPPING the Future of Your Community Programs in the Illinois Institute for Rural Affairs where she also coordinates the Rural Community Development Initiative that helps distressed rural communities identify opportunities to revitalize their economies. She has published extensively on brownfield redevelopment issues and has studied revitalization practices used in local economies. She currently is engaged in an analysis of best practices in entrepreneurship promotion and development used by state and local agencies as well as business succession planning programs to encourage youth to remain in rural communities and continue businesses.

**June Holley**, M.A., was president and founder of the Appalachian Center for Economic Networks (ACEnet), a regional entrepreneurship organization in southeastern Ohio, for more than 20 years. At ACEnet, she pioneered the implementation of many innovative entrepreneurship strategies including business networks, Kitchen Incubators, youth entrepreneurship, regional entrepreneurship networks, policy networks, and cluster-focused initiatives. In 1991, she was inducted by Governor Voinovich into the Ohio Women's Hall of Fame. An avid researcher on entrepreneurship a-nd innovation, she has authored over 40 papers, articles, and books on various aspects of economic networking. June Holley now provides consulting, training, and mentoring to a wide range of organizations around the world that are interested in creating healthier communities through a better understanding of networks, collaboration, innovation, and learning. She is codeveloper of Smart Network Toolkit, a user-friendly network mapping application to help communities and regions identify and enhance their networks, and training and mentoring programs for Network Weavers.

**Ronald J. Hustedde**, Ph.D., is professor in the Department of Community and Leadership Development at the University of Kentucky. He also directs the Kentucky Entrepreneurial Coaches Institute, a unique $1.28 million leadership program designed to stimulate an entrepreneurial culture in Appalachian Kentucky. Hustedde is past president of the Community Development Society and is coeditor of *Community Development: A Journal of the Community Development Society*. He is widely published and his research interests include venture capital and equity capital markets, community economic development and rural entrepreneurship.

**Joseph A. (Jay) Kayne**, Ph.D. holds the Cintas Chair in Entrepreneurship at the Richard T. Farmer School of Business at Miami University. Previously, he served as vice president for community and policy at the Kauffman Center for Entrepreneurial Leadership, during which time he coordinated the development of KCCatalyst, a partnership to encourage and support the emergence of new technology and life sciences companies in the greater Kansas City area, initiated a Governors' Academy on Entrepreneurship with the National Governors Association, and partnered with the University of Missouri–Kansas City (UMKC) to develop the Entrepreneurial Effect: Entrepreneurship for the Economic Development Professional. Before joining the Kauffman Foundation, Kayne spent eight years in Washington, D.C., as director of economic development and commerce policy studies at the National Governors Association (NGA). He served as lead NGA staff in developing the National Rural Development Partnership and the U.S. Innovation Partnership.

**Jason Henderson**, Ph.D., is assistant vice president for regional programs at the Federal Reserve Bank of Kansas City, Omaha Branch. His research includes interests in rural development, agricultural economics, and industrial organization. He has published on rural entrepreneurship, the growth of knowledge-based activity in rural America, the use of electronic commerce in agricultural industries and the location, and growth of value-added food manufacturing activity. He is heavily involved in tracking the rural economy for the bank's monetary policy responsibilities. His work has been widely cited by policy officials, researchers, and leading media outlets, including the *Wall Street Journal*, the *Financial Times*, *USA Today*, and *ESPN Outdoors*.

**Nailya Kutzhanova** is a Ph.D. candidate in the School of Urban and Public Affairs at the University of Louisville. Her research interests include economic development strategies, human capital development, sustainable local economies, and international development. Her dissertation research is on the relationship between entrepreneurial skill development and business performance. She has participated in several Entrepreneurial League System projects and has documented the results.

**Gregg A. Lichtenstein**, Ph.D., is president of Collaborative Strategies, a consulting firm that specializes in working with entrepreneurs, business incubation programs and strategic alliances. Working with Tom Lyons, he designed the Entrepreneurial League System, which is being implemented in several different regions around the world. The purpose of this unique system is to transform local and regional economies by developing entrepreneurs' skills, creating successful companies, and building entrepreneurial communities.

**Scott Loveridge**, Ph.D., is professor of regional development, Department of Agricultural Economics, and state extension leader for community development at Michigan State University. He previously served as director of the Regional Research Institute at West Virginia University and as a member of the faculty of Applied Economics at the University of Minnesota. He is founding editor of the *Web Book of Regional Science,* and a member of the editorial board of *Community Development: Journal of the Community Development Society.* His recent publications have appeared in *Economic Development Quarterly, Public Productivity and Management Review, Socio-economic Planning Sciences,* and *Review of Regional Studies.* He focuses on local economic development policy.

**Sarah Low,** M.S., is a doctoral student at the University of Illinois. Her current research focuses upon entrepreneurship and regional economic asset indicators relating to economic growth. Other recent research involved fiscal impact analyses of state enterprise zones and the economic impact analyses of ethanol plants. She has been active in presenting research to state legislators, fellow economists, and economic development practitioners.

**Thomas S. Lyons,** Ph.D., is Lawrence N. Field Family Chair in Entrepreneurship in the Zicklin School of Business, City University of New York. He is a member of the national Advisory Group to the RUPRI Center for Rural Entrepreneurship. He has written seven books and numerous articles and technical reports on various aspects of state and local economic development, with a focus on the role of entrepreneurship in local and regional development efforts. He, with Gregg A. Lichtenstein, pioneered the Entrepreneurship League System used across the United States and in several other countries.

**Don Macke,** M.A., is codirector of the Center for Rural Entrepreneurship. The Center is a Rural Policy Research Institute national policy and research organization. The RUPRI Center supports research, outreach, and policy work throughout North America. He has more than 30 years of experience in the field of rural community economic development. Previous experience includes serving as a policy advisor in the Nebraska Legislature, executive director of the Nebraska Rural Development Commission, and has consulting experience in 38 states, Canada, and the Caribbean. His current work focuses on community-based strategies to support local entrepreneurs as a core development approach. Along with Deborah Markley and Vick Luther, Don recently coauthored *Energizing Entrepreneurs: Charting a Course for Rural Communities* which along with a companion Website (www.energizing entrepreneurs.org) provides a comprehensive guide for community leaders seeking to build entrepreneurial strategies.

**Deborah M. Markley,** Ph.D., is managing director and director of research with the Rural Policy Research Institute's Center for Rural Entrepreneurship, a national research and policy center. Her focus within the Center is practice-driven research and evaluation of best models for entrepreneurship development in rural places. Prior to her work with the Center, she chaired the RUPRI Equity Capital Initiative and completed a national study of nontraditional venture capital institutions. Her research has also included case studies of entrepreneurial support organizations, evaluation of state industrial extension programs, and consideration of the impacts of changing banking markets on small business finance. She has extensive experience conducting field-based survey research projects and has conducted focus groups and interviews with rural bankers, entrepreneurs, business service providers, venture capitalists, small manufacturers, and others. Her research has been presented in academic journals, as well as to national public policy organizations and Congressional committees.

**Glenn Muske**, Ph.D., is professor in the Department of Design, Housing, and Merchandising as well as the home-based and microbusiness specialist for the Oklahoma Cooperative Extension Service (OCES). His mission is "the development of entrepreneurs and the communities where they live." In this role, he provides assistance and training to current and potential micro and home-based business owners. Much of his support is focused on the start-up business owner and in the area of marketing. His research interests include understanding the development of successful microenterprises. Recently, he and a colleague have studied copreneurs, or couples owning and running a family business as a team. He has published widely in scholarly and professional journals as well as an extensive involvement in the OCES outreach program.

**Craig Schroeder**, B.S., is a senior associate with the RUPRI Center for Rural Entrepreneurship with more than 20 years of experience in rural community economic development and public policy. Most of his recent research has involved studying and implementing successful youth entrepreneurship programs in the Midwest. He has served on several prominent regional, state, and national rural development boards and commissions during his career, including Chairperson and Executive Director of the Nebraska Rural Development Commission. Of particular note is his work in creating the Youth Attraction Formula, a tool for rural communities to use in addressing persistent youth out-migration.

**Norman Walzer**, Ph.D., retired as professor of economics and founding director of the Illinois Institute for Rural Affairs at Western Illinois University. He is Senior Research Scholar in the Center for Governmental Studies at Northern Illinois University. He has contributed extensively to the literature on local public finance and local economic development with a special interest in rural applications. He regularly works with state and local government agencies on issues related to development or finance. His most recent book was on *The American Midwest* and he is currently editing a special issue of *Community Development* on the effectiveness of community visioning and planning programs.

**Stephan Weiler, Ph.D.,** is professor in the Department of Economics at Colorado State University. From 2004 to 2006, he was assistant vice president and economist at the Federal Reserve's Center for the Study of Rural America to lead the center's applied research work. His research has spanned a variety of developments and labor market issues in Africa, Appalachia, Europe, and the American West. His current work focuses on regional economic growth and development, particularly in struggling rural areas, combining theoretical, empirical, and policy analysis in topics such as geographic informational asymmetries, public/private partnerships, industrial restructuring, housing, immigration, entrepreneurship, and the environment.

**Michael D. Woods, Ph.D.,** is a professor in the Department of Agricultural Economics, Oklahoma State University, where he teaches, conducts research, and provides community outreach programs in the area of community economic development. Currently he is developing and delivering programs concerned with economic development options for Oklahoma communities. He has published 21 journal articles, 28 Experiment Station publications, 35 Extension publications, and four textbook chapters. He has served on numerous state, regional, and local committees and boards involving local economic development and business issues.

Made in the USA
Lexington, KY
07 August 2011